The Politics of Possession

T0385567

Development and Change Book Series

As a journal, *Development and Change* distinguishes itself by its multi-disciplinary approach and its breadth of coverage, publishing articles on a wide spectrum of development issues. Accommodating a deeper analysis and a more concentrated focus, it also publishes regular special issues on selected themes. *Development and Change* and Wiley-Blackwell collaborate to produce these theme issues as a series of books, with the aim of bringing these pertinent resources to a wider audience.

Titles in the series include:

Gender Myths and Feminist Fables: The Struggle for Interpretive Power in Gender and Development
Edited by Andrea Cornwall, Elizabeth Harrison and Ann Whitehead

Twilight Institutions: Public Authority and Local Politics in Africa
Edited by Christian Lund

China's Limits to Growth: Greening State and Society
Edited by Peter Ho and Eduard B. Vermeer

Catalysing Development? A Debate on Aid
Jan Pronk et al.

State Failure, Collapse and Reconstruction
Edited by Jennifer Milliken

Forests: Nature, People, Power
Edited by Martin Doornbos, Ashwani Saith and Ben White

Gendered Poverty and Well-being
Edited by Shahra Razavi

Globalization and Identity
Edited by Birgit Meyer and Peter Geschiere

Social Futures, Global Visions
Edited by Cynthia Hewitt de Alcantara

The Politics of Possession
Property, Authority and Access to Natural Resources

Edited by

Thomas Sikor and Christian Lund

A John Wiley & Sons, Ltd., Publication

This edition first published 2009
Originally published as Volume 40, Issue 1 of *Development and Change*
Chapters © 2009 The Institute of Social Studies
Book compilation © 2009 Blackwell Publishing Ltd

Blackwell Publishing was acquired by John Wiley & Sons in February 2007. Blackwell's
publishing programme has been merged with Wiley's global Scientific, Technical, and
Medical business to form Wiley-Blackwell.

Registered Office
John Wiley & Sons Ltd, The Atrium, Southern Gate, Chichester, West Sussex, PO19
8SQ, United Kingdom

Editorial Offices
350 Main Street, Malden, MA 02148-5020, USA
9600 Garsington Road, Oxford, OX4 2DQ, UK
The Atrium, Southern Gate, Chichester, West Sussex, PO19 8SQ, UK

For details of our global editorial offices, for customer services, and for information
about how to apply for permission to reuse the copyright material in this book please see
our website at www.wiley.com/wiley-blackwell.

The right of Thomas Sikor and Christian Lund to be identified as the authors of the
editorial material in this work has been asserted in accordance with the UK Copyright,
Designs and Patents Act 1988.

Wiley also publishes its books in a variety of electronic formats. Some content that
appears in print may not be available in electronic books.

Designations used by companies to distinguish their products are often claimed as
trademarks. All brand names and product names used in this book are trade names, service
marks, trademarks or registered trademarks of their respective owners. The publisher is
not associated with any product or vendor mentioned in this book. This publication is
designed to provide accurate and authoritative information in regard to the subject matter
covered. It is sold on the understanding that the publisher is not engaged in rendering
professional services. If professional advice or other expert assistance is required, the
services of a competent professional should be sought.

Library of Congress Cataloging-in-Publication Data

The politics of possession : property, authority and access to natural resources / edited by
Thomas Sikor and Christian Lund.
    p. cm. – (Development and change book series)
  "Originally published as Volume 40, Issue 1 of Development and Change."
  Includes bibliographical references and index.
  ISBN 978-1-4051-9656-7 (hbk. : alk. paper)

1. Natural resources–Political aspects. 2. Right of property. I. Sikor, Thomas.
II. Lund, Christian.
HC85.P65 2009
333.3–dc22

                            2009036497

A catalogue record for this book is available from the British Library.

Set in 10pt Times by Aptara
Printed and bound in Malaysia by Vivar Printing Sdn Bhd

01   2009

Contents

Notes on Contributors

Sara Berry is Professor of History at Johns Hopkins University, Baltimore, Maryland, USA, specializing in twentieth-century African social and economic history and development studies, with particular emphasis on West Africa.

Rikke B. Broegaard is a project researcher at the Danish Institute for International Studies, Copenhagen, Denmark, with a PhD in International Development Studies from Roskilde University. Her current research interests include inequality and access to natural resources, land tenure security and land markets.

Stefan Dorondel holds a PhD from Humboldt University, Berlin. He is a researcher at the Francisc I. Rainer Institute of Anthropology, Bucharest, Romania.

David Lorenzo is a PhD candidate at Roskilde University, Denmark. He has conducted research in Mexico and Peru on communal land tenure institutions. His PhD research in Andean communities focuses on a variety of topics that shed light on processes of territorialization in stateless places.

Christian Lund is Professor in International Development Studies at Roskilde University, Denmark. His most recent works include Local Politics and the Dynamics of Property in Africa (CUP, 2008) and Twilight Institutions: Public Authority and Local Politics in Africa (Blackwell, 2007).

Monique Nuijten is Associate Professor at Wageningen University. She is author of the book Power, Community and the State: The Political Anthropology of Organisation in Mexico (Pluto Press, 2003), editor of the book Corruption and the Secret of Law: A Legal Anthropological Perspective (Ashgate, 2007) and author of numerous articles on communal land tenure and state-peasant relations.

Nancy Lee Peluso is Professor and Chair of the Division of Society and Environment, Department of Environmental Science, Policy, and Management, University of California at Berkeley, USA. Her research is on forest and agrarian politics in Java and West Kalimantan, Indonesia, focusing on property, resource access and political ecology.

Jesse C. Ribot is an Associate Professor of Geography at the University of Illinois, Urbana-Champaign, Illinois, USA. He was previously a Senior Associate at the World Resources Institute in Washington, DC. He conducts research on decentralization; resource tenure and access; natural resource commodity chains; and household vulnerability in the face of climate and environmental change.

Dik Roth is a social anthropologist and Assistant Professor in the Law and Governance Group of Wageningen University, Wageningen, The Netherlands. Among his research interests are socio-legal studies and anthropology of law, natural resources governance and management, and development policy. He has published, among others, on the politics of regional autonomy in Indonesia, the role of legal complexity in land and water rights, and flood policy in The Netherlands.

Thomas Sikor is Reader in Development Studies at the University of East Anglia, Norwich, UK. His research examines resource property, governance and institutions with a geographical interest in post-socialist countries, including empirical studies in Albania, Romania and Vietnam.

Johannes Stahl is a Ciriacy-Wantrup Postdoctoral Fellow in the Department of Environmental Science, Policy and Management, University of California at Berkeley, USA. His research focuses on human-environmental relations in post-socialist Central and Eastern Europe.

Access and Property: A Question of Power and Authority

Thomas Sikor and Christian Lund

INTRODUCTION: THE ARGUMENT

As larger political economic forces transform rural resources of material or cultural value, access to these resources is often contested and rife with conflict at many levels simultaneously. In societies characterized by normative and legal pluralism such as post-colonial and post-socialist countries, this is particularly evident. The central dynamic is created by people's attempts to secure rights to natural resources by having their access claims recognized as legitimate property by a politico-legal institution. The process of recognition of claims as property simultaneously works to imbue the institution that provides such recognition with the recognition of its authority to do so. This is the 'contract' that links property and authority. Property is only property if socially legitimate institutions sanction it, and politico-legal institutions are only effectively legitimized if their interpretation of social norms (in this case property rights) is heeded (Lund, 2002). The process of seeking authorization for property claims also works to authorize the authorizers and, at the same time, institutions underpinning various claims of access — hence catering for particular constituencies — undermine rival claims to the same resources.

Nevertheless, property is part of a larger picture of access to resources, whether legally recognized or not. While not all forms of access to resources or their benefits are guaranteed by a politico-legal institution, they may still constitute an important element in people's livelihoods. Indeed, the 'grey zone' between what people have rights to and what they merely have access to is terrain worth exploring. In parallel to this, politico-legal authority is only part of a larger picture of power, whether legitimate or not. Not all forms of power to decide who gets access to what resources and benefits, and on what terms, are legitimized with equal effect. Nonetheless, powerful groups and institutional coalitions may still exercise what are essentially political decisions about people's access to resources and benefits. This second 'grey zone' between authority and power — that is, successfully and

The chapters in this volume originate from a researcher training workshop jointly organized by the Junior Research Group on Postsocialist Land Relations, Humboldt University Berlin, and the Graduate School of International Development Studies, Roskilde University, in late 2006. Funding for the workshop was provided by Deutsche Forschungsgemeinschaft and Roskilde University. We thank Sara Berry, Anne Larson and three anonymous reviewers for their constructive comments on this introductory essay. This essay has also benefited from very stimulating discussions with the workshop participants and contributors to this volume.

less-successfully legitimized decisions about how resources are distributed in society — is equally worth investigating. These two sets of relationships, their interconnections and recursive constitution form the object of this chapter.

Two issues are therefore simultaneously at stake: struggles over property are as much about the scope and constitution of authority as about access to resources. To investigate how competition for society's vital resources is organized and structured is to investigate not only how wealth is distributed and how classes of 'haves' and 'have-nots' are made; it is equally to investigate how polities emerge, consolidate and recede through processes of legitimization, inclusion, exclusion and violence. The social, political and institutional landscape is amorphous at close inspection, however (Cleaver, 2002; Douglas, 1986). Nuijten uses a very suggestive conceptualization of a force field to refer to a wider set of diverse powers: 'In a force field certain forms of dominance, contention and resistance may develop, as well as certain regularities and forms of ordering. In this view, the patterning of organizing practices is not the result of a common understanding or normative agreement, but the forces at play within the field' (Nuijten, 2003: 12). Our argument is that within such a force field, organizing practices that concern the distribution of resources are particularly interesting.

This introduction and the chapters that follow in this collection venture to make a particular incision into the recursive constitution of property and institutional authority. By investigating both successful and failed processes of legitimation of access as property, and processes of legitimation of power as authority, we develop a novel interpretation of the distinction between access and property. We argue that issues of access and property are joined to questions of power and authority. People attempt to consolidate their claims to land and other resources in various ways, often in pursuit of turning their access to resources into recognized property. In our argument we bring together two perspectives on resource use that often remain separated, and which have produced two strands in the literature — one on broader access–power relations (such as Berry, 1993; Ribot and Peluso, 2003) and another on the narrower property–authority relations (including Lund, 2002, 2007). In the process, we hope to clear up some of the dynamics generating the ambiguity of property observed in post-colonial and post-socialist settings (cf. Berry, 1993; Verdery, 1996).

Moreover, by investigating how institutional authority and property rights are recursively constituted, we are also investigating governance and state formation processes. The political dynamics of property are the processes whereby rights over land and other natural resources are settled and contested. They are fundamental to how authority is established and challenged among competing politico-legal institutions, thereby allowing the study of property dynamics to facilitate special insights into everyday processes of state formation. The institutional contestants' pursuit of control over natural resources involves them, unavoidably, in the competition for authority, its consolidation, reconfiguration and erosion. This is not necessarily done with the intention of state formation at the local level; it is done to check and overcome their competitors and benefit from the advantages of power. The result is nonetheless, in part, institutional (see Lund, 2008: 3; Tilly, 1985). Recent years have seen the emergence of a rich literature on state formation in post-colonial contexts.[1] Characteristic of this — admittedly very diverse — work is an interest in the almost forensic analysis of political processes that make up state, legitimacy and authority. The key word is process.

This introductory essay seeks to position our argument in relation to the literature and the contributions to this volume. Considering the wealth of research in the two fields, the discussion of the literature is necessarily somewhat eclectic and may appear overly simplistic at times. Yet we intend to sketch out the contours of the larger, theoretical argument pursued in the chapters that follow. The essay begins by discussing the difference between access and property and subsequently looks at legitimacy and legitimizing practices. We then proceed to establish the mutually-constitutive character of property and authority, as legitimacy travels back and forth between the two. As a next step, we look into the dynamics of power and authority to examine the role of property in the making and unmaking of authority. We then return to our interest in the dynamics of access and property, on the one hand, and power and authority, on the other, identifying territoriality as a particularly interesting notion and examining the use of violence in institutions' legitimizing practices. We finish with syntheses of the chapters in this volume, relating them to the discussion in this introductory essay, and some brief concluding remarks.

PROPERTY AND ACCESS: A PARTIAL OVERLAP

Most simply put, property is about relationships among social actors with regard to objects of value (von Benda-Beckmann et al., 2006). Property relations involve different kinds of social actors, including individuals and collectivities. The actors are linked to each other in social relationships, and property takes the form of 'enforceable claim[s] to some use or benefit of something' (MacPherson, 1978: 3). Property relations exist at the level of laws and regulations, cultural norms and social values, actual social relationships, and property practices. Property is therefore legitimized claims, in the sense that the state or some other form of politico-legal authority sanctions them.

---

1. The list is long, but includes Boone (2003); Comaroff and Comaroff (1999); Corbridge et al. (2005); Das and Poole (2004); Gupta and Ferguson (1997); Hansen and Stepputat (2001, 2005); Lund (2007); Migdal (2001); Nuijten (2003); Sivaramakrishnan (1999); Steinmetz (1999); Sturgeon (2005).

Property relations in post-colonial and post-socialist settings are often ambiguous. In post-colonial contexts, property regimes are negotiable and fluid to some degree because of the multiplicity of institutions competing to sanction and validate (competing) claims in attempts to gain authority for themselves (von Benda-Beckmann and von Benda-Beckmann, 1999; Berry, 1993, 2002; Juul and Lund, 2002; Moore, 1998; Shipton and Goheen, 1992). This frequently provides scope for accumulation for the powerful (Peters, 2004). Post-socialist property relations are often equally equivocal as social actors struggle over the very categories and relationships constituting property (Sturgeon and Sikor, 2004; Verdery, 1999).

The utility of property as an analytical lens has been challenged as too narrow by recent emphasis on the multiple mechanisms that open up, influence, hinder and close down access to resources. Property is not the only way by which social actors are able to benefit from resources. Access, by contrast, is broader and includes property. Law or other social norms do not sanction and encompass all forms of possession: it is equally important that social actors gain and maintain access to resources in many ways that do not amount to property (Leach et al., 1999; Ribot and Peluso, 2003). A variety of access mechanisms condition people's access to resources and benefits. In addition to property, these include technology, capital, markets, labour, knowledge, identities and social relations (Ribot and Peluso, 2003: 159–60). The difference between access and property implies that social actors may derive benefits from resources without holding property rights to them. For example, they may derive benefits from an agricultural field — by way of occupation or market exchange — even though they do not hold any rights to the land. It is important, therefore, to 'understand *why* some people or institutions benefit from resources, *whether or not* they have institutionally recognized rights to them' (Ribot and Peluso, 2003: 154; emphases in the original). Access is thus different from property, as access is about 'the ability to benefit from things' (Ribot and Peluso, 2003: 153), making it more encompassing than property, which refers to legitimate social relationships only.

Ribot (1998) provides an illustrative example of the many ways by which social actors enjoy access to resources. He investigates the distribution of benefits along a charcoal commodity chain in Senegal from extraction in the Tambacounda region, through processing, transport, and trade to final use in Dakar. On the way to the capital city, the charcoal passes through the hands of various actors, including villagers, migrant woodcutters, merchants, transporters, urban wholesalers, retail vendors and outlet owners. They are all able to benefit from the charcoal commodity chain, yet they derive their respective benefits in different arenas and by way of different mechanisms. Villagers, for example, enjoy customary property rights to forests, even though Senegal's forests are legally owned by the state and managed by the Forest Service. In contrast, migrant woodcutters derive benefits from charcoal not through direct rights to the forests but by seeking employment with charcoal merchants. They gain these labour opportunities by way of a shared social identity and social ties with the merchants, the stigma attached to the work, and specialized technical skills. Merchants, in turn, reap a significant share of overall benefits, due to their control over labour opportunities and marketing. They work through 'social ties with other merchants, distributors, retailers and state agents, and through credit, misinformation, licenses, quotas and circulation permits' (Ribot, 1998: 328). This analysis demonstrates that multiple mechanisms influence the distribution of benefits from natural resources among social actors. Property is only one of them, in addition to product markets, the institutions governing capital flows, technology, and so forth.

Correspondingly, formal property rights do not necessarily imply that the social actors holding them are able to derive material benefits from the natural resources to which those rights apply. This is very apparent, for example, in local dynamics associated with forest devolution in Vietnam's Central Highlands (Sikor and Nguyen, 2007). Here, the forest department decided to grant villagers use rights to local forests in an effort to improve forest protection and raise living standards. The department and the villagers settled on a relatively egalitarian distribution of property rights among the households belonging to indigenous ethnic groups. Nevertheless, the actual material benefits derived by local households displayed significant variation three years after devolution. The fields that the households had been able to clear in the forests varied in size and harvests, reflecting the influence of differences in the households' labour capacity and wealth. Similarly, households extracted different quantities of poles from the forests, and these differences were due to yet other access mechanisms. Better-off households extracted more poles because they owned the required machinery (chainsaws and tractors), were able to hire additional labour, and simply needed larger quantities of poles in their pepper plantations. Despite the devolution of forest management, access to the forest thus depended on a variety of access mechanisms in addition to property rights. For families who did not benefit from such mechanisms, 'property rights' remained effectively vacuous claims.

This situation is not uncommon; people may hold property rights to some resources without having the capacity to derive any material benefit from them. Cousins (1997) argues that people lack 'real' rights if such rights are promised in law but denied in practice. Verdery (2003) observes a lack of 'effective ownership' by Romanian villagers who find themselves unable to benefit from their land rights. This is exactly what the distinction between property and access is about: property is about claims which are considered legitimate, and access is about the 'ability to benefit'. It demonstrates that property and access overlap partially: property rights may or may not translate into 'ability to benefit'; and access may or may not come about as a consequence of property rights. But 'ineffective' ownership or property rights are distinct from no rights at all, even if they do not translate into ability to benefit. While rights may have no value at a certain point in time, the fact that they are somehow enshrined in legislation or recognized by some politico-legal institution may come in handy if circumstances change. Then it may actually be of great benefit to be able to refer to (historical) rights when vindicating claims (see Lund, 2008; Moore, 1992).

Thus, different processes may be at work simultaneously, leading to variations in social actors' property rights and access. The processes constituting property may be different from those leading to variation in access. Property relations may reflect the influence of a set of laws and norms lending legitimacy to claims on resources. Access, in turn, may be constituted by a different set of processes conditioned by a broader range of social institutions. As a result, property and access may be distributed among social actors in different ways. Going a step further, competition over access can in many ways be seen as the forerunner of property contestations where people try to secure their possession with recognition from a politico-legal institution. This calls for research into the economic, political and discursive practices that actors undertake in a terrain of competing claims when they seek legitimacy for their own (see Broegaard, this volume). Moreover, it suggests the need to investigate the processes whereby property is made and solidified or challenged and, possibly, undone, directing our attention to social practices employed by actors and institutions seeking to legitimize their actions.

LEGITIMACY AND LEGITIMIZING PRACTICES

Legitimization by a politico-legal authority emerges as the distinguishing factor between access and property. Obviously, legitimacy is not a fixed and finite substance: it is a result of processes of legitimization, some with distinct authorship, others as reproduction of mores; some successful, others less so. The point is that competing actors and competing institutions operate to legitimize different forms of possession as property. Hence, different, competing legitimacies are at play in situations of legal and institutional pluralism. The exercise of authority is intimately linked to claims of legitimacy of the particular institution. This often involves a general, historically-based claim as well as a specific claim to legitimacy. Institutions tend to argue or justify their legitimacy in relation to the concrete exercise of authority. But institutions do not embody intrinsic legitimacy; their legitimacy must be actively established.

This notion of legitimacy draws on work by both Moore (1988) and Lentz (1998), who argue that it is not useful to see legitimacy as a fixed, absolute quality against which actual conduct can be measured. It is more fruitful to investigate the processes through which various actors and institutions attempt to legitimize actions and vindications (Fortmann, 1995; Rocheleau and Ross, 1995). What is legitimate varies between and within cultures and over time, and is continuously (re-)established through conflict and negotiation.

This notion of legitimacy also connects us with broader work on legitimizing practices, or 'grounded practices of sovereignty' (Moore, 2005). An important element in this process has to do with social conceptualization; that is, how concepts and 'truths' are established (cf. Agrawal, 2005; Ferguson and Gupta, 2002; Foucault, 1980; Li, 2007). These broader conceptualizations indicate to us that concepts and ideas about property and access are not merely the tools of the analysts. People and institutions actively employ and interpret concepts in their attempts to enact different political projects and interests. Concepts and ideas of different origin thereby enter local arenas and become 'idiomatized'. They are not merely instruments of analysis but are also their object. Thus, in addition to competition over land claims and claims to authority, conflicts also engender an ongoing (re)definition of the very concepts of property we might otherwise tend to see as fixed (Shipton and Goheen, 1992; Verdery, 2003).

It is quite clear that what is considered legitimate property is historically contingent. Although arguments often involve reference to precedent and the past, the right moment for pressing a particular claim depends on the contemporary political constellation of institutions that can recognize claims as valid. What constitutes a good claim at one moment may be less viable at another and may not resonate with what is generally or politically accepted. Similarly, what is perceived as legal or as illegal may change over time without any change in legislation. Government policies, statements and practices can effectively outlaw certain legal practices and nullify established rights. Government may thus effectively turn private property into public land, and the inventive opportunism of farmers may secure them private rights to public infrastructure, contrary to the legislation in place (see Lund, 2008 and this volume).

Local resource politics displays many instances in which the meaning of key terms such as public, private, government, legitimacy, ownership, etc. are effectively questioned. When policy is resisted, embraced, or diverted, such concepts become central reference points in the political debate. They *appear* stable, but in the larger claims for a livelihood and a position in life, people struggle over the local, idiomatic meaning of these concepts. Rather than regretting the inadequacy of the terms in describing the real situation, it is important to see these ideal concepts as integral parts of the political struggle. When, for example, various forms of indigenous land tenure are being translated into one-dimensional ownership in such discussions and debates, it bespeaks a deliberate simplification of a complex composite tenure system. The chapters throughout this volume demonstrate the importance of having a command over the terminology and the process of categorization.

Legitimacy and legitimizing practices, therefore, emerge as a defining element of property. Yet we want to go a step further. We want to use the distinction between access and property as an entry point into the processes constituting authority. We want to ask why and how some actors benefit from resources by way of property and others do not. What practices and processes allow some actors to get their claims to resources recognized as property rights, while other actors gain and maintain access through other mechanisms? More generally, what are the processes setting property apart from access?

PROPERTY AND AUTHORITY: A CONTRACT

As a first step, we propose to recognize that property not only sets up an economic relationship, in the sense that property relations influence the shares of social actors in benefit streams originating from resources; property relations are also political (MacPherson, 1978). In this sense, property rights have something in common with citizen rights as two fundamental aspects of social life: what we have and what we are — *avoir* and *être*. Property rights and citizen rights in their broadest form exist only to the extent that they are produced, endorsed and sanctioned by some form of legitimate authority (see the contributions by Berry, Nuijten and Lorenzo, and Peluso in this volume).

Property is intimately connected with authority, in the sense of legitimate (or rather successfully legitimized) power (Weber, 1976). In other words, authority refers to an instance of power that is associated with at least a minimum of voluntary compliance, making it likely 'that a command with a specific content will be obeyed by a given group of persons' (ibid.: 28). Authority characterizes the capacity of politico-legal institutions, such as states and their constituent institutions, village communities, religious groupings and other organizations, to influence other social actors. Authority thus relates to property because rights, privileges, duties, obligations, etc. require support by politico-legal authority (von Benda-Beckmann, 1995). Similarly, taxes and tributes are significant ways in which institutional recognition of people's claims to property is established and institutions are recognized by fiscal subjects. As authority grants or denies legitimacy to property claims, such claims are intimately bound up with the scope and constitution of authority. The two form a contract of mutual recognition. In situations of institutional pluralism so characteristic of post-colonial and post-socialist societies, however, political authority is not exclusively vested in the state, and moreover, the state is hardly a set of congruent institutions. This complicates the situation significantly, and many competing contracts are formed (Lund, 2006).

The intimate connection between property and authority becomes very apparent when authority relations are overlapping or change over time. For example, pre-colonial property rights in Java were largely determined by local communities connected to local kings in patronage relations (Peluso, 1992). Rural people acquired resources, such as land and trees, through their membership of a local community or, if they migrated, allocation by the local king. Under colonial rule beginning in the nineteenth century, the Dutch introduced a forest service that divided forest land from agricultural land and established a bureaucracy to manage forest land. Yet even then, there were multiple claimants to the forest: 'Local people, regional rulers, and entrepreneurs were engaged in a "layered" system of rights to control or use the forest and its products' (Peluso, 1992: 48). Over time, state control of the forest and forest land increased gradually, as laws eradicated the 'layered' system in 1870, and foresters planted teak in villages and restricted local access in the 1930s. With independence the Indonesian government simply took over the forest service, enforcing control over forest land in ways that were much more militarized and repressive than under Dutch rule. In response, forest-dependent villagers resisted state control either through everyday forms of resistance or outright violence. Yet they did not merely resist state control over labour, land and trees; they also countered the state's ideology of scientific forestry with moralities emphasizing subsistence needs and historical claims on forests. In this way, villagers asserted authority relations rooted in local communities that justified their own claims on forests and challenged the legitimacy of the state's claims (for a case in irrigation see also Roth, this volume).

In Africa there are many examples of how rights to resources have changed because of the changing status of the local authority which grants and guarantees rights. The waxing and waning of chieftaincy power in many societies have solidified or undermined property rights accordingly. Burkina Faso is an interesting example. The socialist-inspired revolution in 1983 did away with the chieftaincy as a political institution and all land was declared state property in 1984. This led to considerable uncertainty about who was entitled to what and with whose authority. Because of central government's limited capacity to conduct, or even oversee, land transactions, these continued in some places under the authority of chiefs, and in others under the auspices of the new local political elite as 'land authorities'. In fact, some members of the emerging elite established their roles by actually distributing land and overseeing land transactions. This way, control over land did not *represent* customary authority; it *produced* it. Current legislation remains basically the same as that of 1984; nonetheless, as the chieftaincy was gradually rehabilitated as a political institution during the 1990s, some chiefs worked to recover some of their control over land, while others who had control over land worked to become chiefs (Lund, 2002). The general resurgence of chieftaincy as an integrated element of the governance structure in Africa will, no doubt, have serious implications for property rights on the continent in future.

The preceding paragraphs demonstrate how property and authority are closely linked. Property relates to authority because property claims require support by politico-legal institutions in a position of authority. When authority relations overlap, social actors are likely to reference their property claims to various politico-legal institutions, making property relations appear

ambiguous to outsiders (Berry, 1993). Ambiguous authority, whatever the
reason, thus attaches itself to the rights themselves and renders them less
than clear. The ambiguity is compounded when social actors make claims
in settings characterized by more fluid relations of authority and power,
settings in which multiple politico-legal institutions compete over authority.
The ensuing dynamic fluidity is the subject of the following section.

DYNAMICS OF POWER AND AUTHORITY

When authority and power relations are contested, politico-legal institutions
tend to compete for authority. They not only struggle to acquire power to
influence others, by whatever means (Weber, 1976); they seek to turn power
into authority by gaining and sustaining legitimacy in the eyes of their
constituency. Simply put, claimants seek out socio-political institutions to
authorize their claims, and socio-political institutions look for claims to
authorize. The relationship is a dynamic one, as illustrated by Keebet von
Benda-Beckmann's notion of 'forum shopping' and 'shopping forums' (von
Benda-Beckmann, 1981). In the presence of competing forums for resolving
disputes, contestants tend to 'shop' for forums for dispute resolution, and
forums actively shop for disputes in an effort to consolidate their authority. Such competition can unfold in many different fields, such as citizen-
ship/belonging, personal security, development and property. Property is,
we would argue, one of the most important fields in which politico-legal
institutions seem persistently to compete for authority in post-colonial and
post-socialist societies (Berry, 2002; Lund, 2002, 2006; Verdery, 1996). The
institutions seek out property claims to authorize in their attempt to build and
solidify their legitimacy in relation to competitors. An institution's success
in this venture is hardly carved in stone, however; once-legitimate institutions may yield this space to other (new or old) institutions more adept at
legitimizing themselves, sometimes with consequences for the very forms
of property.

   In northern Ghana the divestiture of land from the government in 1979
stirred up a hornets' nest of questions about authority. Land was 'returned to
its original owners'. Legislators expected chiefs to re-establish themselves
as the customary authority in land matters as in the rest of Ghana, where
they have comprehensive customary authority in matters of land and law,
and chiefs saw land as an important domain through which to consolidate
their customary authority. Neither had factored in a possible re-emergence
of the earthpriests as ambitious customary authorities. The earthpriests did
not claim authority in general, but restricted themselves to questions of land.
The new legal situation provided an opportunity for reassessing the past,
resettling old accounts, reasserting 'belonging' in terms of prerogatives and
jurisdictions, and renegotiating ownership to land. Chiefs and earthpriests
intensified their competition over control of the land. The justification of

claims to authority was played out in different fashions and forms. In the town of Bolgatanga, earthpriests formed a union to better stand up to the chiefs, who were well organized historically and represented in local governance bodies such as the House of Chiefs. Lobbying with, among others, the Lands Commission over the right to issue land leases and with the Electoral Commission over administrative boundaries, and fighting cases in the High Court over compensation for loss of property, chiefs and earthpriests were struggling to assert their authority to handle land matters. One interesting feature of this process is that not only did chiefs and earthpriests operate as institutions (or 'forums') to grant, sanction and guarantee the property claims of ordinary land users, they themselves shopped around for opportunities to prove their capacity as authorities. Moreover, these aspiring authorities also sought out the endorsement of their claim to authority with other institutions (in particular government institutions) such as the Land Commission, the Electoral Commission, and the High Court (Lund, 2008).

Shifts in authority may even have effects on the form of property in question, as illustrated by Katherine Verdery's writings on post-socialist Romania (see also Sikor et al., this volume). Just as in Ghana, land was returned to its historical owners after 1990, with land restitution seen as a key project for the Romanian state to re-establish its authority on the foundation of a capitalist economy and western-style democracy. Property rights served as signifiers of the break with socialism, new political rights and participation in the economy. In addition, land restitution was crucial in reorganizing the relations between central and local units of the Romanian state. Land restitution, implemented by local land commissions, was one of the primary tasks to be undertaken by local-level institutions within a broader process of decentralization. Yet this also meant that the authority of the Romanian state, in general, and local-level institutions, in particular, was at stake in the course of land restitution. It was no surprise, then, that reports abounded in Romanian newspapers of local cases of corruption in the land restitution process. Central units of the state and other central-level actors were uneasy with the new powers enjoyed by local-level actors and contested their authority by questioning the legitimacy of their dealings (Verdery, 1996). At the same time, local-level state actors weakened the legitimacy of the Romanian state in the eyes of the local population through their corrupt practices. The actions of the mayor of a Transylvanian village discussed in Verdery (2002) impacted not only on the practice of restitution but also on the authority of the Romanian state, when he took advantage of restitution to extract bribes from claimants and carve out favours for his relatives and friends. Similarly, when villagers protested the privatization of a granary they had built under socialism, they resisted the notion of private property embedded in the legislation. They asserted a collective claim to the locally important granary on the basis of the labour they had invested in building it, countering the principles set out in national law to govern the privatization of socialist assets. Their claim even gained the support of a local judge, whose ruling emphasized morality and the question of what constitutes the 'public good' against the procedures specified in national legislation (Verdery, 1999).

As highlighted by Verdery's account, 'the state' is often a key politico-legal institution seeking to establish, consolidate and expand its authority by way of shopping for property claims. 'The state' may be a very important player even where property claims are hotly contested and actual power relations diffuse, as highlighted by Nuijten's research on issues of private and communal property in Mexico (Nuijten, 2003). According to Mexican law, land belonged to the *ejidatarios* (communal property owners), but it was effectively controlled by several private land owners. Nuijten examines the efforts undertaken by the *ejidatarios* to recover land that belonged to their *ejido*. The land conflict had lingered on for decades without resolution, in spite of numerous requests made by the *ejidatarios* to the Ministry of Agrarian Reform to resolve the conflict. Nevertheless, the *ejidatarios* went on fighting for the recovery of the land despite their general distrust of the political system and administrative bureaucracy. Nuijten explains the *ejidatarios'* continuing struggles with their belief in the existence of 'the state' as an imagined centre of control, which could help them to recover the 'lost land'. Their belief in 'the idea of the state' was nurtured by a series of intermediaries who pretended to have privileged relations with state officials and knowledge of state procedures. These brokers presented themselves to the *ejidatarios* as capable of dealing with the state bureaucracy and helping them to recover the 'lost land'. The belief in the idea of the state — and the search for its real-world personification — even made the *ejidatarios* write to the Mexican president with a plea for support. Nuijten concludes that 'the *ejidatarios* are implicated in the process of the construction of the idea of the state' (2003: 118). On the other hand, their belief in the idea of the state was fostered by certain techniques of government, such as maps, documents and procedures. More broadly, one may add, their belief was rooted in the promise of the Mexican state to enforce property rights, which allegedly offered them backing for their claims to the 'lost land'. Property — or to be precise, the 'idea of property' — thus served to consolidate the authority of the Mexican state, and the competition between the *ejidatarios* and the private landowners over how to involve the state as an umpire had consequences for the nature of property.

Property, therefore, may be equivocal in settings characterized by uncertain relations of authority and power. Ambiguous authority attaches itself to property and renders it less than clear. Property relations may be highly uncertain when power relations are diffuse and evident concentrations of authority are absent. In such situations, property relations may not have 'crystallized into practices of exclusion and inclusion within routinized rules' (Verdery, 1999: 55). The underlying diffusion of power and authority prevent this (cf. Sturgeon and Sikor, 2004). This stands in contrast to conventional theories on property rights, particularly the more evolutionary approaches, which argue that as land becomes more valuable, narrower definitions of property emerge and clearer rights ensue (Demsetz, 1967; see also Firmin Sellers, 1996, 2000; Platteau, 1996). While scarcity may indeed promote exclusivity, evidence from the present collection would suggest that where there are many institutions competing for the right to authorize claims to land, the result of an effort to unify and clarify the law might well be to intensify competition amongst them and weaken their legitimacy. Thus, the 'meantime' in evolutionary theory (from an imagined situation with no property rights to an equally imagined situation with perfectly unequivocal rights) seems to characterize all societies (Rose, 1994). Nevertheless, property also attaches itself to authority in the sense that successfully defended property imbues the politico-legal institution with authority. Guaranteeing property claims offers some rewards for institutions with ambitions of authority, but this is a competitive game and does not work by mere administrative *fiat*.

TERRITORIALITY AND VIOLENCE

Guaranteeing property rights for some people logically means denying the same guarantee to others. As we have argued, such processes do not take place in a political vacuum: on the contrary, enforcing certain decisions about property is often met with resistance from those whose rights are eroded in the process. Understanding the processes of guaranteeing and denying property as opposed to access by other means, therefore, requires research on the political and discursive strategies operated by different politico-legal institutions. In other words, if one wants to understand how access claims become property it is necessary to examine the processes whereby authority is formed, strengthened, challenged and unravelled by way of authorizing property rights. Institutions will generally seek to legitimize their exercise of power with reference to law, or custom, precedence, or propriety, or administrative expediency. They thus seek to turn power into authority by authorizing particular property claims and by way of other strategies such as the extension of citizenship.

Institutions undertake a wide variety of activities to legitimize their authority. However, since we are concerned here with property regarding land and other natural resources, the notion of territoriality deserves particular attention. The control of spatial ordering and the control of people in space combine different techniques and policies of classification, registration and mapping (Sack, 1983; see also Walker and Peters, 2001). This not only structures the physical space, it also organizes the political perception of it. Territorializing strategies allow and disallow certain forms of land use and access; they regulate certain forms of mobility; and by differentiating rights to resources they contribute to the structuration of citizenship. The strategies may take the form of internal territorialization when pursued by states to establish control over natural resources and the people that use them (Vandergeest and Peluso, 1995). Following Sivaramakrishnan (1997) and Agrawal (1998), we think this evocative idea might be pushed further. It is not merely states in the form of unitary government structures that employ territorializing strategies. We suggest that generally politico-legal institutions that compete for authority in this field operate to legitimize their undertakings partly through territorial strategies. In fact, territoriality is often a key element in the exercise of authority (Lund, 2006: 693–5). By making and enforcing boundaries, by creating a turf, a quarter, a parish, a soke, a homeland etc., different socio-political institutions invoke a territorial dimension to their claim of authority and jurisdiction whereby even institutions that are not the state or do not represent formal government claim this particular attribute of governance. Territorial markers ranging from national flags through sign-boards, fences, party banners, masks and marches to graffiti on walls — or rubber trees (see Peluso, this volume) — pepper space and render it political. These markers create sometimes contiguous, but more often overlapping and frequently contradictory spaces with different structuring effects on access and property.

However, the repertoire is wide when institutions operate to enforce particular claims and hence particular ideas about property, and it does not exclude the use of physical force. Indeed, force, violence, physical presence, eviction, land grabbing, resistance, attrition, and so on, are at the base or origin of most property regimes. Violence is often an integral or underlying feature in struggles over property, sometimes preparing the ground for new legitimizing practices. Violence, force and deception are powerful instruments in establishing 'settled facts' on the ground (Peluso and Watts, 2001), and fear and risk may be as common motives for compliance as belief in power's legitimacy. Thus, when institutions attempt to sanction claims or undo rights they do not necessarily restrict themselves to peaceful means, thereby exercising their power in ways which can be considered illegitimate. Our proposition is that regardless of the origin of access and power, there is an inherent drive to legitimize the exercise of power; to launder power as authority, as it were. But there is no reason to expect that the quest for legitimacy is conducted by legitimate means alone, especially if one recognizes that what may be illegitimate to some may be seen as legitimate by others.

E.P. Thompson's classic study on the Black Act and the transformation of the forest property system in nineteenth century England shows how violence went hand in hand with legislation and the legitimation of new rights. New laws and draconian penal measures displaced common people's historical use of forest resources from the realm of tolerated customary access to the realm of illegal poaching and infringement as resources were privatized. Brute force exercised by state agents with reference to law and authority

from the courts and government, and attacks carried out by commoners —
'blacks' — with reference to customary rights and the unjust nature of new
property laws marred society with violence and terror (Thompson, 1975).

The more contemporary case of conflict over land and oil revenues in
Ogoniland in Nigeria, analysed by Watts (2001), is another case in point.
The federal government and the petroleum companies argued that oil is
the property of the state and its exploitation was granted to the companies
through concession. Opposition to this reading of the property regime from
the Movement of the Survival of the Ogoni People was met with extreme
violence from the military. Violent intimidation of the inhabitants and their
spokespersons has been intense since the early 1990s. Controversy over how
best to voice the interests of the Ogoni community — their property claims
vis-à-vis the state and the oil companies — has also resulted in violence between Ogoni and neighbouring communities as well as internecine violence
amongst the Ogonis themselves. This example is complicated — though not
uncommon — in the sense that state institutions operated both as stakeholders claiming property rights *vis-à-vis* the local people *and* as the authorizing
institutions deciding on the issue. The opportunities for rent seeking by state
officials under such circumstances are gigantic, and the instrumentalization
of state power to secure property to the powerful is classical.

A final brief example is the violent evictions of smallholders from the communal areas in Vumba, Zimbabwe in the late 1990s, analysed by Hammar
(2002). The evictions actually concerned many more than those for whom
the government had managed to produce summons and eviction orders.
Again, the violence could be seen as the state's exercise of means of last
resort — hence it was legitimate action from the perspective of some. From
the perspective of others, however, the state's resort to legal procedures was
a cover for massive evictions and a ploy to instil fear in anybody who might
have contemplated opposition. The more recent violent seizures of large
farms by 'war veterans' in Zimbabwe would appear also to be condoned by
government and its supporters, although they have little basis in law (see also
Peluso, this volume). We put these examples forward because they demonstrate the double nature of violence and law. While government institutions
may resort to violence as an ultimate means of power, such violence is not
necessarily legitimized successfully in the eyes of all subjects. There are
many examples of violence considered illegitimate; even if efforts to justify
state violence claim the opposite. Also, violence may well be exercised by
other groups in concert or collusion with government agents, or in opposition to them. As argued above, it makes little sense for us to determine what
is legitimate and what is illegitimate violence in absolute terms; our analytical interest lies with how politico-legal institutions may employ violent
means in their quest for legitimacy. The occurrence of violence does not
diminish the need to look at institutions' quest for legitimacy if one wants
to understand the dynamics of property.

THE CONTRIBUTIONS TO THIS VOLUME

The contributions to this volume demonstrate the validity of thinking in terms of access and property, on the one hand, and power and authority, on the other. Moreover, they indicate how property and access to natural resources are intimately bound up with the exercise of power and authority. At the same time, each contribution emphasizes a slightly different aspect of the conjoined processes of authorizing property claims and legitimizing politico-legal institutions.

Sara Berry examines how negotiations over property rights to land intersect with those of social belonging, and how both types of negotiations are part of broader processes constituting authority at local and national levels. Looking at competing land claims in West African localities, she compares case histories of land acquisition and use, connecting local competition over land with national-level politics in Ghana, Côte d'Ivoire and Benin. Land claims, she finds, have been linked historically to claims on authority and social belonging at the local level. At the same time, local contestations over land, social belonging and authority have resonated with claims to citizenship and electoral politics at the national level. As a result, recent neoliberal efforts to privatize land or clarify ownership have intensified debates over citizenship and authority across West Africa, provoking rather than alleviating political conflict.

The intersection of negotiations over property with social identities is also a key theme in Nancy Peluso's analysis of landscape dynamics in West Kalimantan, Indonesia. Peluso examines how the Indonesian state has shaped contestations over property rights to land and the construction of ethnic identities. The Indonesian state emerging from her analysis is much more powerful than the West African states in Berry's account. The colonial state effectively shaped ethnic identities, thereby producing not only Dayak and Chinese but also 'racialized territorialities', that is, territorialities associated with and productive of ethnic identities. Years later, the independent state employs violence to effectively erase prior identity-based claims of the Chinese and to establish the control of new actors over trees, land and legitimate access or rightfulness. Peluso thus makes the important point that violence plays a significant role in eliminating earlier rights, levelling the ground for establishing a new set of property rights and associated legitimations.

Monique Nuijten and David Lorenzo look at the 'performance of authority' in a Peruvian *comunidad campesina*. Their analysis of land administration in the *comunidad* reveals how control over land is enacted and helps to constitute local authority relations. Both leaders and regular members display strong concern with the rules governing the registration and reallocation of agricultural land. The enactment of the rules in the yearly reallocation procedure constitutes a key pillar of the authority attributed to the *comunidad campesina*. There is a glaring gap between the rules that people rehearse in meetings and actual practice in land reallocation and administration. This observation leads Nuijten and Lorenzo to conclude that talk about rules, or 'rule talk', plays an important role in the performance of authority in the *comunidad*, highlighting the significance of legitimizing practices in the constitution of authority.

Jesse Ribot's contribution shares the focus on practices legitimizing authority with Nuijten and Lorenzo. Ribot analyses struggles over authority between two different units of the state in relation to competing claims on forests in rural Senegal. Local people and merchants compete with each other over the distribution of benefits derived from the wood cut in local forests for the production of charcoal, seeking authorization for their claims from the Forest Service and Rural Councils. Decentralization has shifted statutory control over forests from the former to the latter, ostensibly giving the elected councils significant powers. Yet decentralization has not conferred effective control over forest to local governments, as the Forest Service continues to control the exploitation of forests and urban-based merchants maintain their lucrative access to forests. Ribot concludes that local governments are unlikely to gain legitimacy in the eyes of the population as long as they cannot effectively back up their constituents' claims to forest resources.

Christian Lund examines how land resources have been recategorized between the two 'master categories' of public and private in the course of political struggle in northern Ghana. Despite the fact that such master categories may be wholly inadequate in accounting for the actual complexity of property objects, social units and rights, people with something at stake use them actively and bring them into effect. Laws, rules and by-laws are referred to as important markers and fashion the local political struggles over the rights to and control over resources. Lund offers a general account of conflicts and the recategorization of resources in the property system of small-scale irrigation. Here, the logics of the different stakeholders and their positioning is examined, and how different levels of public policy have provided opportunities for such changes is discussed. The chapter also examines the details of a particular controversy demonstrating the social and political powers involved in the recategorization of property.

Rikke Broegaard shifts the analytical lens away from the primary focus on authority in the previous chapters towards the process of authorizing claims to resources as property. Her account of a land registration and land titling programme in rural Nicaragua examines how social actors are differently positioned to gain state endorsement of their land claims as property rights. Land registration and titling do not benefit all people equally; less fortunate households do not register land, and it is mainly the more powerful who obtain land titles. People's ability to get their claims to land recognized depends on their capacity to call upon the state officials involved. Of particular significance are 'local kings' — powerful state officials who take advantage of their position to issue titles to their affiliates in direct contradiction with the law. The local kings also use their leverage on land administration to acquire land titles for themselves. Like Berry, Broegaard thus finds that neoliberal programmes seeking to privatize land or clarify land ownership may aggravate contestations over authority and cause political conflicts.

Thomas Sikor, Johannes Stahl and Stefan Dorondel also focus on local negotiations over access and property. Like Broegaard, they look at negotiations taking place in the context of large-scale land reform programmes, in this case post-socialist land reforms in Albania and Romania. In addition, they examine how local struggles over forests in four localities are conditioned by and feed into national-level politics. There are distinct differences between the Albanian and Romanian cases, particularly in the ways in which local struggles shape the authority attributed to the state. These differences reflect the influence of national politics on local struggles and simultaneously indicate how post-socialist politics have come to follow different trajectories in the two countries. The emergence of customary arrangements challenges the Albanian state as the primary politico-legal institution of authority. In Romania, contestations over authority do not challenge the state as an institution but pitch more personalized forms of exercising authority against those that are more closely governed by law.

Dik Roth finally returns to the primary concern with contestations over authority which are found in the contributions of Nuijten and Lorenzo and Ribot. Roth examines contestations over authority between two kinds of irrigation institutions in a migrant society in Sulawesi, Indonesia. One institution, the water users' association, was established and backed by the Indonesian state. The other institution, the 'traditional' *subak*, was introduced by Balinese migrants. Each institution defines the bundles of rights and responsibilities pertaining to management in a different way, and hence endorses a different set of land and water management norms, rules and practices. The differences cause direct conflict between local state representatives and Balinese irrigators over the scope and degree of legitimacy attributed to these institutions. Yet they also lead irrigators to adjust the rules of both institutions in order to reduce conflict, in the process transforming both the water users' association and the *subak* into completely unique and localized institutions.

BY WAY OF CONCLUSION

Property and access are not predefined categories, but distinctions between property and access are linked to the formation, consolidation, expansion, contestation, contraction and decline of authority. In this essay we have sketched out a complex of relationships between access and property and between power and authority in order to suggest the importance of making the distinctions, identifying the connections and recognizing the recursive constitutions between them. Struggles over property are as much about the scope and constitution of authority as they are about access to resources. Similarly, contestations over authority deal as much with the nature and distribution of property as with issues of power.

The relationships between access and property and between power and authority are dynamic. While individuals and institutions may harbour ambitions of a particular development from access to consolidated property, and from power to legitimate authority, we propose that this is an inherently empirical question. The actual trajectory rarely confirms a simple, predictable evolutionary direction. Just as many people struggle to turn access claims into legitimate property, many are stripped of property rights to their possessions when the institutions that guaranteed them are weakened. Similarly, just as competing institutions attempt to shore up legitimacy for their power, that legitimacy may well be undermined by circumstances in the wider fabric of society beyond their control. Institutional opportunities and strategies are almost as plentiful as historical circumstances, but we suggest that in the attempt to understand the relations between struggles over natural resources, contestations about authority and state formation, attention to legitimizing strategies will be rewarded.

We finally argue that it is useful to think in terms of the concepts of access and property on the one hand and power and authority on the other for another important reason: they offer an analytical perspective on the politics and governance of resources where categories do not define our focus. Rather, attention to the recursive constitution of access and property on the one hand and power and authority on the other help to make the socio-political processes of *categorization* the object of investigation (see Lund, this volume). The grey zones between access and property and power and authority are exactly where categorization takes place. This categorization is, we argue, part of a state formation process made up by competing institutions' quest for authority in different significant domains.

REFERENCES

Agrawal, A. (1998) *Greener Pastures: Politics, Market, and Community among a Migrant Pastoral People*. Durham, NC and London: Duke University Press.

Agrawal, A. (2005) *Environmentality: Technologies of Government and the Making of Subjects*. Durham, NC and London: Duke University Press.

von Benda-Beckmann, F. (1995) 'Anthropological Approaches to Property Law and Economics', *European Journal of Law and Economics* 2: 309–36.

von Benda-Beckmann, F. and K. von Benda-Beckmann (1999) 'A Functional Analysis of Property Rights, with Special Reference to Indonesia', in T. van Meijl and F. von Benda-Beckmann (eds) *Property Rights and Economic Development: Land and Natural Resources in Southeast Asia and Oceania*, pp. 15–56. London and New York: Kegan Paul International.

von Benda-Beckmann, F., K. von Benda-Beckmann and M. Wiber (2006) 'The Properties of Property', in F. von Benda-Beckmann, K. von Benda-Beckmann and M. Wiber (eds) *Changing Properties of Property*, pp. 1–39. New York: Berghahn.

von Benda-Beckmann, K. (1981) 'Forum Shopping and Shopping Forums: Dispute Processing in a Minangkabau Village in West Sumatra', *Journal of Legal Pluralism* 19: 117–59.

Berry, S. (1993) *No Condition is Permanent: The Social Dynamics of Agrarian Change in Sub-Saharan Africa*. Madison, WI: University of Wisconsin Press.

Berry, S. (2002) 'Debating the Land Question in Africa', *Comparative Studies in Society and History* 44(4): 636–68.

Boone, C. (2003) *Political Topographies of the African State: Territorial Authority and Institutional Choice*. New York: Cambridge University Press.

Cleaver, F. (2002) 'Reinventing Institutions: Bricolage and the Social Embeddedness of Natural Resource Management', *European Journal of Development Research* 14(2): 11–30.

Comaroff, J.L. and J. Comaroff (eds) (1999) *Civil Society and the Political Imagination in Africa*. Chicago, IL: University of Chicago Press.

Corbridge, S., M. Srivastava and R. Veron (2005) *Seeing the State: Governance and Governmentality in India*. Cambridge: Cambridge University Press.

Cousins, B. (1997) 'How Do Rights Become Real? Formal and Informal Institutions in South Africa's Land Reform', *IDS Bulletin* 28(4): 59–68.

Das, V. and D. Poole (eds) (2004) *Anthropology at the Margins of the State*. Santa Fe, NM: School of American Research Press.

Demsetz, H. (1967) 'Toward a Theory of Property Rights', *American Economic Review* 57(2): 347–59.

Douglas, M. (1986) *How Institutions Think*. Syracuse, NY: Syracuse University Press.

Ferguson, J. and A. Gupta (2002) 'Spatializing States: Toward an Ethnography of Neoliberal Governmentality', *American Ethnologist* 29(4): 981–1002.

Firmin-Sellers, K. (1996) *The Transformation of Property Rights in the Gold Coast*. Cambridge: Cambridge University Press.

Firmin-Sellers, K. (2000) 'Custom, Capitalism, and the State: The Origins of Insecure Land Tenure in West Africa', *Journal of Theoretical and Institutional Economics* 156: 513–30.

Fortmann, L. (1995) 'Talking Claims: Discursive Strategies in Contesting Property', *World Development* 23(6): 1053–63.

Foucault, M. (1980) 'Truth and Power', in C. Gordon (ed.) *Power/Knowledge*, pp. 109–33. New York and London: Harvester Wheatsheaf.

Gupta, A. and J. Ferguson (eds) (1997) *Culture, Power, Place: Explorations in Critical Anthropology*. Durham, NC: Duke University Press.

Hammar, A. (2002) 'The Articulation of the Modes of Belonging: Competing Land Claims in Zimbabwe's Northwest', in K. Juul and C. Lund (eds) *Negotiating Property in Africa*, pp. 211–46. Portsmouth, NH: Heinemann.

Hansen, T.B. and F. Stepputat (eds) (2001) *States of Imagination: Ethnographic Explorations of the Postcolonial State*. Durham, NC: Duke University Press.

Hansen, T.B. and F. Stepputat (eds) (2005) *Sovereign Bodies: Citizens, Migrants and States in the Postcolonial World*. Princeton, NJ and Oxford: Princeton University Press.

Juul, K. and C. Lund (eds) (2002) *Negotiating Property in Africa*. Portsmouth, NH: Heinemann.

Leach, M., R. Mearns and I. Scoones (1999) 'Environmental Entitlements: Dynamics and Institutions in Community-Based Natural Resource Management', *World Development* 27(2): 225–47.

Lentz, C. (1998) 'The Chief, the Mine Captain and the Politician: Legitimating Power in Northern Ghana', *Africa* 68(1): 46–65.

Li, T.M. (2007) *The Will to Improve: Governmentality, Development, and the Practice of Politics*. Durham, NC: Duke University Press.

Lund, C. (2002) 'Negotiating Property Institutions: On the Symbiosis of Property and Authority in Africa', in K. Juul and C. Lund (eds) *Negotiating Property in Africa*, pp. 11–43. Portsmouth, NH: Heinemann.

Lund, C. (2006) 'Twilight Institutions. Public Authority and Local Politics in Africa', *Development and Change* 37(4): 685–705.

Lund, C. (ed.) (2007) *Twilight Institutions: Public Authority and Local Politics in Africa*. Oxford: Blackwell.

Lund, C. (2008) *Local Politics and the Dynamics of Property in Africa*. Cambridge and New York: Cambridge University Press.

MacPherson, C.B. (1978) 'Introduction', in C.B. MacPherson (ed.) *Property: Mainstream and Critical Positions*, pp. 1–13. Toronto: University of Toronto Press.

Migdal, J. (2001) *State in Society: Studying How States and Societies Transform and Constitute One Another*. Cambridge: Cambridge University Press.

Moore, D. (2005) *Suffering for Territory: Race, Place, and Power in Zimbabwe*. Durham, NC and London: Duke University Press.

Moore, S.F. (1988) 'Legitimation as a Process: The Expansion of Government and Party in Tanzania', in R. Cohen and J.D. Toland (eds) *State Formation and Political Legitimacy*, pp. 155–72. New Brunswick, NJ: Transaction Books.

Moore, S.F. (1992) 'Treating Law as Knowledge. Telling Colonial Officers What To Say to Africans about Running "Their Own" Native Courts', *Law & Society Review* 26(1): 11–46.

Moore, S.F. (1998) 'Changing African Land Tenure Reflections on the Incapacities of the State', *European Journal of Development Research* 10(2): 33–49.

Nuijten, M. (2003) *Power, Community and the State: The Political Anthropology of Organisation in Mexico*. London and Sterling, VA: Pluto Press.

Peluso, N. (1992) *Rich Forests, Poor People: Resource Control and Resistance in Java*. Berkeley, CA: University of California Press.

Peluso, N. and M. Watts (2001) 'Violent Environments', in N. Peluso and M. Watts (eds) *Violent Environments*, pp. 3–38. Ithaca, NY and London: Cornell University Press.

Peters, P. (2004) 'Inequality and Social Conflict over Land in Africa', *Journal of Agrarian Change* 4(3): 269–314.

Platteau, J.-P. (1996) 'The Evolutionary Theory of Land Rights as Applied to Sub-Saharan Africa: A Critical Assessment', *Development and Change* 27(1): 29–86.

Ribot, J. (1998) 'Theorizing Access: Forest Profits along Senegal's Charcoal Commodity Chain', *Development and Change* 29(2): 307–41.

Ribot, J. and N. Peluso (2003) 'A Theory of Access', *Rural Sociology* 68(2): 153–81.

Rocheleau, D. and L. Ross (1995) 'Trees as Tools, Trees as Text: Struggles over Resources in Zambrana-Chacuey, Dominican Republic', *Antipode* 27(4): 407–28.

Rose, C. (1994) *Property and Persuasion: Essays on the History, Theory, and Rhetoric of Ownership*. Boulder, CO: Westview Press.

Sack, R.D. (1983) *Human Territoriality: Its Theory and History*. Cambridge: Cambridge University Press.

Shipton, P. and M. Goheen (1992) 'Understanding African Land-Holding: Power, Wealth, and Meaning', *Africa* 62(3): 307–25.

Sikor, T. and Q.T. Nguyen (2007) 'Why May Forest Devolution Not Benefit the Rural Poor? Forest Entitlements in Vietnam's Central Highlands', *World Development* 35(11): 2010–25.

Sivaramakrishnan, K. (1997) 'A Limited Forest Conservancy in Southwest Bengal, 1864–1912', *Journal of Asian Studies* 56(1): 75–112.

Sivaramakrishnan, K. (1999) *Modern Forests: Statemaking and Environmental Change in Colonial Eastern India*. Stanford, CA: Stanford University Press.

Steinmetz, G. (ed.) (1999) *State/Culture: State Formation after the Cultural Turn*. Ithaca, NY: Cornell University Press.

Sturgeon, J. (2005) *Border Landscapes: The Politics of Akha Land Use in China and Thailand*. Seattle, WA and London: University of Washington Press.

Sturgeon, J. and T. Sikor (2004) 'Post-Socialist Property in Asia and Europe: Variations on "Fuzziness"', *Conservation and Society* 2(1): 1–17.

Thompson, E.P. (1975) *Whigs and Hunters*. New York: Pantheon Books.

Tilly, C. (1985) 'War Making and State Making as Organized Crime', in P. Evans, D. Rueschemeyer and T. Skocpol (eds) *Bringing the State Back In*, pp. 169–91. Cambridge: Cambridge University Press.

Vandergeest, P. and N. Peluso (1995) 'Territorialization and State Power in Thailand', *Theory and Society* 24: 385–426.

Verdery, K. (1996) *What Was Socialism? And What Comes Next?* Princeton, NJ: Princeton University Press.

Verdery, K. (1999) 'Fuzzy Property: Rights, Power, and Identity in Transylvania's Decollectivization', in M. Burawoy and K. Verdery (eds) *Uncertain Transition: Ethnographies of Change in the Postsocialist World*, pp. 53–81. Lanham, MD: Rowman & Littlefield.

Verdery, K. (2002) 'Seeing Like a Mayor. Or, How Local Officials Obstructed Romanian Land Restitution', *Ethnography* 3(1): 5–33.

Verdery, K. (2003) *The Vanishing Hectare: Property and Value in Postsocialist Transylvania.* Ithaca, NY: Cornell University Press.

Walker, P.A. and P. Peters (2001) 'Maps, Metaphors and Meanings: Boundary Struggles and Village Forest Use on Private and State Land in Malawi', *Society and Natural Resources* 14: 411–24.

Watts, M. (2001) 'Petro-Violence: Community, Extraction, and Political Ecology of a Mythic Commodity', in N. Peluso and M. Watts (eds) *Violent Environments*, pp. 189–213. Ithaca, NY and London: Cornell University Press.

Weber, M. (1976) [1922] *Wirtschaft und Gesellschaft: Grundriss der Verstehenden Soziologie (Economy and Society: An Outline of Interpretive Sociology).* Tübingen: J.C.B. Mohr.

2

Property, Authority and Citizenship: Land Claims, Politics and the Dynamics of Social Division in West Africa

Sara Berry

INTRODUCTION

Claims on land have multiplied across West Africa in recent years, pushing up land values, crowding court dockets with land litigation cases and giving rise to frequent altercations, some of them violent, among rival claimants to particular pieces of land. Impelled by population growth, urban expansion and increased use of land for a variety of commercial and productive purposes, rising land values have themselves become a source of further increases in demand for land as a form of speculative investment or insurance against future contingencies. Heightened by fears of potential displacement, rising competition over land has given rise to intense contestation, as people challenge one another's claims, or find that land they had acquired or used in the past has been reallocated or sold without their knowledge by others seeking to take advantage of the expanding market. In recent years, these pressures have been further intensified by legal and administrative initiatives designed to clarify and strengthen property rights in the name of efficient land allocation and use.

Competition over land probably owes less to simple population growth than to the sometimes massive relocations of people that took place under colonial rule and after independence, as people sought out new economic opportunities or fled from war, environmental degradation, state oppression and/or economic decline. In the decades since independence, West Africa has been transformed from an overwhelmingly rural region to one that is likely to become predominantly urban in the near future. Between 1960 and 1990, the number of people living in towns (>5,000 population) rose from 13 to 40 per cent of the region's population, and has been projected to exceed 60 per cent by 2020 (Snrech, 1998: 133). While these figures do not include estimates of rural–rural or urban–rural movements, the case studies discussed below indicate that these too have a long history in the social life of the region, both within and across national boundaries.[1] As

An earlier version of this chapter was prepared for the workshop on 'Property and Access to Resources: Fuzzy Concepts? Fuzzy Realities?', International Development Studies, Roskilde University, September 2006.

1. Among the eleven member countries of the Economic Community of West African States (ECOWAS), international migration rose from 2.5 to 6.8 million between 1960 and 2000,

urban incomes fell during the 1980s following the imposition of austerity
measures under structural adjustment (World Bank, 1986), many newly
impoverished urbanites returned to the countryside, adding to pressures on
rural land (de Bruijn et al., 2001).

Land conflicts reflect more than economic and demographic pressures,
however. In post-colonial societies of West Africa, land is also seen as a
form of political space — territory to be controlled both for its economic
value and as a source of leverage over other people.[2] States exercise power,
in part, through the control of territory, setting conditions for entry into areas under their jurisdiction and regulating conduct within their boundaries.
Local actors — families, village authorities, chiefs, NGOs, and so on —
may emulate these practices, challenging or disrupting state control over
local loyalties and resources, or seeking to enhance their own visibility and
influence in regional or national political arenas (Sikor and Lund, this volume; Juul, 2006; Le Meur, 2006b). Dissident or insurgent groups may seize
territory as a means of challenging state power — ousting ruling regimes,
forcing concessions, or negotiating for access to state resources and/or increased political participation[3] — while economic and political pressures
raise the stakes in acquiring and defending claims to land, intensifying efforts to establish the validity of both proprietary and territorial claims and
heightening fears of dispossession and exclusion for those who fail to do so.

Seeking to convince authorizing officials that their claims to land are as
good or better than anyone else's, many people have turned to the past,
basing claims to land on narratives of origin or ancestry that are difficult, if
not impossible, to refute. Declaring that 'we were here first' implies that 'our'
claims cannot be gainsaid because no-one was there to witness our arrival. In
1994, I listened as a well-educated Ghanaian civil servant explained, without
apparent irony, that his ancestors had descended from the sky to settle on the
land that he and his family hold today (Berry, 2001: 152). Fantastic on the
surface, his story also demonstrated a clear understanding of contemporary
political realities. By denying that his ancestors had travelled from any other
terrestrial site to reach his present location, he implied that no-one, including
the chief, could call him or any member of his family a 'stranger'. In Ghana,
as we shall see, such a claim goes to the heart of contemporary debates over
property, authority and belonging.

As this anecdote suggests, the recent upsurge in claims to land based on
ancestry, origin, or 'custom' has as much to do with politics as with access

and West Africa was home to 42 per cent of all international migrants living on the continent
(Ammassari, 2004). As of 2004, an estimated 3.2 million Africans had fled from their home
countries as refugees, and an additional 12 to 13 million were internally displaced within
their own countries (Black, 2004: 6).

2. For another approach to this issue in a different context, see Peluso (this volume).
3. My thinking on these issues owes a great deal to Bettina Ng'weno's study of property
    relations and territorial claims and conflicts in Colombia (Ng'weno, 2007). I am, of course,
    solely responsible for the arguments expressed in this chapter.

to economic resources. In the decades since independence it has become abundantly clear that, rather than establish clear parameters for self-rule, state institutions and constitutional arrangements that were hastily assembled in anticipation of independence marked the beginning of prolonged struggles over how West Africans would govern themselves in the aftermath of colonial rule. As newly independent regimes moved to eliminate political opposition, or were overthrown by their own armies, the European-style parliamentary institutions left behind by departing colonial officials soon gave way to military or single-party regimes. Consolidating power in the hands of small ruling elites, state leaders enriched themselves from the public treasury and used the coercive powers of the state to put down protests and suppress dissent. Ambitious post-independence plans for economic development foundered on the combined realities of Africa's weak position in global markets, and African leaders' preoccupation with staying in power rather than investing in the public interest.

By the 1980s, economic decline and mounting indebtedness pushed most West African governments to agree to restructure their economies in exchange for foreign loans. State budgets were cut, markets deregulated, public services privatized and state-owned enterprises and assets transferred to private hands. The ensuing sharp contractions in income and employment, public services and state capacity worked widespread hardship on ordinary people, especially in the cities, while ruling elites found ways to evade cutbacks in their own salaries and perquisites, or took control of formerly state-held assets in their capacity as private citizens. By the late 1980s, international financial institutions and donor governments admitted that cutbacks in state capacity were impeding their own efforts at economic restructuring, and concluded that governments as well as markets would have to be restructured. Facing internal as well as foreign pressures for political reform, most states agreed to hold multi-party elections.

As party competition re-emerged and elections took place, some regimes managed to retain their hold on power, at least temporarily; others stepped or were forced aside. Regardless of electoral outcome, however, the reinstitution of multi-party political competition reopened debates over criteria of eligibility for political participation and social entitlement that had been suppressed, or dictated by the state, under authoritarian rule. Just as fears of dispossession intensified in the increasingly active land markets of West Africa's deregulated economies, so newly competitive electoral contests stoked fears of disenfranchisement, as rival candidates and citizens alike re-examined the question of who was eligible to stand for office and/or vote. Like claims to land, competing claims to citizenship frequently turned on questions of historical precedent, giving rise to debates over descent, cultural heritage and territorial origin that both reinforced the salience of these categories as sources of social and political entitlement, and challenged efforts to clarify their significance for contemporary claims to property and authority (see Sikor and Lund, this volume). In the following pages, I present

examples from three West African countries that illustrate the interconnect-
edness of property, authority and citizenship in both local and national-level
struggles over land and power, and raise questions about the implications of
West African experience for the conceptual underpinnings of the neoliberal
paradigm.

DISAPPEARING FRONTIERS: STRUGGLES OVER LAND
AND CITIZENSHIP IN SEVERAL RURAL LOCALITIES

Since the early years of colonial rule, West Africans have brought increasing amounts of land under cultivation, often moving into un- or sparsely
inhabited areas in the process. Migrant farmers pioneered the development
of cocoa growing in semi-humid coastal forests; planted groundnuts and
cotton, for domestic use as well as export, in interior savannas; and played
a major role in expanding production of foodstuffs to feed growing urban
populations across the region.[4] In many areas, local residents welcomed
new arrivals, seeing them as prospective labourers, producers, followers
and/or allies. As more people arrived and land became scarce, however,
later arrivals were greeted more warily, often turning to one another rather
than to members of their host communities for political leadership and social
support. To illustrate the kinds of changes in land and labour relations, local
power structures, and social alliances and divisions that have accompanied
increasing pressure on land, I discuss three localities in which immigration
and agricultural expansion led to the closure of former social and territorial
'frontiers'. I begin by comparing histories of migration, forest clearance, and
growing tension over land and social belonging in the former cocoa frontiers
of southwestern Ghana and Côte d'Ivoire; then look briefly at the savanna
frontiers of central Bénin where migrants coming from different directions
arrived at various times between 1940 and the 1990s, planting annual crops
that varied according to changes in local consumption patterns and market
conditions within and beyond the local area. Settled more gradually than
the cocoa producing areas, as incoming settlers crossed paths with local migrants departing to or returning from Ghana, Côte d'Ivoire and/or Nigeria,
these districts did not begin to experience significant land shortages until the
late 1990s.[5]

---

4. Noteworthy contributions to the large literature on migration and agricultural growth include: Baier (1980); Bassett (2001); Copans (1982); Guyer (1987, 1997); Hill (1963);
   Netting (1968); Swindell (1985); and sources cited below. Watts (1983) and others have
   argued that farmers were sometimes forced, by economic pressure and/or state coercion,
   to substitute export for food crop cultivation, resulting in food shortages that were often
   hardest on the cultivators.
5. In all three cases, I have drawn primarily on studies by other scholars for evidence on
   local histories of migration, farming, frontier development and closure, and accompanying
   transformations in relations of property, authority and social difference. My own field
   research in Ghana was carried out primarily in rural areas of Asante Region where, by the

As world markets recovered and shipping became available for commercial traffic after the end of World War II, migrants streamed into southwestern Ghana and Côte d'Ivoire to establish new cocoa farms on rich virgin forest soils. In both cases, immigrants obtained permission to plant tree crops from local residents, who showed them where to farm; then proceeded to clear forest growth and plant cocoa and food crops, extending their farms in stages until they had used up their initial allotments. When uncultivated land was no longer available in the vicinity of the first farm(s), many migrants moved on, establishing additional farms in as yet undeveloped portions of the forest zone. As long as there were new areas to develop, land shortages and declining yields in older cocoa growing areas were offset by the opening up of new ones, resulting in patterns of aggregate growth that masked cyclical downturns in output from ageing trees (Ruf, 1995). By the 1980s, land scarcity combined with falling world prices, brought on by new supplies from southeast Asia, helped push both countries into debt and forced governments to adopt structural adjustment programmes in order to qualify for debt rescheduling and loans from the IMF and the World Bank.

Although the overall process of agricultural expansion, frontier closure and economic decline followed similar trajectories in both Ghana and Côte d'Ivoire, relations between migrant farmers and their forest hosts developed differently on the two cocoa frontiers. In Ghana, migrants obtained farming rights from local chiefs, whose authority over land had been formally institutionalized under colonial rule, and who used their authority to extract substantial amounts of rent from 'stranger' farmers (Arhin, 1986: 24ff; Boni, 2006: 176–7). As supplies of virgin forest land dwindled, chiefs not only demanded larger payments,[6] but also expanded the category of 'stranger' to include descendants of 'immigrants' who had settled in the southwestern forests long before the process of cocoa expansion began (Boni, 2006: 172ff). Since protests were likely to end up in the chief's court, migrants' ability to resist these demands was limited, unless they were prepared to abandon their farms.

---

late 1940s, local cocoa output was declining and residents were leaving to establish new farms in Brong-Ahafo and the southwest. Sources for the case studies discussed here are cited below.

6. During the first phase of expanding cocoa production in southeastern Ghana in the early decades of the twentieth century, colonial officials accepted the claim that chiefs' customary right to a share of anything valuable 'found' on their stool lands applied to cocoa grown by 'strangers' but not by 'subjects' of the stool. Chiefs were, however, allowed to raise levies from their subjects to cover unusual stool expenses — an interpretation of custom that led to frequent protests from beleaguered stool subjects, and demands, sometimes endorsed by colonial officials, that chiefs be removed from office. See, for example, Berry (2001: esp. Ch. 2). No longer able to assess levies on local 'citizens', in recent years chiefs have taken advantage of rising land prices to sell off land formerly farmed by local families 'to make way for development', such as commercial farms, timber or mineral concessions, or construction. See Amanor (1999: 68–78); Berry (2001: 114–23); Ubink (2008), among others.

In Côte d'Ivoire, the balance of power between hosts and migrants tipped the other way. Before the arrival of migrant cocoa growers, most residents of the southwestern forests lived in small, dispersed settlements, without chiefs or other institutionalized forms of local authority. In most cases, immigrant farmers obtained permission to farm from individual residents or household heads, who not only did not ask for payment, but provided drinks or a chicken for the customary ceremony to welcome the new arrivals and ratify their acceptance into the local community. Viewed as clients rather than tenants, migrants did not pay rent, but 'thanked' their hosts (or *tuteurs*) with occasional gifts of produce, contributions to hosts' family ceremonies, or assistance (loans or help with farm work) in times of need. Rhetorically, these contributions were depicted as spontaneous expressions of migrants' 'gratitude', and *tuteurs* were expected to reciprocate, as needed, out of mutual affection and concern. As time passed and migrants came to outnumber and out-produce their hosts, the fiction of their social dependence and subordination diverged further and further from reality (Chauveau, 2006: 226ff). In contrast to southwestern Ghana, where migrant farmers were exploited by local authorities, in southwestern Côte d'Ivoire, local farmers felt exploited by immigrants whose tree farms put them in effective control of much of the land.

On the savanna frontiers of central Bénin, changes in cropping patterns and immigrant–host relations were more diversified than those that transformed the forest frontiers of southwestern Ghana and Côte d'Ivoire. From the 1940s to the early 1970s, small groups of farmers from Atacora, Bénin's poorest region in the northwest, moved into Savè and Ouessè, growing tobacco and castor oil as well as food crops on land granted to them by local lineages. Beginning in the 1960s, they were joined by Idacha moving northward to settle on the sparsely populated frontiers of northern Zou Province, and later, by Fon travelling by way of Togo from their crowded homelands near Abomey (Edja, 1997: 8–9; 1999; Le Meur et al., 1999: 34–5). Both groups of migrants grew yam and groundnuts for sale as well as local consumption. In some areas, they crossed paths with local residents who had emigrated in the 1950s and 1960s to work on cocoa farms in Ghana and Côte d'Ivoire, or to Nigeria during the oil boom of the 1970s, and were returning to invest in farming and trade in their home communities (Le Meur and Adjinacou, 1998: 125–6). As cotton prices rose in the 1990s, Mahi farmers who had left their home region in central Zou in the 1960s and 1970s to seek opportunities in Nigeria and elsewhere returned to Savè to join Bénin's rapidly expanding cotton export boom. Reminding local residents of their history in the region, some now 'reclaimed' land from immigrants who had arrived during their absence, displacing the latter from lands they had farmed for thirty or forty years (Edja, 1997, 1999).

Control over land in Savè and Ouessé varied from one locality to another. In Savè, land was controlled by lineage or family heads rather than chiefs — an arrangement that is common throughout the Yoruba-speaking regions of southern Bénin and southwestern Nigeria. Royal lineages (who provide candidates and choose successors to the *oba* or king) control their own lands but, unlike Akan chiefs in Ghana and southeastern Côte d'Ivoire, neither the king nor the heads of royal lineages exercise any authority over land held by non-royal lineages (Edja, 1997; Le Meur, 1999, 2002). Early Idacha immigrants established new farming villages and later served as brokers, negotiating with Sabe lineages on behalf of subsequent arrivals, in their capacity as village heads (*bales*) (Le Meur, 2002: 139; Le Meur et al., 1999: 45). Fon immigrants who arrived in the 1980s tended to bypass the *bales*, preferring to negotiate directly with local lineage elders for access to land. In contrast to the forest frontiers of southwestern Ghana and Côte d'Ivoire, where the rapid spread of cocoa growing led to marked social differentiation between migrants and hosts, the ethnically and agriculturally diversified history of migrant farming in central Bénin gave rise to varied, multidirectional shifts in patterns of authority over land, contributing to a proliferation of political actors and informally governing institutions that accelerated under structural adjustment and the return to electoral competition in the 1990s. While differences between migrants and hosts figured prominently as a discursive resource in changing circumstances, they were neither effectively co-opted by chiefs to legitimize their authority, nor collapsed into opposing categories of ethnicized antagonism.[7]

WHO IS A 'STRANGER'?

In all three of the frontier areas described above, 'strangers' were treated differently from 'locals' in terms of access to land. As new immigrants arrived and more land was brought under cultivation, the terms of access changed, but differential treatment of host and migrant populations continued. Rising demand for land and increased production for the market commercialized land transactions and intensified local debates over where to draw the line between 'locals' and 'strangers'. In Ghana, chiefs' authority over land is both proprietary and territorial. Strangers obtained farming rights from a chief or chiefs who claimed jurisdiction over the land in question,[8] making an initial payment for the right to plant and annual payments out of the proceeds of

---

7. Working in collaboration with Thomas Bierschenk and Jean-Paul Olivier de Sardan, Edja, Le Meur, Adjinacou and other Béninese and European scholars have produced a rich corpus of empirical and analytical research on transformations in local governance in post-colonial Bénin. See Bierschenk and Olivier de Sardan (1998); Bierschenk et al. (2000); and numerous papers and reports published separately by participating authors. I am particularly grateful to Pierre-Yves Le Meur for helpful comments on an earlier version of this chapter.
8. Legally, land is 'vested' in traditional offices ('stools' and 'skins') rather than owned outright by their occupants, but in practice it is often hard to tell the difference. Codified under colonial rule, this principle has been ratified in successive constitutions since independence. Article 267(1) of the 1992 Constitution states that 'all stool lands shall vest in

the farm once their cocoa began to yield. A Ghanaian chief is more than a landlord, however. Following independence, chiefs were stripped of the administrative and judicial roles formally assigned to them under colonial rule, and ordinary men and women became 'citizens' of Ghana rather than 'subjects' of the stool to which they had formerly owed allegiance. Colonially sanctioned distinctions between 'subjects' and 'strangers' remained in effect, however, *de facto* if not *de jure*, in part because government continues to recognize 'customary' laws that allow chiefs to collect land rent from 'strangers', but not from members of the local community over which they exercise jurisdiction.[9]

Derived from colonial law and governing practice, the line between locals and strangers in Ghana is fundamentally a political one, drawn on the basis of the historical relationship between an individual's family (matrilineal descent group in Akan communities) and the stool in question and, like all matters of historical interpretation, subject to debate (Berry, 2001: 18–20, 150ff). Articulated through a 'constant and strategic process of forging one's ancestry and its deeds rather than the "true" reconstruction of one's genealogical tree' (Boni, 2006: 170), personal status and access to land remain linked to chiefly jurisdiction in Ghana, whether or not there is any basis for this in contemporary law. Before the colonial era, chiefs exercised authority over people separately from their authority over land. A person did not need to reside or work on stool land in order to be considered a 'subject' of the stool in question, nor did 'strangers' owe allegiance to the stool on whose land they happened to reside. To facilitate the incorporation of 'loyal' chiefs into the apparatus of colonial rule, officials sought to link chiefs' administrative and judicial responsibilities to territorially bounded jurisdictions. Excluded from any formal governing role after independence, chiefs have parlayed their constitutionally recognized authority over stool lands into a level of influence in both local and regional governance that is all the more real because it is entirely informal. No longer 'subject' to traditional rulers, Ghanaians refer to themselves as 'citizens' of Ghana *and* of the local communities to which they belong by virtue of their ancestors' past relations to the presiding stool — a discursive practice that effectively mirrors the incorporation of legally incorporeal 'traditional authority' into the *realpolitik* of contemporary governance.[10]

---

the appropriate stools on behalf of, and in trust for the subjects of the stool in accordance with customary usage'.

9.   As explained in note 6 above. The history and contemporary status of chiefly authority in Ghana has attracted a great deal of scholarly attention. Noteworthy contributions to the literature include Arhin (2001); McCaskie (1995); Rathbone (1993, 2000). The role of chieftaincy in Ghanaian land tenure is discussed, inter alia, in Amanor (1999); Berry (2001); Kuba and Lentz (2006); Lund (2002, 2003).

10. But note that the term 'subject' made its way into the Constitution of 1992, Article 267(1). See note 8 above. Boni refers to stranger farmers' payments to Sefwi chiefs as 'taxes' rather

In contrast to Ghana, where categories of 'citizen' and 'stranger' are constructed in terms of historical precedent and 'customary' jurisdiction, in Côte d'Ivoire, hosts and migrants refer to one another in terms that reflect colonial era imaginaries of differences in the 'potential for "civilization" between ethnic groups' (Chauveau and Leonard, 1996: 179). Invented under colonial rule as a collective term for people living in west central Côte d'Ivoire, the ethnic label 'Bété' has come to be used as an ethonym for people 'indigenous' to the southwestern forests.[11] The cocoa pioneers who moved into west central Côte d'Ivoire in the late 1940s and 1950s came primarily from adjacent savanna areas to the north. Many of the earliest immigrants were Baulé — members of the same ethnic group as President Houphouët-Boigny and leading members of the ruling PDCI (Parti Démocratique de Côte d'Ivoire) (Akindès, 2004; Chauveau, 2006). Although subsequent arrivals spoke different languages and came from different regions in the Ivoirian north, forest residents often referred to them collectively as Jula. Long used in West Africa as a general referent for Mande-speaking Muslim traders, Jula took on ethnic connotations in Côte d'Ivoire under colonial rule, and has been used by southern Ivoirians as a generic label for their northern compatriots in the post-colonial era.

As cocoa production expanded, migrant farmers from northern Côte d'Ivoire were joined by a growing number of immigrant labourers from impoverished neighbouring countries in the Sahel. By the 1980s, over a million people from Burkina Faso were estimated to be living in Côte d'Ivoire — a number that dwarfs the labour force extracted from the 'labour reserves' of Upper Volta under colonial rule. Although they willingly accepted jobs as agricultural labourers in the cocoa farms of the southwest, Sahelian migrants aspired to farms of their own (Blion and Bredeloup, 1997: 715). By the 1980s, many had acquired small plots of land, interspersed among the farms of their erstwhile employers, where they planted food crops and some trees. As national economic conditions deteriorated in the 1980s and 1990s, men and women who had left their parents' cocoa farms to attend school and find jobs in the cities now found themselves unemployed

---

than 'rents', nicely capturing the ambiguous nature of chiefly jurisdiction in contemporary Ghana (Boni, 2006: 176–7; cf. Le Meur, 1999: 189; 2002: 142–3).

11. Dozon (1985, 1997, 2000). Anchored in ideas about differential economic and political capacities, colonial ethnic categories acquired racial overtones — a link that persisted under *houphouëtisme*, Houphouët-Boigny's philosophy of development which conflated his policy of maintaining an 'open door' to Côte d'Ivoire's economy with a belief that the Akan in general, and himself in particular, were innately destined to govern their fellow citizens (Akindès, 2004). The current president of Côte d'Ivoire, Laurent Gbagbo, heads the Front Populaire Ivoirien (FPI), which draws much of its popular support from peoples of the southwest. Outspokenly critical of *houphouëtisme*, Gbagbo became 'a rallying symbol of the Bété populations and a sizeable fringe of populations in the west who considered themselves to have been marginalized in the redistribution of the fruits of growth' under the PDCI (Akindès, 2004: 19).

and struggling to survive in the shrinking urban economy. Heeding the President's advice to 'return to the land', they arrived in their former villages only to discover that their elders had given out the uncultivated portions of their land, and were reluctant to reclaim them from 'clients' whose loans and gifts had become crucial to their own economic survival (Chauveau, 2006: 229–31). Obliged to take menial jobs in order to survive, urban returnees seethed at their perceived dispossession at the hands of 'northerners' — both Ivoirian and foreign-born — and the PDCI regime, whose Baulé leaders were suspected of favouring members of their own ethnic group.[12]

In the frontier areas of central Bénin, relations between hosts and strangers varied from one local area to another. Among each new group of migrants, early arrivals obtained permission to farm from local authorities — lineage heads, village chiefs, 'big men' — depending on the history of the particular locality involved. As more immigrants arrived, their predecessors emerged as a new category of local authority — serving as intermediaries for later arrivals from their own home areas, helping them find jobs, introducing them to local landholders, representing them in dealings with local authorities and, in some cases, allocating land directly to incoming migrants rather than leading them to Savè lineage elders to ask for permission to farm (Edja, 1997: 13).

The accumulation of migrants' requests for land led to shifts in patterns of authority within Savè lineages as well as among the migrants. During the middle decades of the century, migrants arriving from Atacora approached local *bales* (village heads) for permission to settle in their villages and farm nearby. After Kérékou launched his socialist revolution in 1972, 'customary' land claims were sidelined in favour of a uniform national policy that land belongs to whomever puts it to productive use,[13] and land disputes were discouraged, depriving *bales* and lineage elders of a major source of their

---

12. Houphouët-Boigny's own political philosophy rested on a 'legitimating myth' of Akan superiority derived from 'a pseudo-scientific colonial legacy ranking the races on the basis of the existence of the state, and the development of writing and of books' in which Mande peoples were at the top, Kru at the bottom and Akan in the middle (Akindès, 2004: 12). Under *houphouëtisme*, the Akan moved to the top, thanks to 'the self-serving rewriting of history during the period of decolonization and after independence by "an Akan group in the Ivoirian political class"' (ibid.: 12–13, quoting Memel-Fotê, 1999: 24). See also Chappell (1989) and Boone (2004).

13. A similar policy was adopted under President Houphouët-Boigny's avowedly capitalist regime in Côte d'Ivoire. Neither Kérékou nor Houphouët-Boigny attempted to write private land ownership into law. 'Fac[ing] discontent on the part of the customary authorities and the elites dependent on them, Houphouët-Boigny simply announced, in 1963, that "*la terre appartient à celui qui la met en valeur*" (the land belongs to those who develop it). This dictum assumed the force of law, although it completely contradicted the provisions of legislation inherited from the colonial period' (Chauveau, 2000: 105). In Bénin, the constitution (*loi fondamentale*) of 1977 'acknowledged . . . private collective and individual rights over land . . . but the state remained the official owner of the land' (Le Meur, 2002: 137).

authority. As the urban economy declined in the late 1980s, many urban dwellers moved back to the rural areas. Better educated than their rural relatives, and more conversant with state policies and the ways of NGOs, these *ressortissants* took an active interest in community and lineage affairs, joining local Development Associations and promoting public debate over land issues and development projects (Bierschenk et al., 2000; Brüntrup-Seidman et al., 2000; Edja, 1997, 2000; Le Meur et al., 1999).

As cotton production took off in the early 1990s, Savè lineage heads began to ask for money rather than gifts of produce from strangers who farmed on their land.[14] Constituting themselves as auxiliary land committees (*comités d'attribution de terres*) within their own lineages, *ressortissants* drew up land registers (*livres fonciers*) to keep track of their families' tenants, and bypassed village *bales* to negotiate directly with the 'big men' of migrant villages over land allocations to their followers. In a concession to long-established migrants, cash 'dues' were assessed only on land cleared and planted after 1990, and many migrants simply avoided paying them. Commercialization continued, however, as some lineages began to sell off portions of their land. In one village in Savè, 156 ha were sold between 1991 and 1994 — 54 ha to half a dozen immigrant farmers, and 102 ha to five *fonctionnaires d'Etat* (state officials) who lived and worked outside the village (Edja, 1997: 18).

The variety of actors taking part in land transactions, and the shifting divisions of authority among land-givers and land-receivers as well as between them, complicated relations between 'autochthones' and 'strangers' in east central Bénin, forestalling either the kind of polarized opposition that developed in southwestern Côte d'Ivoire, or the consolidation of chiefly authority and exploitation of strangers that took place in southwestern Ghana (Bako-Arifari and Le Meur, 2003). In Savè, Edja found that differential access to land was less pronounced between immigrant and local farmers than between farmers and *fonctionnaires*. In Ouessè, Le Meur and Adjinacou studied one village where tension between autochthones and strangers rose in the early 1990s, after village leaders imposed taxes on migrant farmers, but found that autochthonous residents were also divided by generational and religious differences, personal rivalries, and tensions over chiefly succession (Le Meur and Adjinacou, 1998; Le Meur, 2002: 142–3). While chiefs regained some of the influence they'd lost under Kérékou, their 'come-back

---

14. In 1995, most landholders in Savè collected a standard amount from each migrant farmer, regardless of the size of his/her farm, a practice long followed in Yoruba communities in Nigeria and Bénin. Known as *isakole,* these payments serve primarily to acknowledge local landholders' continued authority over land farmed by strangers, rather than as rent paid for the use of another's property (Edja, 1997: 12–13). As pressures on land increased in the 1990s, landholders in some villages were raising the amounts demanded and, in some cases, linking the amounts demanded to the sizes of migrants' farms (ibid.: 17; Le Meur, 2002: 140). On the history of *isakole* in western Nigeria, see Berry (1975); Francis (1984); Lloyd (1972); and Omotola (1983).

was not institutionalized... [C]hiefs received only potential space to manoeuvre and realise their strategies... [and] success... depended greatly on
the local context' (Le Meur, 1999: 199; also Bako-Arifari and Le Meur,
2003).

Portrayed as a shifting mosaic of fissures and alliances among migrants
(early vs. late arrivals, *bales* vs. other villagers, Fon vs. Idacha), rival
landowners, land buyers, intellectuals, and state officials,[15] the social landscape of the agricultural frontier in the 1990s had not coalesced around
shared antagonisms between autochthones on the one hand and strangers on
the other. In Ouessè, claims to authority over migrants have also figured in
power struggles between different groups of autochthones and among local
authorities (Le Meur, 2006b). Shaped by a 'complex articulation between
labour control, access to land and natural resources, and migration', Le Meur
argues, the occupation of the agricultural frontier was further complicated
by the *Projet de Gestion des Terroirs et Ressources Naturelles* (PGTRN,
originally PGRN) — a multi-faceted programme of rural development, land
reform and decentralization launched by the state, under pressure from international donors, in 1993. Carried out by a number of overlapping and
competing state and non-governmental agencies, the PGTRN aimed to de-
marcate and register both individual land holdings and community *terroirs*,
as part of a larger effort to strengthen rural productivity and sustainable
resource management. Both categories of spatial demarcation presumed a
uniformity of tenure and management arrangements that 'simply did not
exist' in the savannah frontiers of Ouessè and Savè, where the ongoing
history of in- and out-migration, individually-negotiated tenure arrangements and spatially-dispersed social networks and allegiances produced a
'polycentric political [and social] landscape' that eluded the process of villagization envisioned by the PGTRN. To date, decentralization has not been
implemented below the level of the commune (formerly sub-prefecture) (Le
Meur, 2006b: 896, and personal communication; see also Bassett et al.,
2007).

Whether class differences will take on ethnic connotations, or vice versa,
as land pressures increase remains to be seen. With a range of discursive
strategies to draw on, people's frames of reference shifted from one instance
to another. Faced with the loss of land sold by local lineage elders, local youth
joined migrant farmers in invoking 'custom' to argue that lineage lands could
be rented, but not sold (Le Meur et al., 1999: 43). In the 1990s, neither class
nor ethnic categories appeared to be particularly stable. In a telling (perhaps
inadvertent) example of their malleability, Edja summarizes his evidence
on land sales in Boubouh village in a table, labelling six migrant farmers
(*colons agricoles*) who bought 54 ha of land in the village as 'outsiders'

---

15. Officials were 'themselves split... between forestry officers following a conservationist
    policy and agricultural extensionists guided by a concern for development' (Le Meur,
    1999: 197–8).

(*allochtones*), while referring to five 'people from outside the village' — *personnes extérieures du hameau (fonctionnaires d'Etat, originaires ou non de la localité)* — who bought 102 ha as 'indigenes' (*autochtones*) (Edja, 1997: 18).

WHO PARTICIPATES, WHO DECIDES? POWER, TERRITORY AND MULTI-PARTY ELECTIONS

In all three of the cases discussed above, local histories of migration, land acquisition, agricultural growth, and social division and belonging coincided with national economic and political events that both impinged on and reflected changes taking place in the countryside. As Catherine Boone reminds us in her comparative study of the rural foundations of post-colonial state power, during the early years of independence, ruling regimes in Ghana and Côte d'Ivoire relied heavily on the cocoa producing sector for state revenue and foreign exchange. Although both regimes collected cocoa revenue through the marketing boards — state monopolies that controlled the sale of domestically grown cocoa on the world market — rather than directly from the farmers, they kept a close eye on economic and political developments in the cocoa-producing regions (Boone, 2003, 2004). In Bénin's *entrepôt* economy, on the other hand, transit trade in imported commodities was arguably more important than peasant agriculture as a source of revenue for the state.[16] In an effort to diversify and strengthen the tax base as well as the economy, Kérékou promoted cotton as an export crop, constructing a nationwide network of state-owned buying stations and cotton gins, and organizing cotton growers into village co-operatives (*groupements villageoises*, or GVs) to stimulate increased production and monitor the crop from field to final buyer (Igué, 1999: 154ff).[17] Between 1970 and 1990, cotton exports grew fourfold, from 36,000 tons to 146,000 tons, and doubled again in the next ten years as state controls were gradually dismantled under structural adjustment (ibid.: 154; IMF, 2004: 13–15). As we have seen, many of the farmers who sought land in Savè and Ouessè in the late 1980s and 1990s did so in order to grow cotton.

Both Nkrumah's regime in Ghana and Houphouët-Boigny's in Côte d'Ivoire worked to consolidate state power — reorganizing state institutions 'to politically demobilize the rural masses, coopt or sideline rural elites, and intensify taxation of export-crop producers' (Boone, 2003: 366), and Banégas (2003) implies as much for Bénin under Kérékou. If rural social realities set key parameters for states' strategies of political consolidation and

16. Since the early 1970s, the fortunes of Bénin's rulers and merchants alike have tended to rise and fall with those of Nigeria's oil industry (Igué and Soulé, 1992).
17. With no role to play once cotton had left farmers' fields, the GVs were probably more important in mobilizing farmers politically than in promoting economic development.

control, however, the process also worked in reverse. In Ghana, Nkrumah created an elaborate apparatus of governing institutions designed, as Boone demonstrates, to sideline powerful chiefs and rural social elites by extending state and party control directly to the farmers. The President was not above playing the chief himself, however, donning ceremonial robes for public ceremonies, and recruiting chiefly allies by taking sides in their disputes with rival chiefs who opposed the CPP regime (Dunn and Robertson, 1973; Rathbone, 2000).

The succession of military and civilian regimes that governed Ghana after Nkrumah's overthrow in 1966 continued to exclude traditional authorities from any formal role in state or local government but, mindful of Asante support for the National Liberation Movement (NLM) which opposed Nkrumah's rise to power in the 1950s, hesitated to risk opposition by curtailing chiefly prerogatives.[18] In the case of land, the Ghanaian state not only refrained from challenging chiefs' control over 'stool lands' in the south, but the Constitution of 1979 extended the same privilege to traditional authorities in the northern regions, where land had been effectively controlled by the state since the early years of colonial rule (Kasanga, 1996; Kasanga and Kotey, 2001; Lund, 2008). Billed as an effort to rationalize land tenure by applying a uniform standard throughout the country, Article 176 of the 1979 Constitution effectively opened a door to expanded chiefly influence in the northern regions of Ghana, including many localities with little previous history of centralized chiefly rule. Igniting a series of sometimes violent disputes over land and chiefly jurisdiction, this act of state divestment enhanced the influence of 'traditional rulers' across Ghana, raised the stakes in contests over chiefly succession, and helped to destabilize local, if not national, politics in both rural and urban areas (Kuba and Lentz, 2006; Lentz, 2003; Lentz and Nugent, 2000; Lund, 2003, 2008).

In contrast to Nkrumah's strategy of state institution-building, Houphouët-Boigny took an ostensibly hands-off approach to land tenure and rural governance. Indirectly challenging Nkrumah's call for pan-African resistance to neocolonialism, Houphouët-Boigny envisioned a future of regional prosperity based on 'pan-Africanism in one country' (Dozon, 2000: 16; also Akindès, 2004: 9). To stimulate the growth of cocoa and coffee production and increase the corresponding flow of revenue to the state, the President not only encouraged Ivoirians to migrate to the forests of the southwest, but famously declared that Côte d'Ivoire's doors were open to all, wealthy investors and manual labourers alike, regardless of national origin. In 1963, he announced a policy of land-to-the-developer, applicable to residents of

---

18. Arhin (2001: Ch. 4). Arhin also points out that the influence of chieftaincy has risen as increasing numbers of well-educated professionals and business people have succeeded to chiefly office (ibid.: Ch. 5).

foreign as well as Ivoirian origin.[19] To sustain the flow of labour and the growth of output in the cocoa producing areas, the central government encouraged local officials to settle most land disputes in favour of migrants (Chauveau, 2006: 222–23). Already suspicious of a ruling regime dominated by the President's Baulé co-ethnics, many forest autochthones concluded that the PDCI was ultimately to blame for their 'dispossession' at the hands of 'northern' immigrants (Boone, 2004: 220, 229–30). As if to confirm their fears, the government not only recognized foreign as well as Ivorian migrants as owners of the lands they had developed, but also allowed them to vote in national elections. Unsurprisingly, foreign-born immigrants voted overwhelmingly for the party that treated them as virtual citizens. Their role in helping to keep the PDCI in power contributed, in turn, to the growing receptivity of forest 'indigenes' to the xenophobic rhetoric of Houphouët-Boigny's successor, Henri Bédié (Akindès, 2004: 26ff; Blion and Bredeloup, 1997: 727–28; Dozon, 2000).

Unlike Côte d'Ivoire, where the state intervened extensively if informally in rural economic and political affairs, most studies portray the state in Bénin as unable to exercise much control over local politics. When Kérékou took power in 1972, following a series of weak civilian regimes each dominated by a politician from a different region, he sought to downplay regional rivalries by enlisting all sectors of society in a common project of socialist transformation. His efforts were only partly successful: economic development was modest at best, and national political debates shifted from 'tripartite regionalization to a sort of "provincialization"' (*'de la régionalization tripartite a une sorte de "provincialisation"'*) (Bako-Arifari, 1995: 10). By the 1980s, the number of local political actors was increasing, spurred by the decline in official foreign aid, the proliferation of NGOs as alternative channels of access to outside resources, and the corresponding emergence of an informal cadre of 'development courtiers' (*'courtiers en développement'*) — local entrepreneurs whose 'business' was to channel NGO resources to their own communities (Bierschenk et al., 2000).

Local activism intensified following the return to multi-party elections in 1990–91 and subsequent measures to decentralize rural development planning and prepare to register private land holdings, in accordance with donor conditionalities (Banégas, 2003; Le Meur, 1999; Le Meur et al., 1999). Begun as a pilot exercise in participatory research to gather information about customary land holdings at the village level, the Rural Land Use Plan (*Plan*

---

19. Although technically in contravention of Ivoirian law at the time, which prohibited the making of private contracts on any part of 'the national domain', in practice the President's pronouncement governed rural tenure arrangements until it was formally countermanded in 1998. The new rural land tenure law (*Loi no. 98-750 sur le domaine foncier rural*) allowed citizens to register customary rights to land, prohibited foreigners from owning land in Côte d'Ivoire, and stated that land which had not been registered by 2008 would revert to the national domain (Chauveau, 2002, 2006; Kobo, 2003).

Foncier Rural) ran concurrently with the Natural Resource Management Project (*Projet de Gestion des Ressources Naturelles*, 1993–8; amended in 1999 to *Projet de Gestion des Terroirs et Resources Naturelles*, or PGTRN) which assumed that residence, land use and local authority were correlated within bounded local territories (*terroirs*).[20] Together, these legal-administrative initiatives worked to territorialize previously overlapping, mobile relations of local authority and agrarian practice. By the mid-1990s, the *logique de région* that dominated national politics in the early years of independence had given way to a *logique de terroir*. Voters backed candidates whom they deemed most likely to advance the interests of their home area, even if this meant switching parties, and platforms, between local and national elections (Bako-Arifari, 1995, 1998). As a mayor-elect in northern Bénin explained to Bako-Arifari in 1990, 'the time is past when bureaucrats come to tell us what to do in Founougo... Democracy means that everyone should do his work and each village should choose its leaders freely among its sons'.[21]

If local politics were driven by local issues and interests, voters and local activists also took a keen interest in national electoral contests, especially after the reinstitution of multi-party elections in 1991. Based on a system of proportional representation, elections for the National Assembly gave rise to intense intra-party negotiations, with local interests often taking precedence over party loyalty in the selection and placement of candidates on party slates (Bako-Arifari, 1995, 1997; Banégas, 2003; Gbessemehlan and Rijnierse, 1995). In Founougo as in many other communities, voters opted for a local son as delegate to the National Assembly, but changed their strategy when it came to choosing the President. Rather than vote for the candidate who happened to come from a nearby village, or whose party platform most closely reflected their interests, citizens gravitated towards a candidate from their own region.[22] Once the elections were over, voters' attention reverted to local issues until the next presidential election five years later. The brief reappearance of *logique de région* at five year intervals

---

20. Unlike the English term 'territory', which denotes a bounded space, *terroir* connotes 'the fashioning of landscapes by local communities' Bassett et al. (2007: 123). In agropastoral economies where livelihood strategies are predicated on mobility and governing practices vary from one locality to another, bounded village *terroirs* are frequently at odds with political economic realities (cf. Le Meur, 2006a, 2006b; Painter et al., 1994).

21. *'c'est fini la période ou les fonctionnaires viennent nous diriger à Founougo....la démocratie a dit que chacun fasse son travaille et que chaque village choisisse librement ses dirigeants' parmi ses fils'* (quoted in Bako-Arifari, 1997: 28. Cf. Bierschenk, 2004).

22. According to Banégas (2003) and others, this strategy accounts, in part, for Kérékou's surprising comeback from his discredited past as military ruler to win the presidential election of 1996. His victory also reflected widespread popular disenchantment with President Soglo's apparent apathy and the flamboyantly self-promoting behaviour of his wife and her political associates.

underscores the general point that local rather than national issues dominate popular political agendas in Bénin, except during national elections (Bierschenk et al., 1998).[23]

The intermittent pattern of local and state interactions in Bénin stands in contrast to the situation in Ghana, where state agencies and politicians are continually engaged with locally based actors through informal as well as formal channels, and in Côte d'Ivoire, where the concentration of state power under Houphouët-Boigny's long reign helped lay the groundwork for ethno-regionally polarized struggles over state control after his death. Coming on the heels of a decade of economic crisis, the reinstitution of multi-party elections in Côte d'Ivoire did not lead to the stable transition to democracy envisioned by the architects of neoliberal reform. Instead, tensions between autochthones and strangers over access to land in the closing cocoa frontiers converged with emerging lines of conflict over control of the state, helping to create a popular audience receptive to candidates' xenophobic appeals, and reinforcing the country's slide into civil war. Conflicts over land and authority were no less intense in Ghana, but focused primarily on local struggles over land and chieftaincy, rather than reactivating the interregional tensions of the late colonial period that had been sidelined in favour of a unitary state government at the time of independence. Since 1992, when outgoing military ruler J.J. Rawlings succeeded himself as President of the fourth Republic, Ghana has presented the anomalous picture of an ostensibly stable democratically elected national regime presiding over local battlefields where tensions over land and chieftaincy erupt, periodically, into open combat.

CONCLUSION

Since the early 1980s, international pressures on African states to deregulate markets, privatize assets and democratize governance have stimulated some kinds of economic activity, depressed others, and led to widespread changes in governing structures and practices that both enabled and destabilized relations of authority and political participation. In all three of the cases discussed in this chapter, market liberalization and political restructuring have contributed to a proliferation of both individual and institutional competitors for power and resources, and of fora in which people seek access to property and authority — a process that has been underway, in one form or another, since colonial times (Berry, 1993: 56ff, 98–9). In the context of market deregulation and multi-party elections, the multiplication of projects and political actors has raised new questions (or reopened old ones) about the respective jurisdictions of state, customary, and in some cases religious

---

23. The current president Yayi Boni, elected in 2007, comes from central-north Bénin, rather than from any of the formerly dominant regional blocs.

laws and authorities, and intensified debate over who is eligible to decide. Competition over land and authority has given rise, in other words, to struggles over the meanings of 'citizenship' in local as well as national arenas of governance and belonging. Far from dispelling tension and confusion, neoliberal efforts to clarify and enforce rights of ownership have often added to them, heightening fears of disenfranchisement and dispossession, and undermining rather than increasing security of tenure. In Côte d'Ivoire, the state's perceived favouritism toward immigrants led to a backlash against 'stranger' farmers in the former cocoa frontiers that coincided with the increasingly xenophobic tone of national politics in the 1990s to help push the country toward civil war. In Ghana, rising tensions over land and fears of dispossession pitted ordinary citizens against 'traditional' rulers, with the state viewed by both as a potential but unreliable arbiter in disputes over land. In Bénin's 'polyvalent political landscape', rising tensions over land have given rise to varied shifts in local hierarchies and social divisions, while the state, preoccupied in part with capturing rents from the entrepôt economy, has so far proved 'unable to capture ... village society' through the programme of villagization envisioned in the PGTRN (Le Meur, 2006b: 896).

In all three countries, intersecting tensions over eligibility for land access and political participation have contributed to a resurgence of appeals to 'tradition' and historical precedent to validate claims to land and citizenship. Far from substituting 'modern' political economies (in which all citizens are presumed equal before the law) for 'traditional' particularisms, neoliberal interventions appear to have reinvigorated particularity and custom as bases for legitimizing claims to property, citizenship and authority within as well as outside the purview of the state. In each of the cases discussed above, privatization and the proliferation of non-governmental actors in development initiatives have fostered and been promoted by the spread of informal modes of governance in both local and national political arenas. While this is perhaps most obvious in the case of Ghana, where chiefs have built extensive networks of influence and collaboration within as well as outside the state, an analogous argument may also be made for Bénin and Côte d'Ivoire. In Bénin, the relative autonomy of local governance described by Bierschenk, Le Meur and others reflects a complex dynamic of shifting practices, alliances and antagonisms, in which relations between the formal authority of village co-operatives and *sous-préfets*, and the informal authority of village elders, lineage big men, *ressortissants*, and self-made '*courtiers en développement*' are anything but fixed or uncontested. In Côte d'Ivoire, Houphouët-Boigny arguably carried informal governance to the heart of state power — bestowing property and voting rights on foreigners and Ivoirians alike by personal fiat and party practice rather than by law. Following his death, his successor Henri Bédié sought to capitalize on popular resentment against *houphouëtisme* by calling for a politics of '*ivoirité*' that effectively closed Houphouët-Boigny's open door and shifted the basis of citizenship from residence (*droit de sol*) to descent (*droit de sang*) (Dozon, 2000: 18).

The case histories discussed here challenge both ready generalizations about 'weak' African states and neoliberal assumptions about economic and political 'reform'. Both the extent of state power and the ways in which it was manifested varied from one region to another and within each of them over time, intersecting or colliding with local dynamics of resource use and struggles over property and authority in sometimes unexpected ways. Rather than drawing general conclusions about the quality (or quantity) of local and/or national governance, these histories of frontier expansion and closure direct attention to a proliferation of formal and informal authorities that has both animated struggles over property and authority, and linked them to continuing debates over 'citizenship' in post-colonial African nations and localities within them.

Analytically, these histories also raise questions about neoliberal policy analyses that measure economic and political development in terms of 'progress' toward open competition among autonomous individuals, but provide no conceptual vocabulary for delineating economic and political space, or addressing property and authority as social processes rather than legal facts. Searching opportunistically for African 'partners' in their project of neoliberal reform, the architects of the so-called Washington consensus have offered advice and financial support to almost anyone — private contractors, NGOs, religious institutions and traditional authorities — who expressed willingness to participate in efforts to open African markets and governments to outside interests and influence. In the process, donors have not only ended up working with authorities who are neither open nor accountable to their citizens (Uvin, 1998), but sometimes appeared to subvert their own project — for instance, in shifting use of the term 'ownership' from exclusive control over property (as in 'ownership' of land) to a synonym for political commitment (as in exhortations to African governments to 'take ownership' of neoliberal reforms). Perhaps it is time to move beyond imagined standards of apolitical markets and 'transparent' bureaucracies to focus on the kinds of dynamic interconnections between property, authority and citizenship discussed in the present volume.

REFERENCES

Akindès, F. (2004) *The Roots of the Military-Political Crises in Côte D'Ivoire*. Research Report No 128. Uppsala: Nordic Africa Institute.

Amanor, K.S. (1999) *Global Restructuring and Land Rights in Ghana: Forest Food Chains, Timber and Rural Livelihoods*. Uppsala: NAI.

Ammassari, S. (2004) 'From Nation-building to Entrepreneurship: The Impact of Elite Return Migrants in Côte d'Ivoire and Ghana', *Population, Space and Place* 10: 133–54.

Arhin, K. (1986) 'The Expansion of Cocoa Production: The Working Conditions of Migrant Cocoa Farmers in the Central and Western Regions'. (Mimeo.)

42 *Sara Berry*

Arhin, K. (2001) *Transformations in Traditional Rule in Ghana (1951–1996)*. Accra: Sedco.

Baier, S. (1980) *An Economic History of Central Niger*. Oxford: Clarendon Press.

Bako-Arifari, N. (1995) 'Démocratie et logique du terroir. Le Bénin' ('Democracy and the Logic of the *Terroir*. Bénin'), *Politique africaine* 59: 7–24.

Bako-Arifari, N. (1997) 'La démocratie entre norms officielles et dynamiques locales. Dynamiques et formes du pouvoir à Founougo (Bénin)', ('Democracy between Official Norms and Local Dynamics. Dynamics and Forms of Authority at Founougo (Bénin)'. Working Papers on African Societies 6. Berlin: Das Arabische Büch.

Bako-Arifari, N. (1998) 'La démocratie à Founougo (Borgou): paysans et "déscolarisés" en compétition pour le pouvoir local' ('Democracy in Founougo (Borgou): Peasants and "School-Leavers" Competing for Local Power'), in T. Bierschenk and J-P. Olivier de Sardan *Les pouvoirs au village. Le Bénin rurale entre démocratization et décentralization* (*Village Authorities. Rural Bénin between Democratization and Decentralization*), pp. 57–100. Paris: Karthala.

Bako-Arifari, N. and P.-Y. Le Meur (2003) 'La Chefferie au Bénin: Une résurgence ambigué' ('Chieftaincy in Bénin: An Ambiguous Resurgence'), in C.-H. Perrot and F.-X. Fauvelle-Aymar (eds) *Le retour des rois* (*The Return of the Kings*) pp. 125–43. Paris: Karthala.

Banégas, R. (2003) *La Démocratie à pas de caméléon. Transition et imaginaires politiques au Bénin.* (*Democracy in the footsteps of the chameleon. Transition and political imagination in Bénin.*) Paris: Karthala.

Bassett, T. (2001) *The Peasant Cotton Revolution in West Africa: Côte d'Ivoire, 1880–1995*. Cambridge: Cambridge University Press.

Bassett, T., C. Blanc-Pamard and J. Boutrais (2007) 'Constructing Locality: The *Terroir* Approach in West Africa', *Africa* 77(1): 104–29.

Berry, S. (1975) *Cocoa, Custom and Socio-Economic Change in Rural Southwestern Nigeria*. Oxford: Clarendon Press.

Berry, S. (1993) *No Condition is Permanent: The Social Dynamics of Agrarian Change in Sub-Saharan Africa*. Madison, WI: University of Wisconsin Press.

Berry, S. (2001) *Chiefs Know Their Boundaries: Essays on Property, Power and the Past in Asante, 1896–1996*. Portsmouth, NH: Heinemann.

Bierschenk, T. (2004) 'The Local Appropriation of Democracy: An Analysis of the Municipal Elections in Parakou, Republic of Bénin, 2002/03'. Working Paper No 39, Institüt für Ethnologie und Afrikastudien. Mainz: Johannes Gutenberg University.

Bierschenk, T. and J.-P. Olivier de Sardan (1998) *Les pouvoirs au village. Le Bénin rurale entre démocratization et décentralization* (*Village Authorities. Rural Bénin between Democratization and Decentralization*). Paris: Karthala.

Bierschenk, T., J.-P. Chauveau and J.-P. Olivier de Sardan (eds) (2000) *Courtiers en développement. Les villages africains en quête des projets* (*Development Courtiers. African Villages in Search of Projects*). Paris: Karthala and APAD.

Black, R. (2004) 'Migration and Pro-Poor Policy in Africa'. Working Paper C6. Sussex: Sussex Centre for Migration Research.

Blion, R. and S. Bredeloup (1997) 'La Côte d'Ivoire dans les stratégies migratoires des Burkinabè et des Sénégalais' ('Côte d'Ivoire in the Migratory Strategies of Burkinabe and Senegalese'), in B. Contamin and H. Memel-Foté (eds) *Le modèle ivoirien en crise* (*The Ivoirian Model in Crisis*), pp. 707–37. Paris: Karthala; Abidjan: GIDIS.

Boni, S. (2006) 'Indigenous Blood and Foreign Labor: The Ancestralization of Land Rights in Sefwi (Ghana)', in R. Kuba and C. Lentz (eds) *Land and the Politics of Belonging in West Africa*, pp. 161–86. Leiden: E.J. Brill.

Boone, C. (2003) 'Decentralization as Political Strategy in West Africa', *Comparative Political Studies* 36(4): 355–80.

Boone, C. (2004) *Political Topographies of the African State: Territorial Authority and Institutional Choice*. Cambridge: Cambridge University Press.

de Bruijn, M., R. van Dijk and D. Foeken (2001) *Mobile Africa: Changing Patterns of Movement in Africa and Beyond*. Leiden: Brill.

Brüntrup-Seidman, S., A. Floquet and P.-Y. Le Meur (2000) 'Political and Development Arenas in Rural Bénin', in F. Graef et al. *Adapted Farming in West Africa: Issues, Potentials and Perspectives*, pp. 273–82. Stuttgart: Verlag Ulrich Grauer.

Chappell, D.A. (1989) 'The Nation as Frontier: Ethnicity and Clientilism in Ivorian History', *International Journal of African Historical Studies* 22(4): 671–96.

Chauveau, J.-P. (2000) 'La Question foncière et le coup d'état en Côte d'Ivoire' ('The Land Tenure Question and the Coup d'Etat in Côte d'Ivoire'), *Politque africaine* 78: 94–125.

Chauveau, J.-P. (2002) 'Une Lecture sociologique de la loi ivoirienne de 1998 sur le domaine foncier' ('A Sociological Reading of the Ivorian Land Tenure Law of 1998'). Research Unit Working Paper No 6. Montpellier: IRD REFO.

Chauveau, J.-P. (2006) 'How Does an Institution Evolve? Land, Politics, Intergenerational Relations and the Institution of the *Tutorat* amongst Autochthones and Immigrants (Gban Region, Côte d'Ivoire)', in R. Kuba and C. Lentz (eds) *Land and the Politics of Belonging in West Africa*, pp. 213–40. Leiden: E.J. Brill.

Chauveau, J.-P. and E. Leonard (1996) 'Côte d'Ivoire's Pioneering Fronts: Historical and Political Determinants of the Spread of Cocoa Cultivation', in W.G. Clarence-Smith (ed.) *Cocoa Pioneer Fronts since 1800*, pp. 176–194. London and NY: Macmillan and St Martins Press.

Copans, J. (1982) *Les Marabouts de l'arachide: la confrérie mouride et les paysans du Sénégal (Peanut Marabouts: The Mouride Brotherhood and Senegalese Peasants)*. Paris: Le Sycamore.

Dozon, J.-P. (1985) 'Les Bété: une création coloniale' ('The Bété: A Colonial Invention'), in J.-L. Amselle (ed.) *Au Coeur de l'ethnie: ethnie, tribalisme et état en Afrique (At the Heart of the Ethnic: Ethnicity, Tribalism and the State in Africa)*, pp. 49–85. Paris: Editions la Découverte.

Dozon, J.-P. (1997) 'L'Etranger et l'allochtone en Côte-D'Ivoire' ('Foreigners and Non-locals in Côte d'Ivoire'), in B. Contamin and H. Memel-Foté (eds) *Le Modèle ivoirien en crise (The Ivoirian Model in Crisis)*, pp. 779–98. Paris: Karthala; Abidjan: GIDIS.

Dozon, J.-P. (2000) 'La Côte d'Ivoire au péril de l'ivoirité' ('Côte d'Ivoire in Danger of Ivorianness'), *Afrique contemporaine* 193: 13–23.

Dunn, J. and A.F. Robertson (1973) *Dependence and Opportunity: Political Change in Ahafo (Ghana)*. Cambridge: Cambridge University Press.

Edja, H. (1997) 'Phenomènes de frontière et problèmes de l'access à la terre: le cas de la sous-préfecture de Savè en Bénin' ('Frontier Issues and the Problem of Access to Land: The Case of Savè District in Bénin'). Working Papers on African Societies No 12. Berlin: Das Arabische Büch.

Edja, H. (1999) *Colonisation agricole spontanée et milieux sociaux nouveaux. La migration rurale dans le Zou-Nord au Bénin (Spontaneous Agricultural Colonization and New Social Circumstances. Rural Migration in North Zou, Bénin)*. Kiel: Wissenschaftsverlag Vauk Kiel.

Edja, H. (2000) 'Médiateurs traditionnels a l'école du courtage en développement. Un exemple autour des projets du service allemande de développement (DED) a Kalalé au Nord-Bénin' ('Traditional Mediators in the School of Development Courtage. An Example of German Development Projects in Kalalé, North Bénin'), in T. Bierschenk, J.-P. Chauveau and J.-P. Olivier de Sardan (eds) *Courtiers en développement. Les villages africains en quête des projets (Development Courtiers. African Villages in Search of Projects)*, pp. 125–44. Paris: Karthala and APAD.

Francis, P. (1984) '"For the Use and Common Benefit of all Nigerians": The Land Use Decree of 1978', *Africa* 53(3): 3–28.

Gbessemehlan, V. and E. Rijnierse (1995) 'Les Elections en milieu rural: le cas de Ouessè' ('Rural Elections: The Case of Ouessè'), *Politique africaine* 59: 70–81.

Guyer, J. (ed.) (1987) *Feeding African Cities: Studies in Regional Social History*. Bloomington, IN: Indiana University Press with the International African Institute.

Guyer, J. (1997) *An African Niche Economy: Farming to Feed Ibadan, 1968–1988*. Edinburgh: Edinburgh University Press for the International African Institute.

Hill, P. (1963) *Migrant Cocoa Farmers of Southern Ghana*. Cambridge: Cambridge University Press.

Igué, O.J. (1999) *Bénin et la mondalisation de l'economie. Les limites de l'intégrisme du marché* (*Bénin and Economic Globalization. The Limits of Market Integration*). Paris: Karthala.

Igué, O.J. and B.G. Soulé (1992) *L'Etat entrepôt au Bénin: commerce informal ou solution à la crise?* (*The Entrepot State in Bénin: Informal Trade or a Solution to the Crisis?*). Paris: Karthala.

IMF (2004) 'Bénin: Selected Issues and Statistical Appendix'. IMF Country Report No 04/370. Washington, DC: International Monetary Fund.

Juul, K. (2006) 'Decentralization, Local Taxation and Citizenship in Senegal', *Development and Change* 37(4): 821–46.

Kasanga, K. (1996) *The Role of Chiefs in Land Administration in Northern Ghana*. London: Royal Institute of Chartered Surveyors.

Kasanga, K. and N.A. Kotey (2001) *Land Management in Ghana: Building on Tradition and Modernity*. London: IIED.

Kobo, P.C. (2003) 'Une Lecture critique d'une loi ambigué' ('A Critical Reading of an Ambiguous Law'), in INADES *Régards sur. . .Le foncier rural en Côte d'Ivoire*. (*Concerning. . . Rural Land Tenure in Côte d'Ivoire*), pp. 21–43. Abidjan: CERAP and Nouvelles Editions Ivoiriennes.

Kuba, R. and C. Lentz (2006) *Land and the Politics of Belonging in West Africa*. Leiden: Brill.

Le Meur, P.-Y. (1999) 'Coping with Institutional Uncertainty: Contested Local Public Spaces and Power in Rural Bénin', *Afrika Spectrum* 34(2): 187–211.

Le Meur, P.-Y. (2002) 'Trajectories of the Politicization of Land Issues: Case Studies from Bénin', in K. Juul and C. Lund (eds) *Negotiating Property in Africa*, pp. 135–55. Portsmouth, NH: Heinemann.

Le Meur, P.-Y. (2006a) 'Governing Land, Translating Rights: The Rural Land Plan in Bénin', in D. Lewis and D. Mosse (eds) *Development Brokers and Translators*, pp. 75–99. Bloomfield, CT: Kumarian.

Le Meur, P.-Y. (2006b) 'State-Making and the Politics of the Frontier in Central Bénin', *Development and Change* 37(4): 871–900.

Le Meur, P.-Y. and Cyriaque Adjinacou (1998) 'Les Pouvoirs locaux au Gbanlin (Zou) entre migration, commerce et région' ('Local Authorities in Gbanlin (Zou) between Migration, Trade and Region'), in T. Bierschenk and J.-P. Olivier de Sardan (eds) *Les Pouvoirs au village. Le Bénin rural entre démocratization et décentralization* (*Village Authorities. Rural Bénin between Democratization and Decentralization*), pp. 121–66. Paris: Karthala.

Le Meur, P.-Y., T. Bierschenk and A. Floquet (1999) 'Paysans, état et ONG' ('Peasants, the State and NGOs'). Working Papers on African Societies No 33. Berlin: Das Arabische Büch.

Lentz, C. (2003) '"This is Ghanaian territory": Land Conflicts on a West African Border', *American Ethnologist* 30: 501–27.

Lentz, C. and P. Nugent (eds) (2000) *Ethnicity in Ghana: The Limits of Invention*. London and New York: Macmillan and St Martins Press.

Lloyd, P.C. (1972) *Yoruba Land Law*. Ibadan: Oxford University Press.

Lund, C. (2002) 'Negotiating Property Institutions: On the Symbiosis of Property and Authority in Africa', in K. Juul and C. Lund (eds) *Negotiating Property in Africa*, pp. 11–44. Portsmouth, NH: Heinemann.

Lund, C. (2003) '"Bawku is still Volatile": Ethno-Political Conflict and State Recognition in Northern Ghana', *Journal of Modern African Studies* 41(4): 587–610.

Lund, C. (2008) *Local Politics and the Dynamics of Property in Africa*. Cambridge: Cambridge University Press.

McCaskie, T. (1995) *State and Society in Precolonial Asante*. Cambridge: Cambridge University Press.

Memel-Fotê, H. (1999) 'Un Mythe politique des Akans en Côte d'Ivoire: le sens de l'Etat' ('An Akan Political Myth in Côte d'Ivoire'), in P. Valsecchi and F. Viti (eds) *Mondes akan. Identité et pouvoir en Afrique occidentale (Akan Worlds. Identity and Power in West Africa)*, pp. 21–42. Paris: L'Harmattan.

Netting, R. McC. (1968) *Hill Farmers of Nigeria: The Cultural Ecology of the Kofyar of the Jos Plateau*. Seattle, WA: University of Washington Press.

Ng'weno, B. (2007) *Turf Wars: Territory and Citizenship in the Contemporary State*. Stanford, CA: Stanford University Press.

Omotola, J.A. (1983) *Cases on the Land Use Act*. Lagos: Lagos University Press.

Painter, T., J. Sumberg and T. Price (1994) 'Your *Terroir* and My "Action Space": Implications of Differentiation, Mobility and Diversification for the *Approche Terroir* in Sahelian West Africa', *Africa* 64(4): 447–64.

Rathbone, R. (1993) *Murder and Politics in Colonial Ghana*. New Haven, CT: Yale University Press.

Rathbone, R. (2000) *Nkrumah and the Chiefs: The Politics of Chieftaincy in Ghana, 1951–1960*. Accra: F. Reimmer; Athens, OH: Ohio University Press; Oxford: James Currey.

Ruf, F. (1995) 'From "Forest Rent" to "Tree Capital": Basic "Laws" of Cocoa Supply', in F. Ruf and P.S. Siswoputranto (eds) *Cocoa Cycles: The Economics of Cocoa Supply*, pp. 1–54. Cambridge: Woodhead.

Snrech, S. (1998) 'Preparing for the Future: A Vision of West Africa in the Year 2020'. West African Long-Term Prospective Study. Paris: OECD.

Swindell, K. (1985) *Farm Labour*. Cambridge: Cambridge University Press.

Ubink, J. (2008) *In the Land of the Chiefs: Customary Law, Land Conflicts and the Role of the State in Peri-Urban Ghana*. Leiden: University of Leiden Press.

Uvin, P. (1998) *Aiding Violence: The Development Enterprise in Rwanda*. West Hartford, CT: Kumarian.

Watts, M. (1983) *Silent Violence: Food, Famine and Peasantry in Northern Nigeria*. Berkeley, CA: University of California Press.

World Bank (1986) *Financing Adjustment with Growth in Sub-Saharan Africa, 1986–90*. Washington, DC: World Bank.

3

Rubber Erasures, Rubber Producing Rights: Making Racialized Territories in West Kalimantan, Indonesia

Nancy Lee Peluso

INTRODUCTION

'In Dayak gardens all crops are planted mixed; the Chinese separate the crops, their land is clean and divided regularly; the Malays are in between' (Sandick and Marle, 1919: 132)

The contentious relationship between rubber and swidden rice production has long caused dilemmas in Borneo, and is increasingly an issue in other parts of Southeast Asia where rubber has recently been introduced. Swidden rice, a staple food crop with great ritual significance in Borneo, is quite literally losing ground. Rubber (*Hevea brasiliensis*) is not only an alien species, it is inedible. This could have presented a daunting deterrent to its production from the point of view of an early twentieth century smallholder, yet rubber was widely sought after and rapidly became Borneo's most common exotic.[1] By the late 1960s, rubber revenues paid for the daily rice of most households in Bagak Sahwa[2] village, an Indonesian administrative village located on the road leading from Singkawang into the interior of West Kalimantan. Most villagers today identify themselves as Salako Dayak farmers. By 2004, the visible result of nearly a hundred years of local rubber production was a landscape of karst hillsides covered with 'forests' of mostly rubber and fruit trees, and the near elimination of swidden fields and unmanaged fallows. As Michael Dove (1993) has famously written about a different area of West Kalimantan, rubber had clearly 'eaten' the rice.

Rubber has played a pivotal role not only in shaping the landscapes and livelihood strategies of Bagak Sahwa and its environs, but also in

I am grateful to a number of people for providing comments on various drafts of this chapter, including Kate Brown, Mary Somers Heidhues, Denise Leto, Tania Li, Nick Menzies, Kit Olivi, Scott Prudham, Simon Takdir, Peter Vandergeest, Arthur Van Schaik and Hui Few-Yoong. The suggestions of participants in the Bornholm Property Workshop (September 2006), as well as those of colleagues and friends at the University of Toronto and the Ohio State University Geography Department, where I presented earlier versions of this essay, have also had a role in shaping the chapter. The usual disclaimers apply.

1. The rise in rubber production area pre-dates Borneo's oil palm revolution by nearly a century.
2. In this chapter, I use the names Bagak Sahwa and Bagak. Bagak was a historical settlement in the Gunung Raya-Pasi area, dating back to the eighteenth or nineteenth century; when administrative villages were formed in New Order Indonesia, several settlements, including Bagak, were combined in the administrative village of Bagak Sahwa. The name Bagak is still used to refer to the hamlet north of the road.

the production and hardening of ethnic and national identities. Authorities' selective recognition and ignorance of certain production and property practices in everyday life — practices that differed under colonial and contemporary modes of rule — helped construct the notions of 'Chinese', 'Dayak' and 'Indonesian' smallholders as distinctive groups having particular 'ethnic' characteristics and competing interests, though obviously with some overlap acknowledged among them. Rubber production associated with these smallholders generated ethnic, or what I call below 'racialized' territorialities. By both creating rights and justifying their elimination, rubber production rendered some smallholders more visible than others at different historical moments.

Physical violence and the continuing threat of it have further solidified the association of rubber production with racialized territories. Through displacement and dispossession, violence made ethnic identity a life-or-death question in this corner of West Kalimantan. These identities, in turn, have been entangled further with spatialized and violent politics of citizenship in Indonesia and have strongly influenced which smallholders have gained access to land for growing rubber. The socio-natural history of rubber serves as an effective vehicle for exploring the relations between violence, property and the production of ethnicity and landscape history in this notoriously troubled region, because the origins of property often involve violence and enclosure to enable accumulation (Blomley, 2003; Marx, 1967; Thompson, 1975).

POWER RELATIONS WRITTEN ON THE LANDSCAPE

This essay focuses on power relations and landscape production as manifested through *claims, rights* and *territory*. How are rubber territories created through rubber production, fixing place and people in particular ways? Further, which claiming practices, histories and memories have been recognized in the form of rights, and which have helped produce ethnic subjectivities and racialized territorialities? How have the politics of rule affected the racialization of bodies, land and territory?

A major segment of what might be called 'the property literature' often leaves violence out of the discussion when explaining changes in property rights. This may be because, in this segment, the initial political-economic conditions under which property arises are taken for granted. Yet, recent work by political ecologists and political economists has reiterated the supposition that unless the initial conditions of enclosure and property legislation are maintained through time and in space, the benefits of property cannot continue to be realized (de Angelis, 1991; Blomley, 2003; Glassman, 2006; Perelman, 2000).[3] Such conditions, which we might also think of as arenas

---

3. The classics on this, of course, include Marx on violence and primitive accumulation and Weber on structural violence. Some of these debates have been revived and

of opportunity and constraint, frequently entail violence (Peluso and Watts, 2001: 29). This reasoning affirms that property relations and their collective territorial effects, like all social relations, require constant work and investment, or risk replacement by new practices for gaining access to or control of land and resources (Ribot and Peluso, 2003). Thus property studies need to explore political economies of power and accumulation — the forms of access to and control over resources — to clarify the construction of property rights and other forms of resource access (Blomley, 2003; Peluso and Watts, 2001; Ribot and Peluso, 2003).

The manner in which rubber produces rights and creates territory requires an understanding of contemporary and historical regimes of access to land, property and rule. In as much as these social relations and resource practices produce the very contexts in which they are enacted, they need to be understood as socio-spatial (Li, 1999; Massey, 1994; Raffles, 2002). Socio-spatial relations in Bagak Sahwa are considerably different today than they were fifty or a hundred years ago. Nevertheless, the categories that emerged out of colonial legal pluralism continue to influence and reproduce the hardened ethnic categories attached to both bodies and territory. These categories are so embedded in both contemporary and historical practice and understanding that I have not been able to avoid using them to make some of my arguments here; but I am keenly aware that they are problematic.[4] This is particularly the case in using the terms 'Chinese', 'Dayak' and 'Malay', denoting ethnic identity. As explained in greater detail below, these terms are used in everyday practice and are generally unproblematized, yet they refer to people with different associations with or experiences of the specific ethnic heritage, and whether or not contemporary subjects or their ancestors were ascribed by law or self-identified as one of these categories. I will show, in relation to rubber production and rights, how they have been produced and reproduced over history through socio-spatial practice and violence.

The categories became particularly important in the nineteenth century under Dutch indirect rule because one's ascribed ethnicity determined legal status, which in turn determined rights to land and forms of legal jurisdiction. Land rights were racialized under colonial-era legal pluralism in the Netherlands' East Indies (NEI). Initially, only people defined as 'Natives' (*Inlanders*) could legally occupy and use 'customary land'. Chinese were defined as 'aliens', migrants, 'Foreign Orientals', and could not — like Europeans and anyone else not defined as Native — legally own land in the eyes of the colonial state. In the decade following the formation of the Republic of Indonesia (1950s), when the nation was led by President Sukarno,

---

recontextualized, as in, for example, Harvey (2003). Much of the extensive literature on political ecology deals with conflict turned violent: see, for example, Peet and Watts (1996/2004) or Peluso and Watts (2001) for a glimpse into this now extensive literature.

4. For that reason, I use the terms Chinese and Dayak without scare quotes every time, and without adding qualifying phrases such as 'people called. . .'.

land rights were discussed and legislated in terms of Indonesian citizenship and class. Under the 'New Order' government of the second president, Suharto, discussions of class and ethnic conflict were literally outlawed and concealed by emergent discourses on community (Brosius et al., 2005; Li, 1996). Since the fall of Suharto in 1998 and subsequent decentralization, multiple categories of legitimacy, including a revitalization of customary claims to territory, have come back into play.

My analysis of rubber's racialized history in this northwestern area of West Kalimantan allows us to see how people have been produced as rights-bearing, racialized or territorial subjects through complex negotiations and contestations over identity, property and territory (Gordillo, 2005; Maurer, 1997; Moore, 2005). It speaks in some ways directly to recent work by Pauline Peters (2002), who has argued that such significant strides have been made toward 'de-economizing' analyses of property that the broader economic and political *effects* of resource-claiming mechanisms and negotiations are often lost. In particular, she argues, the emphasis on negotiations has deflected attention from the fact that struggles over access to resources produce winners and losers.[5] Negotiations must be fit into larger patterns and processes of resource distribution and differentiation. Adding to the confusion is the often uncritical use of Katherine Verdery's (1998) notion of 'fuzzy' property rights. As Verdery points out, the specificities of access to resources may seem complex and fuzzy to casual observers or short-term researchers but to the people who have lived with and developed them, they have logics of legibility.[6] Moreover, fuzziness can be projected to mask conflict or avoid confrontation. When different parties have incompatible claims to the same resources or land, legitimated by multiple authorities, the idea of fuzziness obscures the terms of difference and power.[7]

The history of rubber production in this corner of West Kalimantan demonstrates that property and territory are not mere products of negotiations. Rubber and associated processes of racialized territorialization have been parts of larger, racialized political economies under Dutch and Indonesian rule. While law and practice alone have been intertwined in negotiations over access to land and rubber production in this area, ultimately neither law nor long-term practice alone determined who was allowed to grow rubber and own the land beneath it. Rubber production thus provides a lens through which to view changing conceptions and practices of claiming, producing

---

5. See also Scott (1998). Perhaps more importantly, it is not only the state that is likely to win; see Ferguson (2005); Ribot and Peluso (2003).
6. Alternatively, locals may construct property and access 'rules' as fuzzy, to keep outsiders or observers from understanding what is actually going on. Scott (1998) makes this point in reference to the messiness of old-fashioned/ancient cities and markets, counterposing the 'order' inherent in intimate knowledge of these with the simplified street grids of contemporary cities and even whole new landscapes of ordered property rights.
7. Verdery mentions all of these in her book. See also MacPherson (1983).

and erasing rights, producing people and territory as racialized or ethnic subjects, and obscuring the violent political conflict that has constituted these
socio-spatial processes.

Rubber Production in Bagak Sahwa

By the last decade of the twentieth century, West Kalimantan had more
rubber trees than any other province of Indonesia. It was one of two Borneo
provinces named 'the heartlands of the industry' (Brookfield et al., 1995:
38; Cleary and Eaton, 1992). Its success is in part due to rubber's flexibility:
if the grower does not tap the trees for a long time, their productivity and
product quality are not affected. Rubber production also requires disciplined
labour but not long hours. In 1990s' Bagak Sahwa, farmers visited fifty to a
hundred or more trees per day, depending on the sizes of their holdings and
their cash needs. Early in the morning, a new cut in the tree's bark would be
made, using a special tool to let a small stream of rubber flow out during the
day. Beneath the cut, collection cups are fixed to catch the oozing latex.

Smallholder production has been acknowledged as the most important
production regime (as opposed to corporate plantation production) for rubber
in West Kalimantan (Dove, 1994; Ozinga, 1940). In 1991, more than 90 per
cent of Bagak Sahwa smallholders grew some rubber. Yet, as detailed in the
next section, rubber smallholders of the past are not the same as those now
and even the idea of who *might* be smallholders and who *could not be* has
changed. Rights and access have shifted with changing political economies,
modalities of rule and the cultural politics of ethnic identity.

Hevea brasiliensis rubber — whether the original varieties brought to
Southeast Asia from Brazil via Kew gardens, or the more recently appearing
high yielding, clonal varieties — is as much a social product as a 'natural'
one, with its own species history involving extensive human intervention.
This socio-natural history is evident in the ways that its biological, ecological and commodity characteristics have all contributed to the stories of its
property rights and its close associations with specific peoples in different
moments. Rubber trees are planted close together — though not always in
monocultures — to facilitate the collection of their sap, which is the valued
latex. Because rubber trees produce for some forty years, their relationship
to landscape and land tenure is important. The agrarian environments where
rubber is grown can be seen as socio-natural territories because of the way
this tree fits into local agroforestry practices.

PRODUCING RACIALIZED IDENTITIES THROUGH LAND RIGHTS

In the eighteenth and nineteenth centuries, people living in western Borneo often identified themselves by the names of the rivers near which they
lived (Harwell, 2001; King, 1993; Pringle, 1970). Some people identified

themselves and each other by the language they spoke (Ba-Nana, Ba-Ahe, Ba-Dameo, Khek), or the regions they were from (Fukien, Guandong, Hainan) (de Groot, 1885). To Dutch administrators under legal pluralism, in Borneo the category of 'Natives' (*Inlanders*) included only those people categorized as 'Dayak' or 'Malay'. The term 'Dayak', as used by colonial administrators, missionaries and scholars, as well as by those who embraced Dayak (or a Dayak language-group's) subjectivity, encompassed many different language-speaking groups living in the interior of Borneo. In this part of West Kalimantan, most of the peoples identified as 'Dayak' spoke Salako (Ba-Dameo) or Kenayatn (Ba-Ahe) and have been differentiated from Malays here by religion: Dayaks are those Dutch-identified *Inlanders* who did not convert to Islam, as Malays, by definition, did.

The Netherlands East Indies colonial state began its indirect rule of the Sultanate of Sambas in Western Borneo (*Westerafdeeling Borneo*) after signing a 'short treaty' in 1849. Dutch administrators and other European observers collapsed people of different language groups from China into a single 'Chinese' category even before they began taking censuses, although when it served their purposes they differentiated them by language group, occupation or ascribed characteristics.[8] By use of the term, they meant people who had migrated to Borneo from China, or their children. Official and non-official visitors to the region in the eighteenth and early nineteenth centuries had often used these categories to refer to local people even before they became formal legal categories (Doty and Pohlman, 1839; Earl, 1837). After Western Borneo became part of the NEI, the usages of these terms by colonial officials, missionaries, historical geographers and anthropologists further reinforced, and hardened, these legal categories (Ellen, 1999).

By legal definition, 'Chinese' were foreign, though not European in origin; hence they were legally categorized 'Foreign Orientals', along with 'Arabs' and 'Indians' (or 'Tamils') — themselves huge categories (see Wolters, 1999). The first waves of Chinese immigrants to western Borneo in the late eighteenth and early nineteenth centuries were all male. These men had come to farm and to mine gold. While some thousands came and went back to China, others chose to settle permanently in the region. Thousands of them married or fathered children with local women.[9] As late as the 1840s, in a report on his travels to Montrado east of Singkawang, van Rees (1858: 49) noted the obvious fact that all early immigrants had Dayak wives, 'resulting in a majority of the population being mixed'. Even after the Kongsi wars of 1850–54, when nearly 25,000 Chinese left the Montrado area, some 24,000 remained, constituting a significant population (Vleming, 1926: 256). By

8. On the British practice of the census, see Cohn (1996) and Shamsul (2004: 123). For a more complete discussion of colonial racial policy in the NEI, see, for example, Fasseur (1994) and Stoler (1995).

9. All sources insist that the women who married Chinese were Dayak not Malay, though an occasional Malay is noted as an exception.

1918, the rural sub-district in which Bagak was located — *Onderafdeeling Singkawang* — housed some 17,410 people classified as Chinese, 16,000 of whom were smallholder farmers (Sandick and Marle, 1919: Appendix BIII: 127).

Local residence or birth in the Indies did not generate Native status for Chinese. Chinese might be referred to as either *totok* (meaning 'pure'), or *peranakan* ('mixed', in Indonesian), but they were still legally treated as foreign. Although *peranakan* means 'mixed', the term was always associated with outsiders, thus '*peranakan Cina*' or '*peranakan Tionghoa*'.[10] It would be odd to say, '*peranakan Dayak*', even though children of such a union would be of both heritages, that is, mixed. However, in the Montrado and rural Singkawang areas, people recognized such distinctions. The children of Chinese fathers and Dayak mothers were called '*Bantangfan*' in Mandarin, a word that meant 'half-chinese barbarians' (Yuan, 2000: 70). The word must have been pronounced in various ways locally, because Veth (1854, Vol 1: 302, cited in Yuan, ibid.) recorded it as '*petompang*'. A Dayak friend told me that some people felt so mixed in Bagak Sahwa and surrounding settlements that they refused to be called 'Chinese' or 'Dayak', preferring '*Pantokng*' instead. As a Salako or Badameo word, therefore, '*petompang*' seems to have been transliterated as '*Pantokng*' (Heidhues, pers. comm., 2008). Yet to the villagers who told me the word means 'mixed', literally, it represented much more than genetic heritage.

Legal classifications were highly gendered, and they generated gendered effects. In particular, the legal ascription of ethnicity or racial identity had to do with men and their children. Dutch administrators categorized the children of a Dayak woman and a Chinese man as 'Chinese'. Dayak women who married or lived with Chinese were said to have *masuk Cina*, 'become Chinese', and if they were formally married to Chinese they were counted on the census as such. Census takers counted unmarried women living with Chinese as 'Native' (and generally noted as Dayak) (Cator, 1936: 30–1).[11]

Of course, there were dimensions of everyday practice that enabled someone to perform or live their lives as Chinese or Dayak or Pantokng, and to be recognized as such in everyday interactions. Second and third generation males might wear queues, for example, to demonstrate 'Chinese-ness', and wear trousers and jackets rather than loincloths. Women married to Chinese men would wear Chinese-patterned sarongs from Java or cotton trousers,

---

10. Suryadinata (1978); Mary Somers-Heidhues (pers. comm., 2007) pointed out that in Java the term '*peranakan Arab*'and in Malaya, the term '*Jawi pekan/peranakan*' refer to mixed descendants of Indian Muslims. Both terms identify outsiders in their respective contexts, but I have never heard this term in West Kalimantan.

11. Census takers apparently were confident they knew which women were 'Native', because Cator provides an exact number — 10,791 — for 'these women' across the whole of the NEI. It would be impossible to know how many of the women married to Chinese, whether counted as Dayak or Chinese, were in fact 'mixed'. Cator (1936: 30–1) cites Census 1930 Vol. VII, p. 33.

rather than the woven cloth and rattan rings worn by Dayak women in this area. Chinese men lived with their wives in *kongsi* houses or single-family houses, often, but not always, along roads; Dayaks tended to live in the hills set back from the roads, in longhouses.

But what of those who were Pantokng? 'Pantokng' did not constitute a clear legal identity category of its own. 'Pantokng' may have been used by local Dayaks to indicate people of mixed heritage living within predominantly Dayak settlements, but was not associated with a clear set of social practices that identified the people calling themselves such.[12] It was much more subtle, varied and contextual — almost a negative category that emphasized what kind of subject they were *not*, that is, not Chinese or Salako, but at the same time, both.[13] It was a discursive category in local circulation, however, and perhaps indicated that those who called themselves such exhibited this mixed-ness in a variety of ways.[14] It was also a category that did not survive in common everyday practice to the 1990s, as I had to be *told* about it, I never heard it used. The reasons for its falling out of public use will come clear below.

The normalcy of some kind of mixing, whatever people called themselves or were called, was also exhibited by the multiple languages or dialects commonly spoken on a daily basis — Dayak languages and various Chinese dialects.[15] Moreover, while a few Dayak women may have been taken by force as wives, as some oral histories have it, so many thousands of women married to Chinese or Pantokng could hardly have been taken against their will. Similarly, even though women married to Chinese men changed many of their daily practices — not least entering into a much more male-dominated domain of everyday life — they did not all move so far away as to have to cut off all ties with their Dayak families. More likely is that many people in the region had more intermingled everyday lives than has been acknowledged in much of the literature. A study of intermarriage between Chinese and Dayaks bears this out, at least tentatively (Tangdililing, 1993). It is very hard to discern the precise historical relations, however, in part because of the gendered historical record — women are barely mentioned in either primary sources or the principal secondary sources of the period.[16]

As the nineteenth and early twentieth centuries progressed, new waves of immigrants from China arrived in western Borneo and took up residence,

---

12. Under the *kongsis*, Chinese considered *Bantangfan* braver and more highly skilled in warfare, but they were looked down upon. For example, the punishment for murdering a *Bantangfan* was the payment of a much smaller sum of blood money than for a native-born or pure Chinese. See Yuan (2000: 70, citing Schaank, 1893: 84–6).
13. I am grateful to Hui Yew Foong (pers. comm., 2008) for encouraging me to clarify this point.
14. The contextual use of the term also requires further local research.
15. According to Heidhues (2003), few 'Chinese' spoke Malay.
16. Even Doty and Pohlman (1839), the missionary couple travelling through the region in 1838, make no mention of women in their report of their trek from Sambas to Pontianak.

including relatively large numbers of women. In the twentieth century, whole families from China migrated to West Kalimantan (Tangdililing, 1993). While this increased the number of local people who might be considered '*totok*', and provided opportunities for local Chinese or Pantokng to marry women of 'purer' Chinese descent, as well as to live more 'Chinese' lives,[17] the numbers of people with mixed Dayak–Chinese descent, and some influence in their lives, would still have been significant at that time.

Race had been territorialized through colonial land laws and policies. The Agrarian Act of 1870, passed in Java and based primarily on the circumstances there, declared that all land was state land except for a few tracts alienated during the time of United East India Company (VOC) rule (on Java). Land over which native or customary rights prevailed was technically state land; however, customary land was considered encumbered (unfree) and subject to what colonial legal experts called 'customary rights of avail' (Burns, 1999). Locally, customary rights to land were called *hak ulayat*, while the territories produced from these laws were and are referred to as *tanah adat*. According to law, *tanah adat* could not be purchased or otherwise transferred to non-Natives. Chinese, therefore, could not legally own or buy 'Native land' because by definition they were 'Aliens'. Chinese and other 'Foreign Orientals' were subject to commercial and civil law just like 'Europeans'.[18] The law was meant allegedly to protect Natives from losing control of the land on which they most depended, but actually limited them to particular tracts. The remaining state lands (the majority of the total land base) were then 'free' to be leased by the state to agricultural enterprises for development.[19]

During the colonial period, some 92 per cent of West Borneo Chinese lived and worked in 'Native States', so-called self-governing Malay sultanates, one of several administrative mechanisms of indirect rule that came out of and reproduced these racial politics (Cator, 1936: 162). Chinese individuals within these states were under the jurisdiction of Chinese Captains and Chinese officials who reported to Dutch administrators, an arrangement that was considered a kind of direct rule — of bodies, not territory — even in Native States which were by definition indirectly ruled territories (Natives living there were indirectly ruled) (Cator, 1936). Chinese subjects' predominance in the western-most parts of West Borneo caused the Dutch to dub Singkawang, Sambas, Mempawah and other nearby areas 'The Chinese Districts', even though technically they were living in Native States (Cator, 1936; Heidhues, 2003). The coining of this name, and the subsequent references to it in official reports and ordinary conversations, helped maintain and shape the racialized territory as largely Chinese.

17. This is what is emphasized in the literature on the Chinese of West Kalimantan.
18. As of 1899, 'European' included Japanese (Anderson, 1983).
19. In Java, the same state territories were used to carve out state forest lands (Peluso, 1992; Peluso and Vandergeest, 2001; see also Burns, 1999)

Though a full explanation of the reasons for and effects of these legal practices is beyond the scope of this chapter, some of their anomalies are worth pointing out. For example, long before the Dutch signed treaties in the mid-nineteenth century with Malay Sultans and constituted the colonial territories called 'Native States', Chinese smallholders in West Borneo had cleared land and improved it by draining swamps or creating irrigation systems. Chinese growers and their Dayak and mixed family members radically transformed the working landscape. According to contemporary informants, when Chinese first arrived, and throughout the times that they opened new forest or swamp for agriculture, contemporary Dayak leaders recognized these practices as constituting rights to the land and made agreements, sometimes involving rents, for their continued use of the land. Even after the passing of the NEI's Agrarian Act, these local precedents of recognition did not subside.

Agrarian legislation recognizing some Chinese rights within the Native States was passed in 1916 but was not implemented until 1921 (Cator, 1936: 163). This regulation stipulated that, 'with official permission, land could be hired [from Natives] by non-Natives for a term of 50 years for coconut or rubber growing', in the Native States.[20] Chinese smallholders' tremendous success in rubber and coconut production had, in part, forced the issue of land tenure regulation and provided the Dutch at least a semblance of control over what was already common practice, that is, Chinese acquisition and transformation of uncultivated or waste land, or their purchase or rental of local growers' ('Native') land (Cator, 1936: 165). There had been unrest in the years immediately prior to the passing of the legislation, unrest that Heidhues (2003: 159, 180–2) connects to Chinese dissatisfaction with Dutch approaches to these agrarian questions.[21] The 1916 law was only a small step, however, as legally these holdings were leases, with the logic of the racialized law still imposing limits on Chinese land rights (Cator, 1936: 164).[22] The leases were easy to obtain, reflecting the state's acknowledgment of its own inability to change this locally sanctioned practice, and perhaps recognizing, in a very small way, a local moral economy regarding land rights. At the same time, opposition to the leases was registered by people who feared the rights of the Natives were not being adequately protected in the wake of the legislation (ibid.: 166).

---

20. A similar regulation was valid in other regions of Government Domain (under direct rule) (Cator, 1936: 163, 164).
21. The Chinese Districts of Western Borneo played a major role in the final nudge toward legislation. Two Chinese officials were murdered near Bengkayang and Anjungan and the unrest among the Chinese community — called 'The Troubles' unfolded (Heidhues, 2003; The, 1966).
22. Moreover, they indicated an acknowledgement of the 'rightfulness' or moral authority of the Chinese smallholders' claims — even though these did not fit with the Dutch way of seeing the broader legal landscape of the NEI.

In response Cator, in particular, and some other Dutch agricultural offi-cials with experience in West Borneo, claimed that the practical differences between Chinese and Native smallholders in West Borneo were insignifi-cant despite their different races.[23] The Regulation of 1916, however, had the contradictory effect of legally recognizing that many smallholders were Chinese, while concretizing the idea, in practice, of a discrete Chinese-ness, here in relation to land use and rights.

After the formation of the Republic of Indonesia in 1950, legal plural-ism was ended. Indonesian citizenship was the important legitimating factor for land ownership — but no agrarian law was in place until after 1960. The agrarian law was manipulated to exclude Chinese from agricultural landholdings.[24] As under colonialism, however, land use practices could be and were used as racial identifiers.[25] Racial categories were not only de-rived from observations of land use practice, but became predictive of it, particularly for rice and tree crop production. It was common practice for anthropologists and other analysts to use subsistence strategies to categorize human–environment relations and to associate ethnicity or race with par-ticular types of resource practices such as hunting and gathering, farming of *sawah* (paddy rice) and swiddens (hill rice and vegetables) (King, 1993; LeBar, 1972; Padoch and Vayda, 1983). In West Borneo, for example, it was assumed that Dayaks grew upland rice in swidden agriculture and Chinese grew wet or paddy rice in *sawahs*. While these assumptions were certainly grounded in local practices and histories, such categorizations reinforced an increasingly strict differentiation between allegedly Chinese, Dayak, Malay and other groups' recognized land uses. But what were the actual land use practices of people of mixed heritage, and what were the influences on land use practice, if any, of Dayak women who married into Chinese families? The answers are difficult to document, in part because practice varied. We have already seen that some Pantokng chose to make swiddens, others grew wet rice in paddies, still others refused simple categorizations and farmed under the influence of multiple traditions and practices.

Assimilation was more difficult for Chinese than for other groups included in the colonial 'Foreign Oriental' category. After Indonesian independence, people of Arab or Indian heritage who married local Malays were assimilated into the category of *'pribumi'* or 'native sons', literally 'sons of the soil'. They came to be treated legally as Indonesian citizens and local. Chinese married to Dayaks and the known children of these unions were not assimi-lated in the same way. Even Chinese who became citizens immediately upon

23. De Groot (1885) argued that Dutch policy toward Chinese was already a mess at the end of the nineteenth century. See also Blusse and Merens (1993: 286–7) and Yuan (2000: 10). Cator (1936) was a huge proponent of changing Dutch policy toward Chinese land tenure.
24. Thanks to Mary Somers Heidhues for pointing this out (pers. comm., 2007).
25. Doing something that went against the grain of these stereotypes also reinforced them. Sandick and Marle (1919), for example, felt it important to explicitly point out that in Bengkayang, Dayaks as well as Chinese had pepper gardens — hundreds of them.

the formation of Indonesia were subjected to a different set of rules. The labels WNI (*Warga Negara Indonesia*, citizens of Indonesia) or WNA (*Warga Negara Asing*, foreign nationals) were marked on their identity cards. Since the term WNI was applied only to Indonesian citizens of Chinese ancestry, it perpetuated a racialized and exclusionary system by signifying that anyone recognized as having Chinese blood was not truly Indonesian. This was discursively reinforced by the terms WNI, WNA or 'non-pribumi', making Chinese identity truly and uniquely 'other'.[26]

Between Indonesia's declaration of independence in 1945 and the passing of the Basic Agrarian Law in 1960, no significant agrarian legislation was adopted. However, nationalists of many political stripes decried legal pluralism as colonial and feudal, and worked toward legislating a unitary land law for all Indonesian citizens, amenable, at first, to those of Chinese ancestry (Heidhues, pers. comm., 2007). Nonetheless, the political tides turned against Chinese in 1959 with the passing of PP10, a presidential decree forbidding foreign nationals to trade in rural areas; it affected Chinese in West Kalimantan, as many had not become Indonesian citizens. Chinese land rights and identities remained ambiguous in practice and legally, even though their roles in generating state revenues through rubber and other tree crop production had long been undeniable. Throughout this process, Pantokng remained largely invisible.

In such mixed and ambiguous social and legal circumstances, what else made smallholders 'Chinese' or 'Dayak'? Rubber production has played a key role in the answer to this question.

Chinese Rubber Smallholders

When rubber was first brought to the botanical gardens of Singapore and the Netherlands East Indies (NEI) in West Java (Bogor) at the turn of the twentieth century, British and Dutch colonial governments attempted to prevent smallholders from growing it (Dove, 1994). They failed. In the late 1930s, rubber produced in West Borneo provided the biggest share of NEI rubber traded on the world market (Ozinga, 1940: 285). By 1931, rubber smallholders in Borneo and Sumatra had planted more land with rubber than all plantation enterprises combined (ibid.: 264). Smallholders in Borneo continued to plant rubber even when restrictions on its export or the financial constraints on its production affected prices (Brookfield et al., 1995; Dove, 1993; Ozinga, 1940: 267). Defying the economic logic of larger enterprises, smallholders produced more rubber during the lean years of the Depression than they had before, *because* the prices were so low (Heidhues, 2003: 154, citing Ozinga, 1940: 262–4, 289–90).

---

26. See Hui (2007) for a detailed and nuanced discussion of West Kalimantan and Indonesian Chinese as 'Strangers at Home'.

Who were these rubber smallholders? By 1940, the majority of rubber smallholders in the whole colonial district of western Borneo were 'Natives'— Dayaks and Malays (Ozinga, 1940: 264). However, in the subdistricts (*onderafdeeling*) of Singkawang and Montrado, the heart of the Chinese Districts, more Chinese than any other population group in this area adopted the crop by the end of its first decade in West Borneo, even though the first smallholder to plant rubber was a Malay (Ozinga, 1940). After these first gardens became productive, Chinese farmers encouraged their Dayak friends, relatives and other associates to grow rubber, distributing seeds and seedlings. Dayak adoption picked up after the decline of forest product prices, which many Dayaks had collected for cash, in about 1915 (Heidhues, 2003: 145, 155). It is not clear when Dayak rubber planters in Bagak started planting rubber, but many explained that it became widespread in the late 1920s and 1930s. They also claim that their ancestors learned how from Chinese friends and family.[27]

Rural Chinese identity in West Borneo became tied up with rubber almost immediately, and this lasted throughout the colonial period. Chinese increased the trade in rubber and other tree crops, and were valued for the revenues they generated. J. Oberman, Resident of West Borneo in the 1930s, stated the predominant assumptions as follows: 'Every Chinese breadwinner has at least two plots, for growing food and a rubber garden'.[28] Sandick and Marle (1919), in their travels around the territory, made a point of differentiating rubber production in inland West Borneo generally and specifically in the Chinese Districts along the island's coast northwest of Pontianak. They point to class differences among the people they call the Chinese, declaring that rubber growers 'get their labourers by using new immigrants [from China]'[29] (1919: 132). This was allegedly because 'most of the natives were not interested in trade or commerce but mainly in subsistence' (Cator 1936: 155). Of course, this characterization depended on the legal fictions that Chinese and Natives were entirely distinct and helped perpetuate that notion. The fact that people of mixed heritage were farming in both 'Dayak swiddens' and 'Chinese rubber gardens' did not even enter into this rhetoric, as indicated by the epigraph at the beginning of this chapter.

Government officials and other observers represented the roadside rubber gardens of the early twentieth century Chinese as highly productive, efficient cropping systems. They wrote about Chinese planting their rubber in discrete single species plots, neat rows of trees unmixed with other trees and crops.

---

27. Cator (1936: 70) also claims that between 1915 and 1925, 'large quantities of rubber-seed and stumps were supplied by [Chinese] to the Natives on the understanding that they should share in the profits of cultivation'.
28. From: Memorandum of transfer, J. Oberman, Resident of West Borneo, 1938, ARA 2.10.39 MvO MMK 265, Appendix II, p. 5 (cited in Heidhues, 2003: 155).
29. Thanks to Arthur van Schaik for pointing out that the use of the word '*halen*' suggests they were active in 'importing' them.

Chinese growers (through a variety of labour arrangements such as share-tapping or wage-labour), hired Chinese labour, and in difficult times, their own family members. Chinese traders in rural areas and in cities dominated the trade in rubber, inside and outside the country, imports as well as exports (Heidhues, 2003: 156–7).

After the formation of the Republic of Indonesia, Chinese smallholders along the Singkawang–Bengkayang Road were still associated with dominance in the rubber trade and in production. A former village head of Bagak Sahwa told me that when he took up his post in 1965, Chinese growers were producing most of the metric tonne of rubber exported daily from Bagak alone. By 1965, a full one-third of Bagak's population were identified in the sub-district office records as Chinese, while according to the census, Chinese constituted nearly half of the neighbouring 'Chinese settlement' of Patengahan closest to the road (Poerwanto, 2005: 146, citing *Kecamatan Singkawang Statistics*, January 1965). Bagak residents sold their latex to any number of Chinese-owned shops along the roadside or to Chinese buyers who would bicycle from Singkawang to purchase it on their daily rounds.

In oral histories collected in the 1990s, older Bagak residents described their memories of the roadsides lined with Chinese rubber gardens. In 2004, during a drive along the road circling the Gunung Raya Pasi Nature Reserve, a Dayak friend affably pointed out places where rubber trees planted by Chinese growers could still be seen in the low hills behind the swath of irrigated rice fields. By this time, however, both sorts of landscapes, once indisputably Chinese, were occupied, owned or farmed by Dayak and other pribumi farmers, or cut down to make way for various 'Dayak' land uses.

The Origins of Dayak Rubber Gardens

Today, a student of property and political ecology dropping into Bagak Sahwa might note that there are three kinds of sites on which Dayaks there and in other villages along the Singkawang–Bengkayang road grow rubber. These different rubber-growing territories have different origins, types of claims and property rights, and 'indigenous' (the general term that has replaced 'Native') or 'nationalist' (Indonesian) associations. They are former swidden fallows, PPKR ('People's Rubber Schemes'), and transmigration areas. The ways these are used and talked about today make it nearly impossible to imagine that Chinese smallholders once farmed these 'Dayak' and 'Indonesian' sites. Contemporary rubber growing is entirely associated with non-Chinese Indonesians, and at many levels conceals the fact that Chinese and Pantokng were the most important early growers and traders of this commodity, buttressing a new racialization of rubber production and affecting general perceptions of racialized territorial and property claims.[30] As I show below, even histories of each type of rubber property disguise the prior occupation of much of this land by Chinese. As they confirm racialized categories of Dayak through associations between Dayak subjectivity and territory, they also mask the extensive mixing of Chinese and Dayak growers/smallholders and their practices that characterized this region.

Swidden Fallow Lands

Until the local introduction of rubber, the hillside landscapes created and managed by Bagak's Salako-speaking Dayaks consisted largely of swidden fields and fallow sites cut into forests of various ages and sizes, dotted with heavily managed, mixed fruit forests. Most grew rice and vegetables, and some maize and cassava in hillside swiddens, a practice which both defined and performed their ethnicity. Increasing needs for cash and the decline of prices for non-timber forest products under colonial rule partially sparked interest in planting rubber. Dutch colonial, and later Indonesian, officials represented Dayak production of rubber, mixed with fruit and other useful trees in swidden fallows, as disorderly and inefficient, similar to the ways they saw Dayak swidden agriculture.

Before the government established and enforced political forests, and before sedentarization was realized in law and practice, creating territorial village boundaries, Borneo swidden cultivators and other small farmers were minimally constrained by access to land locally.[31] Rubber could be planted in swidden fallows and, unless land was a constraint, did not hinder rice production in adjacent swidden fields. When swidden cycles were sharply reduced by political pressures to sedentarize and changes in resident populations occurred, it became more difficult for farmers to cultivate rubber and swidden rice simultaneously, as both crops needed land for a long-term production cycle. As rubber (and fruit) took up more land, swidden fallow times were shortened and rice yields lowered. Families could not produce enough rice to live on for a year. Consequently, farm-dependent families needed to produce rubber to buy rice and other goods (Peluso, 1996).

Salako readily admit the importance of what they and their ancestors learned about planting rubber from Chinese planters. Some had had credit and provision arrangements with Chinese wholesalers, shopkeepers or growers. By the 1930s, they could exchange rubber for government-issued coupons to buy food and other supplies on credit. Still, it was not until Dutch colonial officials forced Salako farmers to move their longhouses

---

30. Mary Somers Heidhues' 2003 book may dispel this kind of thinking about the origins of rubber production, but her work is unlikely to affect Chinese land rights.
31. 'Political forests' are state-authorized and regulated land use zones that are demarcated, mapped, legislated and reserved for long-term or 'permanent' maintenance under forest cover. See Peluso and Vandergeest (2001); see also the Law on Village Authority, 1979.

from the uppermost slopes of their ancestral lands to create a watershed protection area that Bagak Salako became serious about producing rubber. This move was the first in several steps that led to their sedentarization and the end of their 'shifting' when the landscape filled up with useful trees.[32]

Planting trees, or what Salako call 'hard' crops (*tanaman keras*) meant tying up swidden land for longer periods of time than it took to plant a season of rice and vegetables, after which fields could go fallow and then revert back to secondary forest. In theory, all descendants of a forest-clearing ancestor could claim rights to make a swidden in that spot. In practice, family members' claims varied depending on whether they were close or distant kin of the original planters. During cultivation, however, a single household or individual controlled the product and the plot, effectively individualizing commonly held rights for the season.[33] With field crops, the short production seasons restored other family members' access to the land much sooner, obviously, than would productive tree crops.

Over time, a household's labour investment in the production and maintenance of rubber was considerable and lengthened the period of effective individual land tenure. Still, in times of relative local land abundance, old, unproductive rubber trees could be abandoned on a fallowed plot, signalling the land's 'return' to the descent group. Land for swiddening became restricted as more people planted rubber and fruit trees immediately after harvesting a rice crop, laying claim to descent group land for longer periods. By the 1970s, when fallow periods in Bagak Sahwa lasted at most ten years, some rubber planters began to directly pass the gardens on to their children. Alternatively, when forty-year-old rubber trees stopped producing, planters might make a swidden the next year, followed by more rubber or fruit. Previously, these gardens would have returned to the descent group pool. By the 1990s, fallows had been reduced to five to six years, 'empty' swidden fallows had become much less common, and swidden fallows planted with rubber had been effectively privatized. They were called *kabotn getah* (rubber gardens) which had come to indicate not only a land use, but a kind of individualized, territorial or property category.[34]

Salako growers have long viewed rubber production as a way to demonstrate their movement toward modernity (author interviews, 1990, 1991). Rubber's status as solely a cash crop meant that growers were commodity producers. While they had limited success in changing the stereotypes of themselves as 'subsistence cultivators', many hoped to deflect the accusations that Dayaks were 'wild farmers' or 'irrational'. Such colonial

---

32. On this sedentarization process in Bagak Sahwa, see Peluso (1996).
33. On myths about communal and private property rights in swidden agriculture, see Dove (1983). For debates about land tenure among swidden cultivators in Borneo, see Appell (1997); Weinstock (1979); Weinstock and Vergara (1987).
34. In 2004, some people still held on to small (200 m²) plots to plant enough swidden rice for ritual purposes. These were being fallowed only a year or two before planting again.

stereotypes were perpetrated since Indonesian independence largely by Indonesian foresters and large-scale plantation entrepreneurs competing for
the same landscapes during the Suharto regime (1966–98). This move toward modernity changed the kinds of practices that constituted Salako or
Dayak identity, especially land and tree tenure. The process of adopting rubber production helped define Dayaks as 'smallholders' or 'peasants', partly
because it tied them to place in different ways than had their swidden landscape practices. In other words, being Dayak was not restricted to growing
rice in swiddens and sharing access to land with other members of a descent group; it also came to be expressed and interpreted through growing
rubber — a commodity — in old swidden fallows.

In 1979, the passing of the national Law on Village Authority fixed village borders, legally keeping villages, including Bagak, 'in place'. Entire
villages could no longer move to new sites, as they had in the past when
a longhouse's settlement territory filled up with productive and long-living
trees. Easy access to the urban markets of Singkawang and Pontianak, facilitated by the repaving of the road in the 1960s and the entry of Japanese
vehicles (motorcycles and vans) in the 1970s, added additional incentives
for planting trees. By 1991, 85 per cent of the villagers owned productive
rubber trees. People could still move, but they no longer brought place
with them (Li, 1999: Ch. 1; Thongchai, 1994; Vandergeest and Peluso,
1995).

Although still called customary land (*tanah adat*), the uses and tenure
practices on these former swidden lands had changed considerably. So had
the racialized association with rubber; it was becoming a 'native' commodity.
Its adoption all over West Kalimantan by Dayaks (a process begun in the
1920s), was being widely documented and used as part of development
strategies (see, for example, Dove, 1993, 1994, 1998; Ward and Ward,
1974).

PPKR: The People's Rubber

A second type of privatized rights to rubber land associated with Dayaks
came in the early 1980s, through a project/scheme called PPKR — *Proyek
Perkebunan Karet Rakyat*, The People's Smallholder Rubber Garden Project.
Clonal varieties were introduced, and smallholder Dayak families were still
the main growers. Funded by the World Bank through the Indonesian People's Bank, this project was introduced immediately after the formal consolidation of several hamlets into the administrative village of Bagak Sahwa.
The land and tree tenure relations created on project lands were completely
new. Individuals or households, not descent groups, were to become title
holders to discrete plots of land.

There were some conditionalities imposed prior to the assignment of a
PPKR scheme to a village. For example, although the loans and titles were

held individually, the village had to identify a contiguous tract of land for planting PPKR rubber, both to facilitate project administration/surveillance by World Bank personnel and to ensure common adherence to the production regime. This requirement generally meant that villagers had to agree to use customary land, and assumed that in any swidden-based system, 'unmanaged fallow lands' would be extensive. The project also required participants to take credit packages to finance the clearance of the area with herbicides and fungicides and buy the high-yielding seedlings. Finally, though it is not clear that this was actually stated, it was assumed that the land and the loans were *not* for Chinese or non-pribumi. Indigenous Dayaks and other pribumi citizens were defined as the targets of these economic development schemes.

The implementation of these rubber production schemes had major territorial and racializing effects. PPKR rubber became a mechanism for the central Indonesian state to assert authority over village land. From the state's point of view, the status of such land would be effectively changed from customary land (*tanah adat*), a category subject to local authority during the colonial period and immediately thereafter, to private property administered directly by the state.[35] Once the loans were paid off, the land became private property (*tanah milik*) and the owner received a land title. The title was registered with an Indonesian government agency and legally would thenceforth have to be transferred or sold exclusively through state mechanisms. In this way, the state strengthened its local power and presence. By changing the land's status, the villagers' relations to the land itself was changed, with the state recognizing and adjudicating only certain kinds of property rights. *Tanah adat* thus became a commodity, stripped of the social meanings invested in it through its history and genealogy. It was not talked about in this way, but this was effectively what was meant to happen.

Yet curiously, perhaps, the move legitimized a re-racialization of this land. Its legal status had been murky. From local Dayak points of view, the land had always constituted part of their territory. As discussed above, the predecessors of their leaders had given Chinese settlers, living in the region until 1967, permission to convert and farm nearby forest and swamp lands (author's interviews; see also Heidhues, 2003; Jackson, 1970; Yuan, 2000). Before the colonial government took over in 1854 and during the period of Chinese *Kongsis* in this area from the mid-eighteenth to the mid-nineteenth century, Chinese settlers had either asked permission of local Dayak or Malay authorities to gain access to land, or, if no one was using it, simply assumed control and converted it. In those times, if land was abandoned and the user had not designated an heir or a new rights-holder, it would return to *tanah adat* status (Peluso, 1996). As one Salako leader stated, even if the swamp forests and lowlands from which these Chinese settlers had initially carved productive *sawahs* and gardens had been undesirable

---

35. Although in reality, the bank (BRI — People's Bank of Indonesia) owned the trees until the loans were paid off.

to Salako farmers at the time of their original allocation to Chinese, if the current Chinese holders abandoned the land it still could be defined as *tanah adat*. Another added that all village land became *tanah adat* in the eyes of local people when village boundaries were established in 1979. Using this land for PPKR, therefore, served to legitimize Dayak claims to this territory.

The name of this rubber planting scheme offers another clue to the political intentions and racializing effects of this project. The 'R' in PPKR stands for '*rakyat*'. *Rakyat*, meaning 'the people', is a strange word to use in this place and at this time. By 1980 it had become a dated word, associated more with the Sukarno regime than that of Suharto, largely because of its populist and communist associations. Suharto regime programmes tended to use the more depoliticized term '*masyarakat*' to mean 'the people'. Both terms are correct in Indonesian; each is inflected by the discourses of different political eras. Despite these associations, the word *rakyat* under Suharto could be used to mean 'the little people'; it actually differentiated people by class. It also carried a racialized meaning: *rakyat* was *never* used to refer to someone deemed Chinese, no matter how poor. The so-called little people's rubber was not for Chinese in New Order Indonesia.

PPKR was thus for pribumi — non-Chinese Indonesians, sons of the soil, smallholders, little people of West Kalimantan. Some pribumi — local — people who were not Dayak, were granted or bought PPKR plots: Madurese, Javanese, Sundanese, and Malays owned PPKR plots at the time of my 1991 survey. Besides providing land titles and modern agricultural techniques to pribumi, the scheme helped change the representation of Salako farmers from 'shifting cultivators' to 'smallholders', and was intended to end shifting cultivation where PPKR rubber was planted.[36] PPKR produced the place (Bagak Sahwa) as a territory belonging to Indonesia, and the people farming it as pribumi: non-Chinese, Indonesian citizens.

The first PPKR area of 42 ha was planted in Bagak Sahwa in 1981–2; another 87 ha were planted in 1982–3, and a further 80 ha were planted over the following three years — a total of 209 hectares. Finding available contiguous customary land could be tricky in an area that was densely populated, by local standards, by the 1980s. However it starts to become clear how it was possible when we realize that most of the land used for PPKR had previously been the rubber gardens, fallows and vegetable and fruit gardens forcibly abandoned by Chinese in 1967 (see below). PPKR was possible only because of the sheer amount of land left behind by former Chinese or *Pantokng* residents who had left, and in the process left land in fallow.

An unintended effect of the state programme was the enabling mechanism of PPKR — not only enabling an increase in Indonesian state authority and presence, but also enabling 'the people', in this case a Salako *adat*

---

36. Even though the Dayaks of Bagak Sahwa had not shifted for a very long time (Peluso, 1996).

community, to assert customary authority over the land. PPKR thus contributed to the racialization of territory and bodies in Bagak Sahwa, whether Salako or Indonesian state narratives of its history are taken as accurate.

Transmigration Rubber: Post-colonial Citizens and Symbolic Subjects

The third type of site associated with Dayaks and other pribumi growing rubber is the transmigration area. Rubber plantations associated with transmigration became an explicit symbol of Indonesian citizenship, national belonging and a kind of smallholder modernity in many parts of West Kalimantan. Although not on Bagak Sahwa village lands, a transmigration area was established in 1989 on an extensive tract of fallow or abandoned adat land in a neighbouring village with close historical connections to Bagak (Peluso, 1996).[37]

The transmigration project planned to resettle 400 families from West Java and other densely populated areas of Indonesia on 800 ha of land. Such projects incorporated the local resettlement of Dayaks and other villagers willing to give up their land in exchange for 2 ha of project land per nuclear household, to be planted in high yielding varieties of clonal rubber. Dayak residents of this 'host village' were required to join the resettlement scheme, as negotiated by their village leader. Again, access to transmigration land was defined by racialized citizenship. Only pribumi were allowed to participate. This was because transmigration was represented as being for the poor, a characterization which, in Indonesian state ideologies and practices, did not have room for Chinese (Hui, 2007). The public assumption was that Chinese, being 'rich', would not want to participate. Moreover, though transmigration was often represented as symbolic of Indonesia, promoting the mixing of Indonesia's ethnically diverse populations (Elmhirst, 1999), many Dayaks viewed it as a process of losing their land. They also had to take out the same loans as other participants for the inputs necessary to grow clonal rubber and, when it was all paid off, they received a land title.

Again, re-racialization resulted from the establishment of this transmigration area. While Salako Dayaks had long lived in this village, so had Chinese and Pantokng. Dayak swiddens, fallows, rubber gardens and *tembawangs* here were not enough on their own to account for all the fallow land used for transmigration, even if each household was estimated to have had 5–10 ha in various stages of field or fallow. Historical materials show that area's most populous group was Chinese (Cator, 1936; Poerwanto, 2005; Sandick and Marle, 1919). This area constituted the agricultural hinterlands of Buduk, one of the region's earliest and most productive gold mines, and Patengahan, an early agricultural settlement of Chinese (Yuan, 2000). From

---

37. This was the village that some residents leaving Bagak in the 1930s moved to, seeking new farming areas when the Dutch established a watershed protection area on the mountaintop.

my work with maps, local histories and these published historical accounts, I can show that parts of Patengahan were integrated into the administrative village of Bagak Sahwa and adjacent villages when the new administrative villages were being formed. The bulk of the 800 ha came from the hundreds of hectares of productive land abandoned by Chinese and Pantokng evicted in 1967.

The presumption underlying this government project was that by the time land titles were distributed and the loans paid off, the land would be fully commoditized and held by pribumi, a category which did not differentiate Dayaks from other 'native Indonesian' ethnic groups. Yet from local Dayak perspectives, creating the transmigration area both reconstituted the land as Dayak and recognized them as pribumi. Participation in such a project by local 'Dayaks' hid any mixed heritage in their families. When I naively asked the village head in 1991 why he had 'given away' the village land to the transmigration authorities, he said he had done no such thing. He was, rather, acting on behalf of his people, contributing to their development and cementing his authority over the land under the new governance mechanisms (interview, 1991).

Even the process by which this land was slated for transmigration confirmed Dayak authority and territory. When he and other village heads travelled to Jakarta to negotiate transmigration deals, the government in a sense recognized the land as *tanah adat* — Dayak territory under a Dayak leader's authority. By simultaneously ignoring that the land had been leased to and registered by Chinese, it also denied the history of the vast Chinese holdings, and of the forms of colonial state authority over those lands and people. The rights-creating practices of Chinese farmers, recognized by Dayaks and other local authorities during an earlier era, were also erased. Those who had made that long-avoided land liveable and arable, became irrelevant to the historical record.

Land allocation and occupation began in 1989 and, within six years, rubber was produced from the newly planted trees on the 800 ha tract. Like PPKR trees, transmigration rubber varieties were clonal and high yielding and, ironically, like Chinese rubber, were planted in 'orderly' and 'modern' plantation style. Several hundred Javanese and Sundanese families moved into the jurisdiction of this Dayak village head and became rubber smallholders alongside the resident Dayaks integrated into the project. Having lost several hundred constituents and subjects to the 1967–74 evictions and counter-insurgency operations, the village head now had a new and expanded pribumi constituency, simultaneously cementing his position as both a Dayak and an Indonesian leader.

Further assisting in the rewriting of the local history were larger narratives about Borneo rubber, and the other practices around smallholder and Dayak rubber production. By this time, Borneo rubber was already 'known' as a Dayak or 'indigenous' crop, and came to be known more widely as a commodity produced by native growers, as more and more reports by economists and anthropologists came out on other parts of West Kalimantan (such as Dove, 1983, 1993; Ward and Ward, 1974). The story of how the Dutch had tried to monopolize rubber production but had been confounded by their Indonesian rural subjects was a well-known story and a source of pride. Planting rubber in transmigration sites seemed to be a natural, normal extension of local production practices and a true 'Indonesian' crop grown by pribumi migrants and transmigrants and 'indigenous' locals. By deflecting attention from this region's specific history with rubber and Chinese growers, the Chinese role in producing these landscapes was also lost. The final section of this chapter shows that the elimination of Chinese and some Pantokng and the masking of their presence would have been less likely without violence.

RACIALIZED TERRITORIES, VIOLENCE, ENCLOSURE

So where were Chinese and Pantokng rubber producers as these Dayak histories came into being? We have already seen that PPKR and transmigration required contiguous land, and that the Chinese smallholders discussed in the previous section were no longer part of the rural land-use conversation in New Order Indonesia, as non-pribumi. This is because physical violence and eviction underlie today's rubber landscape; indeed it is hidden also by rubber production in those same spaces. Violence generated by the change of regime politics between Sukarno and Suharto, in the period from 1965 through 1974, hardened the differences between people considered or self-identified as Chinese or Dayak, and led definitively to the decline of the public use of the term and also to the subjectivity of people who had lived their lives as Pantokng.

To connect these events to the property and landscape outcomes of these changes, I need to explain the geopolitical context, however schematically. Briefly, West Kalimantan in the 1950s and 1960s was a site where global and national conflicts were both staged and played out. Indonesia's first president, Sukarno, took an anti-colonial stance to the formation of the Federation of Malaysia and launched his *Ganjang Malaysia* (Crush Malaysia) campaign from West Kalimantan. In the course of this, the province became heavily militarized. The turnabout of Sukarno's political fortunes by an alleged coup attempt in 1965, and the appointment of Suharto as second President, led to the criminalization of the Communist Party and other leftist organizations and a transformation of Indonesia's positioning in Cold War politics. Despite the extremely complex circumstances on the ground, the official position in West Kalimantan became that all rural Chinese were either illegal communists or their supporters, and therefore enemies of the new Indonesian government (Coppel, 1983; Soemadi, 1974: 92).[38]

---

38. I can only provide a schematic account here of this highly complex and relatively long period of conflict in West Kalimantan. For more in-depth analysis of the 'Confrontation' in English,

The famous Indonesian massacres of communists, other leftists, and alleged associates in 1965–66 in Java, Bali and Sumatra were followed by
pogroms against Chinese in major cities of Java and Sumatra. Anti-Chinese
violence in West Kalimantan followed in 1967–8, with a different twist.[39]
This was not spontaneous anti-Chinese action. The military was clearly
behind the event called *Demonstrasi Cina* (by Dayaks today) or *Demonstrasi Dayak* (by government and journalistic accounts then) (Davidson and
Kammen, 2002; Peluso and Harwell, 2001). From late 1967 to early 1968,
Dayaks and other local residents responded to organized and pre-planned
provocations by Indonesian soldiers and intelligence officers, with the assistance of some Dayak leaders, to evict Chinese from their rural homes and
businesses.

According to local and military sources, Indonesian Special Forces alerted
Dayak leaders of the impending order to mobilize collectively against the
Chinese. Once the plan was known, Dayak villagers in Bagak and several
other villages told their Chinese and Pantokng friends and relatives what they
heard was going to happen. In Bagak, what were thought by some would be
temporary evacuations took place peacefully; no-one was killed. This was
the case in some other villages in the early days as well (Heidhues, 2003).
These Chinese were accompanied to Singkawang in the days preceding the
actual 'Demonstration',[40] another indication that it had been planned.

The signs to begin the Demonstration and other aspects of the violence
were explicitly racialized as Dayak: in addition to a radio announcement
from the former Dayak governor of West Kalimantan, the red bowl (*mangkok
merah*) a Dayak symbol for war, was to be circulated. The red bowl sum-
moned Dayak men and boys to perform as headhunters and warriors. They
wore red headbands, bark bracelets and loincloths — things not done for
decades. For weapons they used elongated bush knives (*mandau*) of ancient
headhunting renown, and homemade hunting guns. As the bowl arrived in
each village, gongs were sounded and people went into action. One village
head from a settlement in the hills behind Montrado market said he and his
'troops' (villagers) were told to descend into Montrado market, evict the
Chinese shopkeepers, kill people who refused to leave, and take over the
shops and the Chinese *sawahs*. He used the Sukarno-era phrase '*Ganjang*'

---

see Coppel (1983); Mackie (1974); Poulgrain (1998). In Indonesian, see, for example,
Kustanto (2002). On the period after *Konfrontasi*, see, in English, Coppel (1983); Davidson
and Kammen (2002); Peluso (2003); Peluso and Harwell (2001); and in Indonesian, Effendy
(1995) and Soemadi (1974).

39. One of the best discussions of these politics is still Coppel (1983).
40. van Hulten (1994) and author's interviews. How many people actually died during the
worst violence and in the aftermath is difficult to ascertain. Most estimates of deaths ranged
from 300 to 500. Many thousands more became refugees: Feith (1968: 134) reported some
53,000 of them by the end of December. Later estimates are much higher. Soemadi (1974)
estimated about 75,000; Douglas Kammen (pers. comm.) has estimated nearly 117,000.

(crush) to describe what they had been told to do: '*Ganjang Cina*'.[41] The evictions spread from Sambas to Pontianak and Sanggau districts, engulfing all settlements where Chinese lived and becoming increasingly violent as they moved further inland (Coppel, 1983; Feith, 1968; Soemadi, 1974).

But who was Chinese and who was Dayak? The very mixed nature of this district, as we have seen in the term 'Pantokng', often made it difficult if not impossible for troops — most from Java, Sumatra and other external places — to separate the two groups. In many cases, political affiliations and a family's explicit orientation to a political position or organization made it clear; Chinese not only acknowledged and performed their identities as such, but were recognizable to military and government officials through social practices and ways of life. For some, more recently migrated people — those who had come over the past few decades — it was not too difficult for military to decide that they were Chinese; many did not even speak Indonesian. Stereotyped views of agrarian practice had became indicators of racialized identities: 'Chinese worked *sawah* and Dayaks made swiddens' was one way the military and officials differentiated them, though Pantokng were involved in both. The creation of a pre-Demonstration panic in the months before can be understood also as a psychological warfare tactic meant both to mobilize people and to differentiate 'Chinese' from 'Dayaks'. The military's plan was to compel Dayaks to enact racialized violence and evict Chinese from the former Chinese Districts.[42] But they still needed help, in large part to root out the Pantokng — a term which had no meaning to the military, as they would have defined any *peranakan/Pantokng* as Chinese.

Pantokng thus had to choose an ethnicity, if there were any doubts. Dayaks both in Bagak and elsewhere (see Tangdililing, 1993) say that, as far as possible, they protected anyone with a close Dayak family connection — a wife, a child or parent married to Dayaks, practising a Dayak way of life — who wished to stay in the village. Ten or more families chose to stay in Bagak. Yet whoever stayed had to depend for their very safety on their neighbours not giving them away. A few Dayak men whose wives were Chinese or Pantokng who appeared Chinese talked about hiding their wives for the duration of the violence (interviews, October 1998).

People today maintain that it was never clear that Chinese would *not* be allowed to return. Chinese farmers, shopkeepers and householders asked Dayak friends to watch out for their farms, shops, houses, stores of rice and other supplies, while they went to Singkawang or stayed with relatives until things cooled down. In the end, however, most were not allowed to return, reclaim, or sell their homes, shops, agricultural land and rubber gardens. Even if friends had not *planned* on taking over their property for the long term, national and regional politics left Chinese land and shops in their

---

41. He told me this in an interview in 1998; this same term was used by Soemadi (1974).
42. Soemadi (1974) discusses these strategies explicitly. See also Kustanto (2002) and Davidson (2002), as well as Davidson and Kammen (2002) and Peluso (2003).

hands for good.[43] The land was either expropriated by the state or directly appropriated by Dayaks and other local Indonesians of Madurese, Malay and other ethnic backgrounds.

The politics of the years following the Demonstration were a politics of racialized fear. While most of the evictions had ended by mid-1968, the military (now purged of its Communist and other left-leaning soldiers) continued to occupy barracks and houses in interior villages (including two or three encampments in Bagak) until 1974, to 'root out' alleged communist guerrillas — now all formally defined as Chinese — who had hidden in the forest.[44] During this time, Dayak villagers were taken as 'trackers' into the forest — again, due to racialized notions of their 'forest expertise'. Refusal to take part was interpreted as complicity. The military commander appointed Dayak villagers to decide who would go into the forest with the soldiers each day. Other villagers were assigned to guard Chinese communist prisoners and patrol the village at night. Special Forces tortured Dayaks who refused to participate in forest operations.[45] To be Chinese or sympathetic to Chinese meant women could be subject to rape by soldiers, and men to other forms of torture and sometimes death, often on a soldier's whim.

Caught in the middle of all this were those of such mixed heritage that they had long ago stopped calling themselves Chinese or Dayak — they were simply farmers or peasants — *petani*. Dayak farmers or leaders perceived by occupying forces as too sympathetic to Chinese could find themselves hung by the ankles or partially drowned until they gave up the names or hiding places of 'Chinese' or called Pantokng neighbours 'Chinese'. Some Pantokng families who chose to remain in the village paid a heavy price. One Pantokng farmer I met had had a Dayak mother and was married to a Dayak woman. He had been tortured by electric shock, interrogated and jailed. He survived but today is one of the poorest people in the village. Another has a shop on the main street. He worked with the military during the searches, translating for captives and guarding the village perimeter with the military and local village patrols. Other Pantokng villagers, some of whom I did not know until very recently, had Chinese or Pantokng ancestry, literally became Dayak: making swiddens, learning rituals, studying healing, and so on.

After the months of violent evictions, and then through their long subsequent absence, the agrarian Chinese of West Kalimantan, as either wet rice or rubber-growing smallholders, literally disappeared as a possible identity.

43. For much more detailed discussions of these events, see Davidson and Kammen (2002); Heidhues (2003); HRW (1997); Peluso and Harwell (2001); conflicting accounts by 'eye-witnesses' include Coppel 1983; Effendy (1982); Feith (1968); van Hulten (1994); Soemadi (1974).
44. See the dissertations by Hui (2007) and Davidson (2002) for a discussion of the shifting alliances and compositions of the military arms of PGRS, PARAKU and PKI during this fraught time.
45. Soemadi (1974) claims the military had 'finished' by 1970 in the western parts of the province.

The use of the term Pantokng also ended. It was no longer safe to be mixed. A six-year military undertaking had been necessary to wrest control of their rural homes, their land and their rubber, followed by a continued threat of violence in West Kalimantan under Suharto. West Kalimantan's heavy police and military presence, enabling continued national surveillance of the area said to have a 'Chinese problem', helped wipe out those hybrid identities.[46] The violence of Chinese and Pantokng eviction was hidden from view, but this also helped protect those Pantokng who had stayed and re-identified as Dayak. Pantokng, Bendi, Peranakan in all their local iterations were literally rendered 'people without history' (Wolf, 1982) — because history was no longer safe.[47] Ironically, both then and a hundred years earlier, violent states mobilized previously sympathetic people who had no stake in the idea of Chinese as a competitive political or economic category, to fight them.

Despite some assumptions to the contrary, Dayaks were not the only pribumi to acquire Chinese land. Indeed, as the stories of property rights and rubber land uses reveal above, the re-racialization of this land was not a practice by 'Dayaks' alone, but as much a move to embed pribumi — Indonesian citizens — in the local landscape. The comment of a village head in Montrado sub-district was telling: 'the Madurese came to Montrado market at the same time as us (Dayaks) in 1967. Before that, it was all Chinese' (author's field notes, October 2004). Bagak's village head allocated shares of abandoned Chinese land to anyone he considered 'local'. Madurese and Malays appropriated abandoned houses and land; they were attracted to rice paddies more than most Dayaks, though many Dayaks were given *sawah* 'shares', which they attempted to farm, dispose of, or hold. Even with all these allocations, a great deal of land was 'left over' and went into fallow. The transformation of this land into pribumi property under rubber production has been described above.

Of course, the extent of 'Chinese land' abandoned would have been known locally but not made obvious to the wider Indonesian public. Some 50,000 to 100,000 people from rural areas of West Kalimantan had been expelled; we can assume that hundreds of thousands of hectares were abandoned. Estimates of the amount of land in West Kalimantan under *sawah* alone, harvested in 1967–71, ranged from 171,000 ha to 186,000 ha (Ward and Ward, 1974). While a small portion of this land was probably created by Dayak and Malay farmers (see, for example, Padoch et al., 1998), we have seen that the majority of it was constructed by Chinese and their *peranakan*

---

46. For more details of these events, and greater historical depth on this period, see sources mentioned in previous footnotes. However, racialized territorialization is not discussed by these other authors.
47. Heidhues (2003: 252) ironically points out that this was the first time a real 'quarter system' — living areas designated racially — was in full force, except for a few years under a particularly 'pugnacious' colonial official.

or Pantokng offspring during and after the *Kongsi* period. Some 80,000 ha had been covered by the short leases for rubber and coconut production land, and much more remained beyond the government's reach (Cator, 1936). In Bagak Sahwa, 209 ha of land were 'available' for PPKR, which had required contiguous land. In the neighbouring village, 800 ha of contiguous, fallowed land were given over to some 350 transmigrant families. These local projects in two small villages accounted for a limited area of the former Chinese Districts.

The 1967–8 evictions and expropriations were not written into the Indonesian history books available for the first ten years of my research in this area (from 1990 to 2000). Nor was it permissible to ask about ethnic origins on national censuses. At best, in *Kompas* newspaper, West Kalimantan Chinese were referred to as 'refugees', and after their resettlement and dispersal, the Indonesian press spent minimal ink on the subject. To the best of my knowledge, the question of compensation or land rights has never been raised formally by or for them.

CONCLUDING THOUGHTS: THE RACIALIZATION OF RUBBER TERRITORIES

The history of rubber in Bagak Sahwa has shown how rubber has both created rights and facilitated erasures in different ways and in different eras. The violence discussed above has been obscured by a 'naturalness' ascribed to contemporary patterns of indigenous people's and pribumi's rubber growing. This chapter is not meant to deny that Dayaks and Malays have grown rubber for a very long time in West Kalimantan. However, the undifferentiated representation of rubber production in economic statistics and in terms of a national development that excludes hundreds of thousands of former smallholders has obfuscated a deeper understanding of rubber production and property rights in this important rubber-producing region.

As we saw above, Chinese smallholders were major revenue producers for the colonial government in Western Borneo but also an administrative anomaly. Local Malays and Dayaks recognized their holdings. Yet, Dutch agrarian law initially had no appropriate category for them as landholders, even though their practices had created rights by local reckonings. After a period of stop-gap Dutch legislation recognizing lease rights, the issues of Chinese land rights and citizenship were not resolved in the first decades of the Indonesian Republic. With the rise of the New Order, Chinese were evicted, many violently, and not allowed to return to rural areas. Government transmigration and PPKR schemes thereafter eliminated the long period of ambiguity regarding Chinese lands: they literally covered up the fact that Chinese had lived there and were forced out. Just as clonal varieties were brought in to replace the traditional varieties of rubber, the growers themselves were also replaced.

Historically, in this part of Kalimantan, rubber was racialized as Chinese, and Chinese were racialized as rubber smallholders. In the Chinese Districts, rubber expanded most rapidly among Chinese smallholders from Pontianak to Singkawang and into the interior beyond, often travelling through Chinese connections to Dayak growers. Rubber subsequently created private rights to land for Dayaks in three ways, within and outside their descent group holdings. The longevity of rubber, compared to the longevity of the field crops replaced by rubber, combined with the changing political ecologies of the region, facilitated *de facto* privatization when farmers repeatedly planted traditional varieties of rubber in their swidden fallows on customary lands. Rubber-growing on PPKR lands and on transmigration plantations generated land titles [private] for both indigenous-pribumi and other pribumi growers. Constraining access to these schemes racialized these territories. The development schemes reinforced the inclusion of local people in a larger territorial and political entity, the Indonesian nation, while inserting the nation quite literally and symbolically into the landscape itself. Planting clonal rubber in evenly spaced rows, treating it with chemicals, and making land a commodity with a title, could be understood as the creation of a new Indonesian frontier.

While producing rights and territories, rubber concurrently produced erasures of people, types of land use, and other systems of rights. Perhaps surprisingly, many Indonesians and Indonesianists remain unaware of this history. Recent NGO and development writings about 'jungle' rubber (for example, Penot, 1995) and PPKR rubber have reinforced the generic indigenous associations, making them seem like a natural history. The history-making narratives of development have thus helped over-determine the ways rubber production and rubber smallholders have been represented, produced and perceived.[48] Stereotypical thinking about 'the Dayaks of Borneo' across regions conflated practices and histories in the interior with those of the former Chinese Districts.

Since the 1967–74 violence, the 'blood and fire' that lay beneath these 'lands filled with tears'[49] has been rendered invisible in the quietest, most subtle ways.[50] Rubber helped erase people, practices and landscape history — at least from the most visible layers. Territory — and even a crop — once racialized as Chinese was reinscribed as simultaneously

---

48. The Ward and Ward (1974) piece is particularly important because of its timing, just as the violence against Chinese and communists in the forests was coming to an end and development as a counter-insurgency measure was being put into place. One line in that piece states, 'Since 1967, most Chinese rubber smallholders have left their former holdings, some of which have been occupied by Malays or Dayaks' (ibid.: 36).
49. A name given the abandoned land by a woman in Bagak Sahwa (interview, 1991; Peluso 1996).
50. Davidson and Kammen (2002) tellingly refer to it as 'Indonesia's Unknown War'.

Indonesian and Dayak. So were the people, as smallholder Pantokng who had remained in the village after the Demonstration and practised their lives largely as Dayaks had little incentive to claim differently: it was life-threatening not to perform as such. In this way, amidst heated academic and policy debates about Dayak rights and marginalization, themselves extremely critical issues, the idea of the dispossessed Chinese smallholder was, at least for a time, lost to New Order social history. To be Chinese under Suharto was *not* to be a farmer. Chinese smallholders of West Kalimantan were relegated to a distant colonial past.

In this contribution, I have delineated connections among property, territory, violence and identity, using the production of rubber as a lens through which to see. In the process, I have shown how the commodity and production histories of rubber helped to create territories and entrench racialized identities and associations with territory. Violence ultimately played a larger role in erasing prior claims, in associating these claims with people of particular 'ethnic' or 'racial' categories, in establishing the control of selected old and new actors over trees and land, and in legitimating access or recognition. In fact, the use of race-cum-citizenship as a condition for access to land affected not only notions of territoriality but the very understanding of ethnicity or racialized bodies and citizenship. Violence subsequently transformed the racialized associations of this landscape, while rubber erased its history.

Examining rubber-growing practices and their changing associations with Chinese and Dayaks might have led to a conclusion that both ethnicity and property rights in this region were 'fuzzy', much as they often are to either outsiders or to policy makers and government officials who have had to deal with them (Verdery, 1998). Histories of rubber production and land rights could also be represented as 'negotiated' (Juul and Lund, 2002; Peters, 2002), if we narrow our view and map rubber production in the Singkawang hinterland and past across 'Native' or 'pribumi' spaces, with 'foreigners' redefined over time from Chinese, to migrants and transmigrants. All these analyses could be seen as accurate or 'true'. What is striking, however, is not how closely Chinese were once identified with rubber, but how rapidly and completely this association disappeared. There was nothing 'fuzzy' about this transformation: they were *made* to disappear, removed from the landscape and the history.

REFERENCES

Anderson, Benedict (1983) *Imagined Communities: Reflections on the Origin and Spread of Nationalism.* London and New York: Verso.
de Angelis, Massimo (1991) 'Marx and Primitive Accumulation: The Continuous Character of Capital's "Enclosures"', *The Commoner* (September). http://www.thecommoner.org
Appell, George N. (1997) 'The History of Research on Traditional Land Tenure and Tree Ownership in Borneo', *Borneo Research Bulletin* 28: 82–98.

Blomley, Nicholas K. (2003) 'Law, Property, and the Spaces of Violence: The Frontier, the Survey, and the Grid', *Annals of the Association of American Geographers* 93(1): 121–41.

Blusse, L. and Ank Merens (1993) 'Nuggets from the Gold Mines, Three Tales of the Ta-kong Kongsi of West Kalimantan', in Leonard Blusse and Harriet T. Zurndorfer (eds) *Conflict and Accommodation in Early Modern East Asia: Essays in Honour of Erik Zurcher*, pp. 284–321. Leiden: KITLV Press.

Brookfield, Harold, Lesley Potter and Yvonne Byron (1995) *In Place of the Forest: Environmental and Socio-economic Transformation in Borneo and the Eastern Malay Peninsula*. Tokyo: UNU Press.

Brosius, Peter J., Anna Lowenhaupt Tsing and Charles Zerner (2005) *Communities and Conservation: Histories and Politics of Community-Based Management*. Walnut Creek, CA: Altamira Press.

Burns, Peter (1999) *The Leiden Legacy: Concepts of Law in Indonesia*. Leiden: KITLV Press.

Cator, Writser Hans (1936) *The Economic Position of the Chinese in the Netherlands Indies*. Chicago, IL: University of Chicago Press.

Cleary, Mark and Peter Eaton (1992) *Borneo: Change and Development*. Oxford and New York: Oxford University Press.

Cohn, Bernard (1996) *Colonialism and its Forms of Knowledge: The British in India*. Princeton, NJ: Princeton University Press.

Coppel, Charles (1983) *The Indonesian Chinese in Crisis*. Oxford: Oxford University Press.

Davidson, Jamie (2002) 'Violence and Politics in West Kalimantan, Indonesia'. PhD dissertation, University of Washington.

Davidson, Jamie and Douglas Kammen (2002) 'Indonesia's Unknown War and the Lineages of Violence in West Kalimantan', *Indonesia* 73: 1–31.

Doty, E. and W.J. Pohlman (1839) 'Tour in Borneo, from Sambas through Montrado to Pontianak, and the Adjacent Settlements of Chinese and Dayaks, during the Autumn of 1838'. *Chinese Repository* VIII(6): 283–310.

Dove, Michael R. (1983) 'Theories of Swidden Agriculture and the Political Economy of Ignorance', *Agroforestry Systems* 1: 85–99.

Dove, Michael (1993) 'Rubber Eating Rice, Rice Eating Rubber'. Paper presented in Agrarian Studies Seminar series. New Haven, CT: Yale University.

Dove, Michael R. (1994) 'The Transition from Native Forest Rubbers to Hevea Brasiliensis (Euphorbiacae) among Tribal Smallholders in Borneo', *Economic Botany* 49(4): 382–96.

Dove, Michael (1998) 'Living Rubber, Dead Land, and Persisting Systems in Borneo: Indigenous Representations of Sustainability', *Bijdragen* 154(1): 20–54.

Earl, George Windsor (1837) *The Eastern Seas or Voyages and Adventures in the Indian Archipelago, in 1832–33–34, Comprising a Tour of the Island of Java, Visits to Borneo, the Malay Peninsula, Siam*. London: W.H. Allen and Co.

Effendy, Marchus (1982) *Sejarah Perjuangan Kalimantan Barat*. Pontianak (self-published).

Effendy, Marchus (1995) *Penghancuran PGRS-PARAKU dan PKI Kalimantan Barat*. Jakarta (self-published).

Ellen, Roy (1999) 'Forest Knowledge, Forest Transformations: Political Contingency, Historical Ecology and the Renegotiation of Nature in Central Seram', in Tania Li (ed.) *Transforming Indonesia's Uplands*, pp. 131–58. Australia: Harwood Academic Publishers.

Elmhirst, Rebecca (1999) 'Space, Identity Politics and Resource Control in Indonesia's Transmigration Programme', *Political Geography* 18(7): 813–35.

Fasseur, Cornelius (1994) 'Cornerstone and Stumbling Block: Racial Classification and the Late Colonial State in Indonesia', in Robert Cribb (ed.) *The Late Colonial State in Indonesia: Political and Economic Foundations of the Netherlands Indies, 1880–1942*, pp. 31–56. Leiden: KITLV Press.

Feith, Herbert (1968) 'Indonesia: Dayak Legacy', *Far Eastern Economic Review* 27: 134–5 (January).

Ferguson, James (2005) 'Seeing Like an Oil Company: Space, Security, and Global Capital in Neoliberal Africa', *American Anthropologist* 107(3): 377–82.

Glassman, James (2006) 'Primitive Accumulation, Accumulation by Dispossession, Accumulation by Extra-Economic Means', *Progress in Human Geography* 30(5): 608–25.

Gordillo, Gaston (2005) *Landscapes of Devils: Tensions of Place and Memory in the Argentinean Chaco*. Raleigh, NC: Duke University Press.

de Groot, J.J.M. (1885) *Het Kongsiwezen van Borneo: Eene Verhandling over den Grondslag en den Aard der Chineesche Politieke Vereenigingen in de Kolonien met eene Chineesche Geschiedenis van de Kongsi Lanfong*. s'Gravenhage: Martinus Nijhoff.

Harvey, David (2003) *The New Imperialism*. Oxford: Oxford University Press.

Harwell, Emily (2001) 'The Un-Natural History of Culture: Ethnicity, Tradition, and Territorial Conflicts in West Kalimantan, Indonesia, 1800–1997'. PhD Dissertation, Yale School of Forestry and Environmental Studies, Yale University.

Heidhues, Mary Somers (2003) *Goldiggers, Farmers, and Traders in the 'Chinese Districts' of West Kalimantan, Indonesia*. Ithaca, NY: Cornell University and Southeast Asian Program Publications.

Hui, Yew-Foong (2007) 'Strangers at Home: History and Subjectivity among the Chinese Communities of West Kalimantan, Indonesia'. PhD Dissertation, Cornell University.

van Hulten, Herman Josef (1994) *Hidupku diantara Suku Daya*. Jakarta: Pt Gramedia Widiasarana.

Human Rights Watch (1997) 'Indonesia: Communal Violence in West Kalimantan', *Human Rights Watch/Asia Report* 9(10) (December).

Jackson, James C. (1970) *The Chinese Gold-Fields of West Kalimantan: A Study in Cultural Geography*. Hull, UK: University of Hull.

Juul, Kristine and Christian Lund (2002) (eds) *Negotiating Property Rights*. Portsmouth, NH: Heineman.

King, Victor (1993) *The Peoples of Borneo*. London: Blackwell.

Kustanto, Johannes Baptis Hari (2002) 'The Politics of Ethnic Identity among the Sungkung of West Kalimantan, Indonesia'. PhD Dissertation, Yale University.

LeBar, Frank M. (1972) *Ethnic Groups of Insular Southeast Asia*. New Haven, CT: Human Relations Files Press.

Li, Tania Murray (1996) 'Images of Community: Discourse and Strategy in Property Relations', *Development and Change* 27(3): 501–27.

Li, Tania Murray (ed.) (1999) *Transforming the Indonesian Uplands*. Australia: Harwood Academic Publishers.

Mackie, J.A. (1974) *Konfrontasi: The Indonesia–Malaysia Dispute, 1963–1966*. Kuala Lumpur and New York: Oxford University Press, for the Australian Institute of International Affairs.

MacPherson, C.B. (1983) *Property: Mainstream and Critical Positions*. Oxford: Basil Blackwell.

Marx, Karl (1967) *Capital*. New York: International Press.

Massey, Doreen (1994) *Space, Place and Gender*. Cambridge: Polity Press.

Maurer, Bill (1997) *Recharting the Caribbean: Land, Law, and Citizenship in the British Virgin Islands*. Ann Arbor, MI: University of Michigan Press.

Moore, Donald (2005) *Suffering for Territory: Race, Place and Power in Zimbabwe*. Durham, NC, and London: Duke University Press.

Ozinga, Jacob (1940) *De Economische Ontwikkeling der Westerafdeeling van Borneo en de Bevolkingsrubbercultuur*. Wageningen: Zomer en Keuning.

Padoch, Christine and A.P. Vayda (1983) 'Patterns of Resource Use and Human Settlement in Tropical Forest', in F.B. Goley (ed.) *Tropical Rain Forest Ecosystems: Structure and Function*, pp. 301–13. Amsterdam: Elsevier.

Padoch, Christine, Emily Harwell and Adi Susanto (1998) 'Swidden, Sawah, and In Between: Agricultural Transformation in Borneo', *Human Ecology: An Interdisciplinary Journal* 26(1): 3–20.

Peet, Richard and Michael Watts (eds) (1996) *Liberation Ecologies*. Oxford: Blackwell (2nd edition 2004).

Peluso, Nancy Lee (1992) *Rich Forests, Poor People: Resource Control and Resistance in Java*. Berkeley, CA: University of California Press.

Peluso, Nancy Lee (1996) 'Fruit Trees and Family Trees in an Anthropogenic Forest: Property Zones, Ethics of Access and Environmental Change in Indonesia', *Comparative Studies in Society and History* 38(3): 510–48.

Peluso, Nancy Lee (2003) 'Weapons of the Wild: Strategic Uses of Wildness and Violence in West Kalimantan', in Candace Slater (ed.) *In Search of the Rainforest*, pp. 204–45. Berkeley, CA: University of California Press.

Peluso, Nancy Lee and Emily Harwell (2001) 'Territory, Custom, and the Cultural-Politics of Ethnic War in West Kalimantan Indonesia', in Nancy Lee Peluso and Michael Watts (eds) *Violent Environments*, pp. 83–116. New York: Cornell University Press.

Peluso, Nancy Lee and Peter Vandergeest (2001) 'Genealogies of Forest Law and Customary Rights in Indonesia, Malaysia, and Thailand', *Journal of Asian Studies* 60: 761–812.

Peluso, Nancy Lee and Michael Watts (2001) 'Introduction: Violent Environments', in Nancy Lee Peluso and Michael Watts (eds) *Violent Environments*, pp. 3–38. Ithaca, NY: Cornell University Press.

Penot, Eric (1995) 'Taking the "Jungle" out of the Rubber: Improving Rubber in Indonesian Agroforestry Systems', *Agroforestry Today* (July–December): 11–13.

Perelman, Michael (2000) *The Invention of Capitalism: Classical Political Economy and the Secret History of Accumulation*. Durham, N C: Duke University Press.

Peters, Pauline. E. (2002) 'The Limits of Negotiability: Security, Equity and Class Formation in Africa's Land Systems', in K. Juul and C. Lund (eds) *Negotiating Property Rights*, pp. 45–66. Portsmouth, NH: Heineman.

Poerwanto, Hari (2005) *Orang Cina Khek dari Singkawang*. Depok: Komunitas Bamboo.

Poulgrain, Greg (1998) *The Genesis of Konfrontasi: Malaysia, Brunei, Indonesia 1945–1965*. Bathurst, Australia, and London: Crawford Publishing House.

Pringle, Robert (1970) *Rajahs and Rebels: The Ibans of Sarawak under Brooke Rule, 1841–1941*. Ithaca, NY: Cornell University Press.

Raffles, Hugh (2002) *In Amazonia: A Natural History*. Princeton, NJ: Princeton University Press.

van Rees, W.A. (1858) *Montrado Geschied- en krijgskundige bijdrage betreffende de onderwerping der chinezen op Borneo, naar het dagboek van een Indisch Officier over 1854–1856*. 's Hertogenbosch, Netherlands: Muller.

Ribot, Jesse and Nancy Lee Peluso (2003) 'A Theory of Access', *Theory and Society* 68(2): 153–81.

van Sandick, J.C. F. and V.J. van Marle (1919) *Verslag eener Spoorwegverkenning in Noordwest-Borneo*. Vols 1–3. Batavia: Albrecht.

Schaank, S.H. (1893) 'De Kongsis van Montrado. Bijdrage tot de geschiedenis en de kennis van het wezen der Chinesche vereenigingen op de Westkust van Borneo', *Tijdschrift voor Indische Taal-, Land- en Volkenkunde* 35: 498–612 (Batavia).

Scott, James C. (1998) *Seeing Like a State: How Certain Schemes to Improve the Human Condition Have Failed*. New Haven, CT: Yale University Press.

Shamsul, A.B. (2004) 'Texts and Collective Memories: The Construction of "Chinese" and "Chineseness" from the Perspective of a Malay', in Leo Suryadinata (ed.) *Ethnic Relations and Nation-Building in Southeast Asia: The Case of the Ethnic Chinese*, pp. 109–44. Singapore: ISEAS.

Soemadi (1974) *Peranan Kalimantan Barat dalam Menghadapi Subversi Komunis Asia Tenggara: Suatu Tinjauan Internasional terhadap Gerakan Komunis dari Sudut Pertahanan Wilayah Khususnya Kalimantan Barat*. Pontianak: Yayasan Tanjungpura.

Stoler, Ann Laura (1995) *Race and the Education of Desire: Foucault's History of Sexuality and the Order of Things*. Raleigh, NC: Duke University Press.

Suryadinata, Leo (1978) *Pribumi Indonesians, the Chinese Minority, and China: A Study of Perceptions and Policies.* Kuala Lumpur: Heinemann Educational Books (Asia).

Tangdililing, Andreas Barung (1993) 'Perkawinan antar Suku Bangsa sebagai salah satu Wahana Pembauran Bangsa: Studi Kasus Perkawinan antara Orang Daya dengan Keturunan Cina di Kecamatan Samalantan, Kabupaten Sambas, Kalimantan Barat'. PhD dissertation, Universitas Indonesia.

The Siauw Giap (1966) 'Rural Unrest in West Kalimantan: The Chinese Uprising in 1914', in W.L. Idema (ed.) *Leyden Studies in Sinology* 15. Leiden: E.J. Brill.

Thompson, Edward P. (1975) *Whigs and Hunters: The Origins of the Black Act.* London: Allen Lane.

Thongchai, Winichakul (1994) *Siam Mapped.* Honolulu, HI: University of Hawaii Press.

Vandergeest, Peter and Nancy Lee Peluso (1995) 'Territorialization and State Power in Thailand', *Theory and Society* 35: 385–426.

Verdery, Katherine (1998) 'Fuzzy Property: Rights, Power, and Identity in Transylvania's Decollectivization', in Joan M. Nelson, Charles Tilly and Lee Walker (eds) *Transforming Post Communist Political Economies*, pp. 101–16. Washington, DC: National Academy Press.

Vleming, J.L. Jr. (1926) *Het Chineesche Zakenleven in Nederlandsch-Indië.* Weltevreden, The Netherlands: Landsdrukkerij.

Ward, Marion and R. Ward (1974) 'An Economic Survey of West Kalimantan', *Bulletin of Indonesian Economic Studies* 10(3): 26–53.

Weinstock, Joseph Aaron (1979) 'Land Tenure Practices of the Swidden Cultivators of Borneo'. Masters Thesis, Cornell University.

Weinstock, Joseph and Napoleon Vergara (1987) 'The Land or the Plants? Approaches to Resource Tenure in Agroforestry Systems', *Economic Botany* 41(2): 312–22.

Wolf, Eric (1982) *Europe and the People without History.* Berkeley and Los Angeles, CA: University of California Press.

Wolters, O.W. (1999) *History, Culture and Region in Southeast Asian Perspectives.* Ithaca, NY: Cornell Southeast Asia Program.

Yuan, Bing Ling (2000) *Chinese Democracies.* Leiden: KITLV Press.

4

Ruling by Record: The Meaning of Rights, Rules and Registration in an Andean *Comunidad*

Monique Nuijten and David Lorenzo

INTRODUCTION: PRACTICES OF ACCESS AND 'RULE TALK'

This chapter discusses local forms of governance and control over land in a peasant community in the central highlands of Peru. Usibamba was established as a *comunidad indígena* (indigenous community) in 1939; in the 1970s the term *comunidad indígena* was replaced by *comunidad campesina* (peasant community) under the Peruvian Agrarian Law. Usibamba has 3,640 hectares of land under communal tenure. A large part of the land is divided into individual plots, but the use of the whole falls under communal regulation. This chapter will show how the strict regime of governance in Usibamba goes hand in hand with continuous internal discussions about the principles of community organization and the hierarchical classification of villagers. The general assembly of all *comuneros* (members of the *comunidad*) is the highest authority at the local level; it gathers every month to make decisions on a wide range of matters. One of the responsibilities of the general assembly is the annual reallocation of vacant plots, every September. This study examines the function of the meticulous registration and quantification of land in this yearly procedure.

Most studies on common property management assume that explicit rules exist about the members of a local community and their rights to land. The inventory of all these rules together is taken to be the 'system of property rules'. Contrary to such a 'rights-based' approach, we use a 'practice force field approach' for the analysis of property relations in Usibamba (see Nuijten, 2003; Nuijten and Lorenzo, 2006). Rather than trying to establish rights, a practice approach studies the ways in which access to land is organized (cf. Ribot and Peluso, 2003). In anthropology and socio-legal studies, property is commonly defined as a bundle of rights and relationships between persons with respect to valuable goods. It is also generally accepted that property is not a relationship between people and things but between people *about* things. This explains the intricate connections that exist between property relations, family obligations, community life and power relations (Sabean, 1984). Property is also linked to a vast array of cultural and social relations within which collective identities are

The title of this contribution was inspired by the book by Richard Saumarez Smith, *Rule by Record: Land Registration and Village Custom in Early British Punjab* (Oxford University Press, Delhi, 1996).

shaped (Hann, 1998: 5). Because of this intermingling of property relations with multiple other dimensions of life, we contend that property relations cannot be studied as a separate set of principles (Sabean, 1990: 33).

Scholars working from a rights-based approach are the first to acknowledge that property rules are flexible and that situations on the ground can deviate markedly from the letter of the law. They explain this by the fact that rules can be negotiated and that legal-institutional property regimes are never fully internally coherent. Some authors therefore choose to make the distinction between property relations in theory and practice, or what von Benda Beckmann et al. (2006) call 'categorical property relations' and 'concretized property relations'. However, in a practice perspective we do not consider this distinction useful, as it still contributes to the definition of property relations as a separate set of principles, leading to the reification of rules.

From a practice perspective, we argue that property relations are shaped in a field of force. Following Bourdieu and Wacquant (1992) we see the field as the locus of relations of force and not of rule. Every field has its own logic and regularities shaped by the configuration of forces. The coherence, ruling and regularities that may be observed in a given state of the field emanate from continuous processes of struggle, competition and accommodation. For this reason, we systematically study the distribution and use of land, as well as transactions and conflicts over a long period of time.[1] In our research we quantify sets of data on land and try to establish patterns in practice and their underlying dynamics without seeing them as based on the application of a set of rules.

Thus rules, rights and laws do not have a preferential position in the analytical framework of a practice approach. We do give a central place, however, to 'rule talk', the ways in which people claim rights to land, frame their explanations of property relations in normative terms, and express themselves about categories of villagers with different privileges and obligations. We argue that rather than referring to a set of rules, 'rule talk' is a way of producing order out of the quite chaotic world of property relations. Rule talk also plays an important part in explaining and justifying decisions and situations. As Reed convincingly points out about the role of story-telling, 'the creation and recreation of stories are a way of ordering our world, making sense of it, justifying specific situations and our decisions' (Reed, 1992: 114; see also Law, 1994: 52).

A second reason for giving 'rule talk' a central role in our analysis is the fact that access to and control over land go hand-in-hand with particular forms of domination and the definition of different categories of people. In our view, these forms of domination and the accompanying reactions

---

1. The material for this study was collected during twenty months of fieldwork in four periods between December 2003 and June 2008. Pseudonyms are used for all people appearing in the text.

of contention and resistance are reflected in daily dialogues, reflexive talk, and irony (Pigg, 1996, 1997; Tsing, 1993). An important difference with rights-based approaches is that a practice approach does not fear inconsistencies and contradictions in the stories that people present. On the contrary, 'shifting, multistranded conversations in which there never is full agreement' may show important areas of contestation and struggle (see Tsing, 1993: 8).

Rose describes these forms of framing as 'discursive fields characterized by a shared vocabulary within which disputes can be organized, by ethical principles that can communicate with one another, by mutually intelligible explanatory logics, by commonly accepted facts, by significant agreement on key political problems' (Rose, 1999: 28). In this view, 'rule talk' is not secondary to governance, it is constitutive of it: 'Language not only makes acts of government describable; it also makes them possible' (ibid.). The important point here is to recognize that these discourses and vocabularies are conflicting and ambivalent and can be drawn upon in a variety of ways to express differing positions and claims. Our aim is to find out how these discourses and moral repertoires relate to the governance of people and communal resources.

LAND TENURE AND DIFFERENTIATED LOCAL CITIZENSHIP

Usibamba is located at an altitude of 3,800 meters in the central highlands of Peru and has approximately 2,500 inhabitants (INEI, 1993). The *comunidad* Usibamba — the legal entity which owns the land — has approximately 450 members. As the majority of households in the village include at least one person who is a member of the *comunidad*, most households have access to an individual plot of land and the right to use the communal pastures. Yet, as we will show, the percentage of families without access to land is growing. Most members of the *comunidad* are men. Widows and female heads of households with children (i.e. single mothers) may become members but women hold a subordinate position in the *comunidad*. Life in the village is harsh because of the poverty, lack of basic infrastructure, and climatic conditions. The villagers seek comfort by drinking liquor, chewing coca leaves and holding numerous festivities. Migration to regional cities, as well as to the capital, Lima, and the USA, is central to the local economy.

Peasant communities in the Peruvian highlands such as Usibamba are known to operate according to strict disciplinary regimes in which *comuneros* have to obey many rules and fulfil many responsibilities and obligations in order to enjoy certain rights. The state is mostly absent in these remote regions and it is the *comunidad* that fulfils the role of public authority and takes responsibility for the organization of civic works for the village, such as cleaning roads and rivers, building bridges, looking after the local burial-ground, and so forth. The *comunidad* draws on the unpaid labour of the *comuneros* for making up communal work parties (*faenas*) and for carrying out these many public functions.

The *comunidad* operates in accordance with the communal regulation (*el estatuto*), a written document that has been developed and adapted over the years. The communal regulation as a local convention with recognized legal value was introduced by the government of Velasco (1968–75). The oldest version of the communal regulation found in Usibamba dates from 1991. But in addition to the regulation, the *communidad* also operates in line with established practices that have not been recorded on paper, and on the basis of broad principles of fairness and justice. Several written rules, for example concerning the number of hectares that *comuneros* are entitled to, are quite specific, but others are fairly abstract and can be interpreted in a variety of ways. For example, according to the communal regulation, decent moral conduct is a central criterion for the allocation of land, but it is hard to predict what will be taken into account in the evaluation of the conduct of *comuneros*. Adultery, the maltreatment of women and children, public drunkenness and several other actions might be presented as evidence of lack of good moral conduct — but they might equally well be ignored. In other words, there is no definition of 'decent moral conduct' even though it is a key concept in the regulation around which much discussion takes place.

The communal regulation is enforced by the executive committee, which is responsible for the daily management of the *comunidad*. The highest authority of the *comunidad* is the general assembly of all *comuneros*, which elects a new executive committee every year on 1 January. Every month a general assembly takes place during which a wide variety of issues are discussed and decided upon. Minutes of the communal meetings are carefully recorded and filed in notebooks. These monthly meetings may last for many hours: it is common for a meeting to start at 09.30 and last until 18.00 hours. For *comuneros* who have cattle to look after and multiple other duties to see to, these lengthy meetings are an ordeal. The fact that the authorities put their whips on the table to show their determination to secure the smooth running of the meeting symbolizes the *comunidad's* passion for discipline, rules and punishments.[2]

On the basis of their relation to the *comunidad* different categories of villagers are distinguished with distinct entitlements and obligations. These are flexible and controversial categories that are the object of continuous discussion and redefinition, but in broad lines amount to the following. A *comunero activo* (active community member) is a full member of the *comunidad*, which implies that he is obliged to participate in all communal work parties, attend every assembly, and is expected to fill public positions and behave in a dignified way. A *comunero activo* has voting rights at the general assembly and is entitled to the maximum amount of land, 5.5 ha —

---

2. As a shepherd community, in Usibamba the whip is an instrument commonly used for tending flocks.

2 ha of irrigated land and 3.5 ha of rainfed land. Women are entitled to half a hectare of irrigated land less. We could say that the *comunero activo* is the 'full citizen'. A *comunero pasivo* (passive community member) is somebody who has retired after twenty-five years of service to the community (or twenty years in the case of women). A *comunero pasivo* has no obligation to participate in communal work parties; he has no right to vote, but is allowed to speak during assemblies in order to give advice. He is entitled to a reduced amount of land, 4 ha. In other words, a *comunero pasivo* is a citizen who has gone into retirement and is respected because of his past commitment to the *comunidad*. A *comunero no-calificado* or *comunero no-agricola* is a resident in the village who is not a member of the community. In the village/local parlance he is also called *no-comunero*. He has no right to vote, but does have the right to speak, although he is less respected and will receive considerably less attention than a *comunero pasivo*. A sharp social distinction exists between *comuneros* on the one hand and *no-comuneros* on the other. A *no-comunero* has fewer obligations to participate in communal work parties, but on the other hand, he has neither voting rights nor entitlement to land; he is a type of 'non-citizen'.

COMMUNAL LAND AND COMMUNITY DISCIPLINE

Young married men from the age of eighteen can become *comuneros* and gain access to a private plot of land upon payment of an entrance fee.[3] Land tenure in the *comunidad* is extremely fragmented and it is common for a *comunero* with a total of 3 ha of land to have ten tiny plots in different ecological zones. Because of the high number of *comuneros* and the scarcity of land, many young men who enter the *comunidad* receive only a small plot, or no land at all. Over the years they try to complete their share by asking for plots of land that come free. In order to have any chance of success in this, it is important to be deemed a good and committed member of the community.

Every year reallocation of the plots of *comuneros* who have died, retired or been punished by the community authorities takes place. The basic principle of land distribution is that land is handed out to *comuneros* according to their personal record. Being a *comunero* is a social process during which continuous commitment to the community should be shown by attending assemblies, working in communal work parties, educating one's children, taking public positions, not being drunk while discussing community affairs and not being an adulterer. The list of duties is long. In building up the personal record of service to the *comunidad*, every *comunero* also has to fill a series of public posts (*cargos*). Their record of service is the only means by which community members can become entitled to larger amounts of land. This record is not written down but consists of publicly-known information

---

3. In 2008 the entrance fee was 250 Nuevos Soles (US$ 85).

Table 1. Possession of Communal Land by Active Comuneros in Usibamba in 2004

Active community members	Irrigated land		Unirrigated land	
	Maximum allowed (ha)	Average possession (ha)	Maximum allowed (ha)	Average possession (ha)
Male	2.00	0.98	3.50	2.60
Female	1.50	0.52	3.00	1.98

that is taken into account and used in negotiation when land falls vacant and is reallocated among *comuneros*. In the *comunidad* no inheritance of communal land is allowed, but there is a so-called 'system of preference'. This means that if a *comunero* dies, the land is normally passed to his sons or other relatives if they are members of the *comunidad*, have a good personal record of service to the *comunidad* and have not yet acquired the maximum amount of land.

The community disciplinary regime demands high moral standards, and if the members do not behave accordingly, they are punished. Money collected in fines forms one of the major sources of income of the *comunidad*. The importance of this regime of punishment is also illustrated by the fact that *comuneros* establish the fine for those who do not participate in collective work parties or any other communal task before any chore starts. A common and much-dreaded punishment is the confiscation of communal plots on a temporary or permanent basis.

On the basis of the registration in the *comunidad* we made a calculation of the total area of land that each active *comunero* had access to in 2004. Table 1 shows that on average the active *comuneros* are far from reaching the maximum number of hectares to which they are entitled. Apart from there not being enough land for all *comuneros* to have their full allocation, another serious problem is the fact that the *comunidad* cannot offer land to new members. For young *comuneros* the situation is gloomy, as they must fulfil all the community obligations but may have to wait for many years before land becomes available for them. Many of them will never acquire the total area of land they are entitled to because of the scarcity of land. As one *comunero* remarked: 'We will arrive at such a difficult situation that we even wish for the death of our parents. That has become the only possibility for receiving land in the community' (field notes, 6 November 2005, at the office of the community).

BECOMING A *COMUNERO* . . . OR NOT?

As we saw, control over land is thus the mechanism through which *co-muneros* are rewarded or punished for their functioning and acts as the pillar of the local regime of governance. This begs the question of why anyone should become a *comunero*, with all the sacrifices implied, when they cannot even make a living on the basis of their access to communal land. This is a question that many villagers are asking themselves today. Naturally, there are other considerations besides access to land that play a role in the decision to become a *comunero*: the *comunidad* stands for local control and authority, and being a member brings prestige. Many old *comuneros* try to persuade their sons to join, even though they are aware of the drawbacks. Being a *comunero* is part of an identity and stands for a form of local belonging and lifestyle. Although the majority of men in Usibamba still are *comuneros,* a growing number of men decide not to enter the *comunidad*.

The growth in the number of *no-comuneros* means that an increasingly large percentage of villagers does not fall under the regulation of the *comunidad*. *No-comuneros* cannot be controlled as easily, since they do not possess land, the main and most effective instrument of punishment. This makes it important for the *comunidad* to find other mechanisms for steering the 'free' villagers, for example through controlling access to plots for houses in the residential area of the village. As all land belongs to the *comunidad*, everybody who wants to build a house has to request land from the communal authorities. If a *no-comunero* asks for a plot of land to build a house he has to show that he is not an 'idle' citizen and that all his children are being educated at the Usibamba school. Otherwise it is impossible for him to get a plot of land from the *comunidad*. These are territorial strategies to control the *no-comuneros*, but they are less influential than control over agricultural land.[4]

What bothers *no-comuneros* greatly is that many decisions affecting the entire village are taken by *comuneros* during their assemblies where *no-comuneros* are not allowed to vote. They feel subordinated to the *comunidad* as they are excluded from the political arena where decisions are made. The members of the *comunidad* are very aware of their position and feel superior to the landless villagers. Hence these community-based modalities of governance go along with forms of differentiation and exclusion.

In Usibamba one finds two discursive registers which at a first glance seem contradictory but together characterize the central dimensions of local governance and control in the *comunidad* particularly well. In other words, these contradictory discursive registers express the conflicting meanings and functions of the *comunidad* in the lives of individual people and the collectivity. On the one hand, it is common to hear *comuneros* complain that they are 'slaves of the community'. They have to carry out official duties and occupy public positions, participate in many *faenas* and attend endless meetings, and in return they only receive access to a tiny piece of land. This image of a regime of slavery is reinforced by the fines that are levied

---

4. In 2005, the housing plots were privatized and no longer fall under the control of the *communidad*.

when *comuneros* do not accomplish their many tasks. The *comuneros* are tired of working as 'slaves' of the community and of being dependent on the arbitrary will of the communal assembly.

In contrast, the second discursive register stresses the importance of the *comunidad* in maintaining public order and safeguarding civic responsibilities. This register emphasizes that participation in the community and collaborating in its many tasks is an important duty, a public responsibility towards the collective project. In this discursive mode, *comuneros* argue that there is no greater honour for an Usibambino than to serve his village/community and contribute selflessly to the development of the community. They express their pride in serving (or obeying) an authority and argue that the disciplinary communal regime allows them to be organized and behave like responsible Peruvians. It is this second discursive register that expresses the moral superiority of *comuneros*. The *comunero* is considered to be the 'responsible citizen', whereas the *no-comunero* stands for an 'idle, worthless person'. *No-comuneros* do not have to follow the rules of the *comunidad* and are 'free', but this freedom also makes them uncivilized.

THE MYTH OF ORDER

From the start of our research we were taken by surprise by the Usibambinos' passion for order: everything in the *comunidad* is registered, numbered, counted and listed. For example, the communal administration and management of land is based on two types of books: the directory of communal plots and the allocation notebooks. In the directory every one of the 3,640 ha of communal territory is numbered and classified according to its location, size, type (rainfed or irrigated) and quality.[5] Each hectare may be divided among two, three or even four *comuneros,* whose names are entered next to the plot in the directory. Hence the directory works as a written map of the *comunidad* land. Table 2 shows an example of registration in the directory. The allocation notebooks work the opposite way and list all the *comuneros* with the different plots they possess (see Table 3).

Surprised by this zeal for listing, we were curious to compare the data from the directory with the allocation notebooks, which in theory should show an exact correspondence. For this, we limited our inquiry to the irrigated land, the most valuable communal resource. According to the directory, the total amount of irrigated communal land is 525 ha, divided into 625 plots. With respect to 268 plots (43 per cent of the total number of plots) the information in the directory was the same as that in the allocation notebooks. In the case

---

5. These 3,640 ha constitute the territory of the community of Usibamba, but also include two terrains held under a private property regime: Fundo de Huallancayo (667 ha bought by 229 villagers of Usibamba in 1964) and the urban area of housing plots (139 ha) privatized in 2005.

Table 2. Data from the Directory of the Comunidad of Usibamba, 2005

Zone	Plot no.	Type	Quality	Area (m^2)	Name
Cruz Pata	387	Irrigated	2nd	10,000	Huaire de la Cruz, Juana
Cruz Pata	388	Irrigated	2nd	10,000	Díaz Inga, Benedicto
Cruz Pata	389	Irrigated	2nd	5,000	Inga Aquino, Flaviano
Cruz Pata	389	Irrigated	2nd	5,000	Inga Astete, Demetrio
Cruz Pata	390	Irrigated	2nd	5,000	Camposano Huaire, Héctor
Cruz Pata	390	Irrigated	2nd	5,000	De la Cruz Quinto, Mauricia
Cruz Pata	391	Irrigated	2nd	10,000	Quiñones Llanto, Valeriana

Table 3. Data from the Allocation Notebook of the Comunidad of Usibamba, 2005

Name	Plot no.	Location		Quality	Real area (m^2)	Useful area (m^2)
Inga Huayas, Raul	75	Molino-Pampa	Irrigated	Good	10,000	10,000
	372	Cruz Pata	Irrigated	Good	5,000	5,000
						15,000
	66	Huamachuco	Unirrigated	Good	5,000	5,000
	76	Huamachuco	Unirrigated	Good	5,000	5,000
	85	Huamachuco	Unirrigated	Good	10,000	10,000
	413	Pacila	Unirrigated	Regular	10,000	4,000
	2,456	Quishar Uclo	Unirrigated	Regular	10,000	3,000
						27,000

of 106 plots (17 per cent), however, the size of the plot registered in the allocation notebooks was greater than the size of the same plot registered in the directory. This means that according to the notebooks the *comuneros* concerned possess more land than according to the directory.

For the reallocation procedure, it is the notebooks which are most consulted. Hence, the disadvantage for the *comuneros* with more land in the notebooks than in the directory is that they soon arrive at the maximum number of hectares and will not be able to claim more land. This phenomenon of having more hectares in the notebooks than in the directory is more common among female community members, who are thus discriminated against in land distribution.

In the case of 251 plots (40 per cent) the opposite occurs: the allocation notebooks register a smaller sized plot than the directory. This practice is more common among male *comuneros*. The fact that it is common for men to be registered with less land in the notebooks and women with more, is a manifestation of the structurally subordinate position of women in the *comunidad*.

The phenomenon that the same plot is recorded with different sizes in the two books is known locally as the 'accordion effect', referring to the way in which plots seem to grow or shrink according to the book used. These

Table 4. Data from the Directory of the Comunidad of Usibamba, 2005

Directory of irrigated land

Zone	Plot no.	Name	Quality	Real area (m²)	Useful area (m²)
Cruz Pata	42	Inga Reyes, Pablo	1st	5,000	5,000
Oluncuto	315	Inga Reyes, Pablo		2,500	2,500
Teja Cruz	41	Inga Reyes, Pablo	1st	10,000	10,000
Litigio	480	Inga Reyes, Pablo	2nd	2,500	2,500
					20,000

Directory of unirrigated land

Zone	Plot no.	Name	Quality	Real area (m²)	Useful area (m²)
Colpa	1,014	Inga Reyes, Pablo	Good	5,000	5,000
Verap	2,230	Inga Reyes, Pablo	Good	5,000	4,000
					9,000

expressions are the source of much laughter and irony during communal meetings. A frequent joke by the *comuneras* when they are registered with more land than they really possess, is: 'Is my plot pregnant or what?'

Another phenomenon that came to light during the comparison of data from the directory and the notebooks was the discovery of sixty-three 'blank' plots covering 45 ha. By this we mean plots that are registered in the directory but without being allocated to anybody. These plots are not recorded in the notebooks. Locally people refer to this phenomenon as 'flying plots', meaning plots that are in use by people without being registered, and thus able 'to fly around'. For the *comuneros* who use this land it means that they can ask for more land as these 'flying plots' are not taken into account in calculating the total amount of land they possess.

Only in the case of serious conflicts is the information in the notebooks checked against that in the directory. In the case of discrepancy between the two books, the information in the directory is decisive. In this context it is interesting to consider the case of Pablo Inga Reyes. Tables 4 and 5 compare information about him in the two books. According to the directory, Pablo possesses a total of 29,000 m²; however, according to the allocation notebooks, his land amounts to 57,000 m². While according to the allocation notebooks the amount of irrigated land that he owns (22,000 m²) exceeds the maximum allowed by 2,000 m² (the maximum allowed extension is 20,000 m²), this figure has been 'corrected' in the directory, where he only possesses the maximum of 20,000 m². Pablo probably 'corrected' these figures himself when he was one of the authorities in the *comunidad* in 2005. As a member of the administrative board of the *comunidad* it was easy for him to consult the books and 'correct' the information. For Pablo this change is crucial, as based on the 'corrected' information in the directory he will receive a larger part of the land of his recently deceased parents. Although

Table 5. Data from the Allocation Notebooks of the Comunidad of Usibamba, 2005

Name	Plot no.	Location		Quality	Real area (m²)	Useful area (m²)
	41	Teja Cruz	Irrigated	1ˢᵗ	10,000	10,000
	42	Cruz Pata	Irrigated	2ⁿᵈ	5,000	5,000
	315	Oluncuto	Irrigated	1ˢᵗ	5,000	4,500
	480	Litigio	Irrigated	2ⁿᵈ	2,500	2,500
						22,000
Inga Reyes, Pablo	273	Salvio Loma	Unirrigated	Good	5,000	4,000
	640	Chuclla Uclo	Unirrigated	Good	10,000	1,500
	829	Angasnio	Unirrigated	Poor	10,000	10,000
	1,014	Colpa	Unirrigated	Good	5,000	5,000
	1,183	Salvio Ladera	Unirrigated	Good	5,000	5,000
	1,360	Otutuyo	Unirrigated	Poor	10,000	2,500
	2,027	Salvio	Unirrigated	Regular	5,000	3,000
	2,203	Verap	Unirrigated	Good	5,000	4,000
						35,000

normally only the notebooks are consulted, Pablo will certainly demand that the information is checked with the directory. As the information in the directory overrules that of the notebooks, Pablo has secured his access to part of his parents' land.

The fact that there are local expressions and jokes to refer to the different types of errors in the books shows that people are well aware of the inaccuracies of the local registration systems. Although *comuneros* may complain about it, and complaints are certainly taken into account by the authorities in their decisions, the books remain the ultimate sources on which land allocation decisions are based.

THE SACRED REGISTRATION BOOKS

The directory and notebooks are treated with much respect. They are kept in the office of the *comunidad* and every *comunero* is allowed to inspect them, but only in the presence of a member of the executive committee; they are never left on their own with the books. The *comuneros* love to riffle through the pages of the books in order to discover how many hectares other people possess. Officially, the secretary of the executive committee is the only person who is allowed to make changes to the books, under the supervision of the president of the *comunidad*. Ideally, the books — both the dictionary and the notebooks — are brought up to date every year after the completion of the reallocation procedure. However, as these corrections are made by hand, this is a very time-consuming activity and therefore only the notebooks are updated.

With every change of the executive committee on 1 January the directory and notebooks are officially handed over to the newly-elected administration during an official ceremony. If the books are stained, if pages have disappeared or in the case of other irregularities, the leaving secretary is held responsible and has to pay a fine. The books are stamped and numbered before being handed over to the new authorities.

The *comuneros* are aware that numbers may 'change' during recording in the notebooks. In fact, the notebooks are full of errors. For that reason, in the case of conflicts or doubts the directory is considered to be the 'ultimate source of truth' and has 'the last word'. As the secretary of the *comunidad* used to say: 'The directory condemns you', or: 'The directory orders'. At the same time everybody knows that the directory lags behind with respect to actual land possession. The revision of the directory only takes place when the *comuneros* feel that the book has become too dirty.

The *comuneros* are exasperated by the inaccuracies in the books. Even trying to find simple information is difficult. The authorities have to spend hours turning the leaves in search of the necessary data. The process of consulting the books is tiresome, as data are difficult to collect and it often takes hours of browsing through the thousands of pages. As Laureano, the *cumunidad* president in 2005, remarked: 'Errors in the numbering of the plots . . . the secretary must have been drunk when he was writing it down'. At another moment he moaned: 'Every year there is a movement of plots. Every year the books are worse. Plots that get lost. We are never going to restore order. When are we going to restore order? I'm sick of those errors' (field notes, 14 October 2005, at a meeting of the authorities).

During one of the assemblies in 2005 people were discussing the poor state of the directory and the notebooks. The *comuneros* opined: 'The numbers of the directory don't coincide with those of the notebooks. It's a terrible amount of work to get the books in order again'; and: 'It is not exact, the measurements aren't exact. There is no sense of responsibility' (field notes, 26 October 2005, at a general assembly). Looking through the archives of the *comunidad* we found that complaints about the state of the books and requests to update the information have been a recurring theme during communal assemblies.

So it is not surprising that the *comuneros* were thrilled when on the anniversary of the *comunidad* on 9 May 2005 they received a computer from the mayor of the district. Much hope was invested in the new instrument that would finally sort out the chaos. Pointing at the computer, Laureano, the president of the *comunidad*, said: 'This instrument can help a lot to investigate what we are doing with the land' (field notes, 6 November 2005, at a general assembly). When we assisted the communal authorities with entering data into the computer, we noticed that they were not surprised at the inconsistencies that were revealed, nor did they try to resolve them. We realized that their aim with the computer was not to 're-establish order' but something else. The computer facilitated their work by allowing fast access to the data of individual plots and *comuneros*. With the computer it was no longer necessary to go through endless pages in order to find the information they were looking for. Whether or not this information was correct was not the central issue.

Although the *comuneros* are annoyed by the lack of order in the registration of land, they also say that exact registration and management of land are impossible: 'Land cannot be weighed and cut like a cheese'[6] is a standard local expression. It also embodies the idea that it is impossible to exactly compare and quantify plots of land in different zones with totally different characteristics. The number of hectares plays a role in decision making, but this information is always weighed against other criteria, and land distribution is shaped by multiple forces that together constitute the force field around the communal land.

The registration of land in the books of the *comunidad* is thus much less accurate than is suggested by the formality and reverence that surrounds them and by the importance given to the directory as the ultimate source of truth in the case of conflicts and the yearly reallocation procedure. We will turn now to the role of rules and registration in the most important communal procedure: the annual reallocation of plots.

THE REALLOCATION PROCESS: RULING BY RECORDS?

Every year before the first rain starts and the fields are being prepared for sowing (around September, or end of October at the latest) the reallocation of communal plots takes place. The formal process takes a couple of days, but the preparations and negotiations start a long time before this. The 'vacant land' concerned consists of plots that belonged to *comuneros* who have died, been penalized or gone into retirement. In 2005, 6 ha of irrigated land were to be redistributed. There were also 22 ha of rainfed land available for distribution, but nobody expressed interest in these plots because of their poor quality or their location a long way from the village. There was even a problem finding the plots; this land had usually been put to use already by other *comuneros*, who obviously offered little support in helping their fellow *comuneros* to find the plot.

Only *comuneros* who do not possess their maximum allowance of hectares can request part of the vacant land. However, since this applies to most *comuneros* this means that there are always many applicants for each plot. This is the period of the year that the directory and notebooks are most consulted. The distribution of 'free land' is a complicated process, as multiple factors are taken into account. *Comuneros* who possess little land have

---

6. Locally manufactured cheese is one of the main sources of income of almost every household in Usibamba. Cheese is made and collected during the week and sold every Thursday at the local market to merchants from the cities of Lima and Huancayo.

greater entitlement to the vacant plots than *comuneros* who have nearly reached their complete share, but factors related to the *comuneros'* personal records are also important — the time they have been a *comunero* (their years of service to the *comunidad*) and whether they have been responsible persons, actively participating in collective work parties and fulfilling public functions 'with dignity'. The evaluation of a person's participation and dignity is of course a subjective matter and open to negotiation, but general principles of justice and fairness are also taken into account in the decision-making process. For example, *comuneros* in precarious livelihood situations or who are going through a rough time in their lives may receive preferential treatment in the reallocation procedure.

In the case of a *comunero* who has died, these principles are over laid by kinship relations. It has become standard practice that the claims of relatives of the deceased *comunero* get priority. However, as the deceased *comunero* normally has many relatives in the *comunidad*, this has become the most delicate part of the reallocation procedure. As Laureano explained to us: 'The lands are communal. You lose the land the day you die. Nobody takes the land with them when they pass away.... Yet, when a *comunero* passes away, all of a sudden thousands of grandsons appear who during his life never remembered him' (field notes, 6 November 2005, at the office of the community).

Every year before the reallocation procedure starts the communal authorities make up a list of plots that have come available. They investigate whether any relatives have legitimate claims to these plots. After this list has been established, and before the public discussion at the general assembly takes place, the authorities organize a meeting together with other local office holders to distribute part of the land amongst themselves as compensation for their work during their period of administration. As Laureano explained: 'The members of the executive committee have made an enormous effort to fulfil their tasks and they are entitled to something. A little compensation for so much effort' (field notes, 21 October 2005, at a meeting of the authorities).

This preferential allocation of land to office holders is standard practice but is not mentioned in the communal regulation. Even during these informal arrangements certain standards are followed. The office holders only take land if they have not acquired their full share. Furthermore, the authorities know that they cannot grab too much land, as this would cause trouble at the general assembly. In other words, the authorities take priority, but within certain limits. Communal authorities are keenly aware that they are only in office for a year, and then return to being one among hundreds of *comuneros*, so they are careful not to anger their social group. Hence, although one might expect the authorities to use this meeting to take a large part of the free land, this is not the case. The person who has to manage this process is the president of the *comunidad*; he has to manoeuvre carefully, as he must satisfy his fellow office holders but at the same time control their greed in order not to arouse the anger of the *comuneros*. *Comuneros* often complain about the authorities taking too good care of themselves.

During the 2005 reallocation procedure the nine members of the executive committee and eight presidents of the neighbourhoods were invited for the preliminary meeting in which the authorities distribute land among themselves. As there was little land available for distribution and the majority of plots were reserved by relatives, Laurcano did not want to hand out more than a quarter of a hectare of irrigated land to each of the authorities that did not have their complete share of land. Laureano addressed the authorities during this meeting:

> We have to act according to the regulation. Here we respect the word of the regulation. Otherwise we would be working incorrectly. As you all know, this year not much land is available for distribution, with few deceased persons and disqualifications. There is very little land; we have to share one bread between all of us; each of us can only have a quarter [of an irrigated hectare]. For rainfed land the same, the maximum that we will assign is half [a hectare].

Commotion and tumult arose among the directives present because of the small amount of land Laureano was prepared to give them. Laureano responded:

> I will be firm even though my staff [the local authorities] will be resented. We have to follow the regulation even though it hurts us. Next year any of you can become president and see that it is not easy. With all diplomacy, I have to take a quarter. So that they [other community members] won't say that we, members of the executive committee, have arranged everything for ourselves. I, as president, am taking a quarter of irrigated land. There must be equality. The reallocation is our task; we have to do a decent job. (Field notes, 6 November 2005, at a meeting of the authorities)

In the distribution of land to the authorities Laureano took several considerations into account. For example, before the meeting he had had a heated discussion with his vice president, who wanted his deceased father's land but already possessed the maximum number of hectares allowed. Laureano could have been 'flexible' and not taken this maximum into account, but he was disappointed by the lack of support his vice president had given him during his term. So he refused to be 'flexible' and instead firmly applied the rules. He told his vice president that he could only receive his father's land if he returned part of his other land to the *comunidad*. With the other office holders similar negotiations had taken place beforehand, so during the meeting itself there was very little discussion.

After this first distribution the authorities convene one or two days of meetings with the parties interested in the remaining land. Every *comunero* who is interested in one of the free plots can visit the authorities. Some *comuneros* arrive at the building with the numbers of the free plots written on their arms. Although the list of vacant plots is not made public, *comuneros* know about plots that have become available through a variety of information channels in the village.

During these meetings the authorities try to arrive at an agreement with the applicants by considering their actual land possession and personal record as a *comunero*. At the 2005 meetings, the first thing the *comuneros* wanted to know was whether the plot they were interested in had already been claimed by office holders or relatives. Rather than asking whether the land was available they asked the secretary whether the plot was reserved or not. Most *comuneros* and *comuneras* who came to the communal office to claim some land had to return home empty-handed.

One of the biggest difficulties in the reallocation process occurs when several relatives all claim the land of a deceased *comunero*. In 2005, up to ten relatives went to the communal office claiming to have the first right to a particular plot. Laureano had to sort out these requests and establish priorities. During one of these 'difficult cases' in 2005, Laureano said: 'Call the relatives in, the legitimate relatives, the original ones. Land of the deceased is claimed by everyone. I accept even sons or grandsons, but nephews, no' (field notes, 6 November 2005, at the office of the community).

Nowhere in the communal regulation does it say that nephews are not entitled to the land of a deceased *comunero*, but the authorities know that the general assembly will give priority to closer relatives. In many cases the plots of deceased *comuneros* are divided in order to satisfy the requests of several relatives.

Each of these family cases is dealt with individually, and Laureano produced solutions as he went along. He frequently got fed up with the quarrelling relatives in his office and called them to order. In one of the cases he told the relatives: 'Try to understand each other within the family. You come here with your stories, the other one with his lies. Whom should I believe? Who is the liar? You've been insulting each other. What example are we giving to our children and our family?' (Field notes, 29 September 2005, at the office of the community).

In exceptional cases in which the relatives cannot arrive at an agreement, the land is given to a non-relative. The allocation of plots can also be decided by drawing lots among *comuneros*. If the parties do not agree with the decision proposed by the authorities during these two days of deliberation, the case is moved to the general assembly of all *comuneros*, which will make the ultimate decision.

THE GENERAL REALLOCATION ASSEMBLY: FAIRNESS VERSUS RULES

As much preparation has taken place in the weeks before the general assembly, most proposals by the executive committee are immediately accepted, despite some complaints, criticism and grumbles in the background. Conflicts that have not been resolved are decided by the general assembly: in

2005, one such case was that of Carmen, and the land of her deceased mother. Since more and more people are deciding not to enter the *comunidad* in Usibamba, an increasingly common phenomenon is that of *comuneros* who die, but whose children are not *comuneros* and therefore not entitled to their land. *No-comuneros* have no right to receive the land of their deceased parents. This can give rise to awkward situations around the 'night-watch' and funeral of the deceased, when distantly-related *comuneros* suddenly appear, making great displays of concern at the bereavement, but actually only interested in the land.

Carmen had looked after her mother, who was a *comunera*, since her father died. Carmen never married and never became a *comunera*; she has a little shop in the village and for many years worked the communal plots of her mother, especially when the latter was too old to work them herself. When her mother died Carmen was very upset by the distant relatives who suddenly 'remembered' her mother and became extremely active during the preparations for her funeral. The relatives knew that as a *no-comunera* Carmen had no right to keep her mother's land.

Carmen also realized that under the community regulation she could not claim the land that she had worked on all her life. Nevertheless, she asked Laureano, the president, if the *comunidad* could at least leave her a family garden (*huerto familiar*). The family garden is a plot of 1.5 ha of communal land, which under special conditions is given to the children of deceased *comuneros* or disabled people. Laureano decided to let Carmen keep her family garden.

At the meeting of the authorities Laureano had to convince the others of his decision and drew on general principles of justice. But he also stressed the point of making a contribution to the village:

I applied fair justice. I would be a heartless authority if I did not leave Carmen anything of her mother's land. . . . Carmen lives in the village and contributes to the development of the village. She does her share, she is on time with all her payments. She doesn't hurt the development of the village. . . . She lives here, we all know her. What harm does it do to give her a plot of land? Although the regulation doesn't allow it, we gave it to her for humanitarian reasons. (Field notes, 30 November 2005, at a meeting of the authorities)

The other authorities were in agreement with Laureano but Carmen's relatives did not agree with the decision, wanting to claim all the land for themselves, so they took the case to the highest authority, the general assembly. During the assembly meeting, Laureano defended his decision:

To be honest I am acting against our communal regulation. As a *no-comunera* Carmen cannot even claim a square centimeter. . . . The family garden is meant for disabled people or orphans until they have attained adulthood. But we all know Carmen's life. . . . I took the case to the board of authorities [executive committee], I didn't decide on my own. We have to give preference to the people who need it. Among the relatives there is jealousy. What can I do to silence the relatives? (Field notes, 11 December 2005, at a general assembly)

Her relatives argued that as a *no-comunera* Carmen had not contributed to the development of the village. They used the discourse of the 'duties and sacrifice' of the *comuneros* against the 'idle life' of *no-comuneros*. They knew that these are weighty principles in the *comunidad*.

Finally the *comuneros* voted, and by a majority it was decided that Carmen could keep a family garden. In this case, notions of justice were successfully used in support of a *no-comunera* and against the communal regulation. This is not very common, but Carmen is a well-known and much respected woman in the village. Interestingly, it was stressed that although she is a *no-comunera*, she nevertheless contributes to the development of the village, as if this is exceptional for *no-comuneros*. In this conflict the communal rules were set aside for principles of fairness and compassion.

The difficulties the communal authorities have to go through in the re-allocation procedure are expressed in the payment of *chuc-cho*[7] by those who receive a new plot. This is a fixed amount per hectare which symbolically compensates the members of the executive committee for the headaches that the reallocation process causes them. As soon as the reallocation process has come to an end the money collected through *chuc-cho* payments is spent on cane alcohol and beer for the members of the executive committee.

Land reallocation can thus be a complex procedure in which many factors are taken into account and in which the authorities play a vital role. In the next section we analyse this process from the perspective of the *comunidad* president.

THE PERFORMANCE OF AUTHORITY

Although to the uninformed outsider the *comunidad* authorities appear to operate in a well-ordered institution, organized according to fixed rules, stable routines and dependable procedures, from the perspective of the authorities themselves a different reality becomes clear (see also Wagenaar, 2004: 651).

The executive committee of the *comunidad* is elected every year on 1 January. The position of president of the executive community is prestigious, but at the same time very demanding. Occupying such a high public position affords a *comunero* much respect and many rights, but it is also an unremunerated job — *ad honorem* — that takes up a great deal of time and can give rise to many conflicts with fellow *comuneros*. The reallocation procedure is considered to be the most delicate act of governance in the year as communal president. As Laureano said: 'The adjudication of plots is a never-ending story and the worst nightmare of every president during his mandate' (field

---

7. The *chuc-cho* is a symbolic amount of money that is fixed every year by the Executive Committee. It is a very small amount; in 2008 it was 3 Nuevos Soles (US$ 1) for each irrigated plot and 2 (US$ 0.7) for each rainfed plot. Although it is a small amount, its payment formalizes the land transfer.

notes, 17 September 2005, at a general assembly). Each president dreads the annual reallocation of plots. Although the public adjudication process only takes a couple of days, the physical (visiting plots) and especially the mental demands on the *comunidad* president, both before and after, are heavy. During this process, he will make friends and enemies for life. Although there is certainly some room for preferential treatment for himself, his friends and his relatives, most of the work involves tedious quarrels and careful manoeuvring over tiny plots of land.

Since the president takes many factors into account in his decisions, and knows that he will be judged on his performance, the adjudication is a serious responsibility and a major task. Every case is 'characterized by novelty, . . . uncertainty, and the requirement to act on the situation, to find some kind of resolution that is both feasible and acceptable' (Wagenaar, 2004: 648). The president also knows that when there is disagreement with his decisions, the general assembly of *comuneros* has the last word through its members' votes.

For each case, the president must identify the key elements of that specific situation: rather than following guidelines or applying rules, the reallocation procedure should be seen as an active, ongoing process in a world in which important principles and experiences of the members of the *comunidad* are shared (cf. Wagenaar, 2004). Laureano did not know the articles of the community regulation by heart but he did know the context within which he was operating. He had never been an authority before but he had been a *comunero* for many years. Following Wagenaar's practice approach to administration and management (2004: 651), we argue that, in most cases, the president of the *comunidad* must make his judgement without any obvious way of determining which rule is the most relevant to the situation at hand and what the right decision should be. These are inherently dialogical and interactive processes. To be effective implies that the *comunidad* authorities must be willing to understand and be influenced by the point of view of other members of the *comunidad*. Hence, good management of the *comunidad* is not just an individual achievement or a particular faculty of the mind but expresses some commonality of a collective (ibid.).

Nevertheless, a president will refer regularly to the regulation of the *comunidad* and the registration books when defending a judgement: 'Although it hurts us, we have to follow the *comunidad* regulation' is a common refrain. As Rose points out: 'To govern, one could say, is to be condemned to seek an authority for one's authority' (Rose, 1999: 27). Laureano did not control the land conflicts that came to him nor did he have a formula to resolve them. When he thought that he had resolved a conflict, he would repeat the phrase: 'In this life everything is aptitude' (*En esta vida todo es habilidad*) (field notes, 28 August 2005, 26 October 2005 and 30 November 2005). He made decisions as the process evolved, listening to different opinions and gathering pieces of information. Seldom did he open the regulation book lying on his desk, but if he did, it was decisive in the verdict. A similar dynamic took place around the incomplete directory and notebooks. When we joked with Laureano about how he could make decisions on the basis of the directory, which in fact is no accurate reflection of land possession, he would just laugh.

One month after the reallocation of 2005, Laureano told us: 'Land isn't easy ... You don't arrive at a solution to the land problems, not even in 50 per cent of the cases. It's quite delicate.... They're looking for "a cat with five legs"' (field notes, 6 November 2005, at the office of the community). In Laureano's view an authority figure should be firm in his decisions and not look back. The *comunidad* president is judged for his capacity to be capable, firm and just. He should learn from mistakes and continue. An authority cannot back down on a decision. It is the role of an authority to take decisions, defend them and ensure that they are respected. Laureano summarized his position on reallocation thus:

> In the reallocation procedure there has been resentment and also those who have left satisfied. That is part of the process. An authority, like a father, does not give everything; he gives in a limited way. It is important that an authority takes on the position knowing that he will cause resentment among the *comuneros*. The highest of all [God] will pass judgement. That is the only one to whom we finally have to render account.... In life nothing is free. We have to correct, educate our *comuneros*. Our intention is to change, correct ourselves. (Field notes, 30 November 2005, at a meeting of the authorities)

This quote reflects the idea that 'mentalities of government contain a strangely utopian element. To govern is to do something rather more than simply exercise authority. It is to believe and make believe that government is possible. It is to suppose that government can be effective, that it can achieve its desired ends' (Dean, 1999: 33). This utopian aspect of accountable and just administration is very apt for the situation in Usibamba. Registration and quantification play a central role, making governance possible. Yet even in its apparently most bureaucratic and managerial form, the administration in Usibamba refers to its utopian element, its striving for a better village, society, way of doing things and way of living (cf. Dean, 1999: 33).

CONCLUSION: ON RULES, NUMBERS AND DEMOCRACY

In Usibamba power and governance are largely based on territorial strategies, meaning that control over area is used 'to affect, influence, or control resources and people' (Sack, 1986: 1, 2). In this process, different categories of villagers are defined through a dialectical process of inclusion and exclusion.

In the *comunidad*, land is governed on the basis of written and unwritten rules and procedures. General principles of fairness, equality and justice also play an important role in local governance. Hence *comuneros* employ a variety of legal and moral principles in the management of their land and people. For this reason we argue that property relations in Usibamba are not based on the existence of a set of property rules but are shaped in a force field in which moral and legal discursive registers are drawn upon as explanatory and justifying mechanisms. We argue that this continuous talking about the rules, making reference to numbers and reflecting on notions of responsibility, public duty and justice, is what constitutes the *comunidad*.

The communal regime of discipline and punishment draws on elaborate systems of land registration. On the basis of the discrepancies and errors that we found in the land registration systems it would be easy to arrive at the conclusion — as experts on natural resource management and policy makers commonly do — that the community of Usibamba needs support in improving its local surveying and registration system. They would argue that their governance is undemocratic and unaccountable because of the many errors in the registration. They would say that the result of incorrect registration easily leads to manipulation by local power holders. However, we argue that such an evaluation is based on an erroneous view on governance in general and the role of numbers for management in particular. It is certainly true that land possession and redistribution in the *comunidad* are not equal and are related to historical power differences among *comuneros*. It is also true that women are systematically subordinated to men in the *comunidad*. The local people are well aware of these existing practices of differentiation and exclusion. At some moments they will fight against them while at others they resign themselves to established practices. Although the directory and notebooks are highly valued and central in decision-making procedures, everybody knows the errors they contain. Although they are treated with much respect they are also the object of irony, and local expressions have grown up around the most common inaccuracies in the registration. Yet, within the existing force field, the local practices of differentiation and exclusion are not unlimited and are balanced by other values with respect to justice and responsibility. Land distribution in the *comunidad* is not equal, but it is not very unequal either.

It is in this context that the role of the rules, registration and numbers used for local management has to be analysed. Technologies of government are always heterogeneous and hybrid assemblages. Rose (1999) argues that numbers, despite their inevitable imperfections, are of central importance to modern democracies. They have an unmistakable political power within technologies of government. Numbers determine who holds power, and whose claim to power is justified. Yet numbers also make modern modes of government judgeable. According to Rose there is a constitutive relationship between quantification and democratic government. Democratic power is calculated power, and numbers are intrinsic to the forms of justification that give legitimacy to political power in democracies. Democratic power needs citizens who calculate power and numeracy, and a numericized space of public discourse is essential in building self-controlling democratic citizens (Rose, 1999: 197–200). Following this line of analysis, the numbers and quantification used in the management of land in Usibamba makes the exercise of a certain democratic form of government possible. The numbers give legitimacy to the local authorities but also make it possible for *comuneros* to hold those authorities accountable for their decisions. Registration and quantification can never be complete or accurate, but that is not the same as being completely inaccurate and false. Democracy is always a 'limited democracy'.

REFERENCES

von Benda-Beckmann, F., K. von Benda-Beckmann and M. Wiber (2006) *Changing Properties of Property*. New York and London: Berghahn Books.
Bourdieu, P. and L. Wacquant (1992) *An Invitation to Reflexive Sociology*. Chicago, IL: University of Chicago Press.
Dean, M. (1999) *Governmentality. Power and Rule in Modern Society*. London: Sage Publications.
Hann, C. (1998) *Property Relations: Renewing the Anthropological Traditional*. Cambridge: Cambridge University Press.
INEI (Instituto Nacional de Estadística e Informática) (1993) 'Resultados definitivos de los Censos Nacionales: IX de Población y IV de Vivienda realizado el 11 de Julio de 1993'. ['Final results of the National Censuses: IX of population and IV of housing, executed on 11 July 1993']. Lima: INEI.
Law, J. (1994) *Organizing Modernity*. Oxford: Blackwell.
Nuijten, M. (2003) *Power, Community and the State: The Political Anthropology of Organisation in Mexico*. London: Pluto Press.
Nuijten, M. and D. Lorenzo (2006) 'Moving Borders and Invisible Boundaries: A Force Field Approach to Property Relations in the Commons of a Mexican Ejido', in F. von Benda-Beckmann, K. von Benda-Beckmann and M. Wiber (eds) *Changing Properties of Property*, pp. 218–42. New York and London: Berghahn Books.
Pigg, S. (1996) 'The Credible and the Credulous: The Question of "Villagers' Beliefs" in Nepal', *Cultural Anthropology* 11(2): 160–202.
Pigg, S. (1997) 'Found in Most Traditional Societies: Traditional Medical Practioners between Culture and Development', in F. Cooper and R. Packard (eds) *International Development and the Social Sciences*, pp. 259–90. Berkeley, CA: University of California Press.
Reed, M. (1992) *The Sociology of Organizations: Themes, Perspectives and Prospects*. New York: Harvester Wheatsheaf.
Ribot, J. and N. Peluso (2003) 'A Theory of Access', *Rural Sociology* 68(2): 153–81.
Rose, N. (1999) *Powers of Freedom: Reframing Political Thought*. Cambridge: Cambridge University Press.
Sabean, D.W. (1984) *Power in the Blood: Popular Culture and Village Discourse in Early Modern Germany*. Cambridge: Cambridge University Press.
Sabean, D.W. (1990) *Property, Production, and Family in Neckarhausen, 1700–1870*. Cambridge Studies in Social and Cultural Anthropology. Cambridge: Cambridge University Press.
Sack, R. (1986) *Human Territoriality: Its Theory and History*. Cambridge: Cambridge University Press.
Tsing, A. (1993) *In the Realm of the Diamond Queen: Marginality in an Out-of-the-Way Place*. Princeton, NJ: Princeton University Press.
Wagenaar, H. (2004) '"Knowing" the Rules: Administrative Work as Practice', *Public Administration Review* 64(6): 643–55.

5

Authority over Forests: Empowerment and Subordination in Senegal's Democratic Decentralization

Jesse C. Ribot

INTRODUCTION

'One gives us the head without the tongue' (Soninke saying)
(Rural Council President, Tamba Atelier, 14 February 2006)

Decentralization should involve the redistribution of power from central government to actors lower in the political-administrative hierarchy. Senegal's decentralization laws gave Mr Weex Dunx,[1] the Rural Council President (PCR) of Nambaradougou in the forested Tambacounda Region, the power to manage the forests in his jurisdiction. Weex Dunx's story illustrates the practices through which the laws that transfer control over forest down the hierarchy are attenuated in the service of initial power holders. The elected rural council is left without the material basis on which to develop as a legitimate local politico-legal institution. Weex Dunx and his rural community have no access to lucrative opportunities in forestry.

Senegal's 1996 decentralization law establishes new domains of 'competence' for rural councils. The rural council is an elected local government of a Rural Community, which is the smallest political-administrative jurisdiction in Senegal. To conform to the decentralization, Senegal's 1998 forestry code attributed significant powers of forest exploitation, use and management to rural councils. Sectoral laws, such as the forestry code, give elected rural councils the material substance — power — with respect to which they can represent the population in their Rural Community. Control over land and other resources — forests in this case — can produce authority (Chanock, 1991: 64; Lund, 2002; Ribot, 1999a; Sikor and Lund, this volume; Watts,

Many thanks to Jakob Trane Ibsen, John Heermans Ahamadou Kanté, Tomila Lankina, Christian Lund, Amy Poteete and Thomas Sikor for their constructive comments on this chapter. Sincere thanks to the Dutch Royal Embassy in Dakar, and especially to Franke Toornstra, for supporting the research behind this chapter. I would also like to thank the Max Planck Institute for Social Anthropology for providing an inspiring setting in which a portion of this chapter was composed.

1. 'Weex Dunx' in Wolof means 'plucked white'. A weex dunx is a scapegoat. Rural Council presidents felt blamed for everything wrong in their communities. Fictive names such as Weex Dunx have been assigned to the interviewees in this chapter. The name of the Rural Community, Nambaradougou, is also made up — it means 'problem village' in Soninke. For a film version of Weex Dunx's story see http://www.vimeo.com/599291/ or http://video.google.com/videoplay?docid=-3498292104301059460 with English subtitles, or http://www.vimeo.com/617574/ or http://video.google.com/videoplay?docid=-3367756256067936009 for French.

1993). The empowerment of the elected councils therefore should set the conditions under which effective and legitimate democratic local authority might emerge.

Senegal's rural councils have effective property rights over forests in their jurisdictions: they can exclude others, exploit the resource and allocate access. But in practice they cannot begin to exercise these rights. The residents of Senegal's Rural Communities remain unable to benefit from commercial forest exploitation. The elected rural councils of each Rural Community are pressured, intimidated and coerced into giving away access to their forests. The new rights inscribed in law have generated unenforceable claims. The councillors making the claims have no means to enforce them, while the Forest Service and sub-prefect charged with implementing and enforcing these new laws have no interest, incentive or intention of translating them into practice. Without the backing of superior politico-legal institutions the laws that give rural councils new powers are ineffective.

In Senegal, as in most developing countries, there are two kinds of zones to which decentralization laws apply: those under development projects, protected and supported by external actors; and those not in project areas and which are subject to the laws legislated by the government as government agencies apply them in ordinary practice. In project areas supplemental funding and technical advice can produce showcase outcomes of decentralized natural resource management. These areas can be sold as demonstration projects or testing grounds for innovation. But they cannot be sold as examples of how the nation's laws work in practice. Law in action can only be observed outside of project areas — in those ordinary places where development scrutiny is rare.

Anyone interested in studying environmental policy or policy writ large must train their attention on the non-project zones in which the government treats people as if nobody from the outside were looking. There we can see what government — and policy — does. Forestry projects in Senegal cover a significant portion of the country's commercially productive forests and are held up as the future of decentralized forestry practice. In Senegal, there are large forest management projects run by the World Bank, USAID and GTZ. Others have examined these projects (Bandiaky, 2008; Boutinot, 2004; Faye, 2006); this chapter will only briefly return to what happens in project areas, where projects are breaking laws and merchants and foresters are also systematically recentralizing control of lucrative forestry opportunities. Rather, the chapter will tell the story of Weex Dunx's ordinary Rural Community experience in the non-project zone of Nambaradougou.

Outside of forestry project areas, Senegal's Forest Service and its merchant allies retain control over forest resources via a repertoire of well-trodden methods (see Larson and Ribot, 2007; Ribot and Oyono, 2005). They disable forest dwellers and enable urban-based patrons to benefit from the forests via misrepresentation of the law, selective application of the law and continued enforcement of abrogated laws. They exclude rural councils from decisions and rural people from benefits by creating an uneven playing field of entry barriers that privilege their allies — all justified by discourses of national good and lack of local capacity. They use bribes and threats while taking advantage of the inability of rural populations to access and influence actors higher up in government. In their efforts to subordinate rural councils, the foresters stand side-by-side with forest merchants and are supported by the central government's local administrators, the sub-prefects. In Nambaradougou, contrary to new laws, the Forest Service continues to allocate access to commercial forest resources, giving access to urban-based merchants.

Many PCRs in the forested zones tried to use their new jurisdiction over forests to negotiate for benefits and better management with the Forest Service and merchants, but their attempts were defeated. The struggle over forests undermines elected rural councils' authority. Authority and property, following Lund (2002: 14–15), are mutually constituted; authorities want to be asked to authorize property claims since they cultivate legitimacy through the welcome exercise of enforcement powers. Claimants want their claims authorized to protect their wealth or livelihoods. In the process both authority and property are reinforced. In the case of Nambaradougou, the material claim that rural councils want to authorize is the power to control forest use, a power transferred to the rural councils by law. The story of PCR Weex Dunx focuses on one such power: the power to decide whether or not charcoal production will take place in the Rural Community forests. This power was transferred by law from the Forest Service to the rural council by giving the rural council jurisdiction over forests and requiring the signature of the PCR before any commercial forest exploitation can take place (RdS, 1998). In effect, the rural council 'owns' the forests.

While the Forest Service and the PCR have legal authority in the local arena, these institutions do not appear to actively 'seek out property claims to authorize in the attempt to build and solidify their legitimacy in relation to competitors' while claimants shop for authorities to authorize their claims (Sikor and Lund, this volume). Rather, this is an access struggle between two politico-legal institutions with different bases of legitimacy. Foresters look upward to the political-administrative hierarchy while the PCR looks to the population in its jurisdiction and to the party that included them on its electoral list. The foresters and PCRs are related by their struggle over forest access — a struggle in which the PCR is subordinated to the foresters. While the law says otherwise, the PCR is the claimant begging the foresters to allow him to exercise his rightful role. The foresters are not seeking claimants here, and the PCR should not have to be seeking authorization.

The PCR–Forest Service relation could be framed as a struggle over authority in which the ability to authorize control over forests hinges on gaining legitimacy. But first and foremost, it appears to be a simple struggle over access to lucrative forest resources (see Ribot and Peluso, 2003). In Nambaradougou the different people involved have significant financial interests in controlling forest access (Ribot, 1998, 2006). Legitimization or marginalization of the two authorities appear to be secondary phenomena. Perhaps desire for legitimacy fuels this power struggle, but it seems that the struggle is primarily about who will profit from the forests. In the struggle, the PCR is unable to fight the hierarchy. He gives in,[2] gaining a small payoff and consequently compromising his local legitimacy. This lack of legitimacy may then weaken his ability to make claims in the next round — but the claim is being made in order to gain financial benefits.

The PCR's benefit is reduced from direct control over forest use to a power to negotiate a bribe in exchange for his signature. When he signs, he receives some cash and gives up any ability to manage the forests in the longer term and for higher stakes, or to respond to the needs and aspirations of his population. The PCR is unable to stop production or to profit from and tax the lucrative resources being extracted from his community's forests. He does not lack legal title to the resource, and he certainly does not lack an interest in stopping forest exploitation. He lacks the ability to challenge the Forest Service and the charcoal merchants who are backed by the foresters and prefects. The rural councillors are given a title; they are elected as the representatives of the people, but they 'have no tongues'.

This chapter, based on the author's intermittent field research in the Tambacounda Region of Senegal from 2002 to 2006, focuses on PCR Weex Dunx's signing of the order to open his Rural Community's forests to exploitation in 2006. The first section provides background on struggles over forest control in Nambaradougou and the broader decentralization of forestry in Senegal, before subsequent sections tell the story of how a signature was coerced out of PCR Weex Dunx.

FORESTRY DECENTRALIZATION IN NAMBARADOUGOU

Nambaradougou is a Rural Community of around 30,000 people in the Soudano-Sahelian open-canopy forests of the Tambacounda Region of Senegal.[3] Its roughly seventy villages and fifteen hamlets depend primarily on peanut and millet farming. Like other neighbouring Rural Communities, Nambaradougou has been a site of charcoal production for over thirty years (Kanté, 2006; Ribot, 2000). To supply the city of Dakar with cooking fuel, migrant woodcutters from Guinea work for urban-based merchants called *patrons charbonniers* ('charcoal patrons' or 'patrons' from here on), cutting and turning Nambaradougou's trees into charcoal through controlled partial burning.

---

2. All the PCRs in the production zones are male.
3. Personal communication with Ahamadou Kante, June 2008.

Local Resistance to Charcoal Production

Almost all residents surveyed in Senegal's charcoal production region oppose production around their villages (Kanté, 2006; Ribot, 2000; Thiaw, 2003, 2005; Thiaw and Ribot, 2005). All but one of fourteen rural council presidents surveyed told us emphatically that the population did not want production in their area (Faye, 2006; Kante, 2006; Ribot, 2000; Thiaw, 2003, 2005; Thiaw and Ribot, 2005; and interviews with eight PCRs by author, 2004–06). In addition, the majority of foresters we talked with also acknowledged that rural populations are against charcoal production (interviews with foresters, 2002–06).

Villagers are against charcoal production due to conflicts with migrant labourers, damage to their forests, and because they do not want outsiders to profit from their forests if they cannot (Kanté, 2006; Ribot, 2000). Resistance to charcoal production in Nambaradougou dates back to at least the early 1990s (Diallo, n.d.; Kanté, 2006; Ribot, 2000). Despite complaints about woodcutting, two out of every ten villages surveyed in Nambaradougou in 2002 had residents who were engaged in charcoal production (Thiaw and Ribot, 2005: 322). Households within these villages are happy to host the migrant charcoal makers, providing them room and board for extra income (Ribot, 1998).

In the early 1990s, Nambaradougou's village chiefs[4] and rural council confronted the Forest Service and patrons, asking them to stop charcoal production. Between 1991 and 1994 local people asked for charcoal production to stop or to be carefully managed; the Forest Service promised to help, but production continued as usual. Rural people were frustrated. In 1993 the first 'participatory' forestry code gave rural councils the right to manage surrounding forests. But under this code the Forest Service continued to give quotas to patrons and permits to their migrant labourers. They continued to cut the forests of Nambaradougou. Some villages chased woodcutters away with threats of violence. Others accepted them. The residents of these villages gained rent by housing woodcutters while their village chiefs got a few small bribes from charcoal patrons. Frustrated and angry, most local people resigned themselves to business as usual (Kanté, 2006; Ribot, 2000; Thiaw and Ribot, 2005).

Regulatory Policy Before 1998

Until 1998 forest management in Senegal was highly centralized. Rural Communities had no say in management or rights in production or exchange. Under this system, a national quota for charcoal production — the total

---

4. Village chiefs are officially administrative authorities dependent on the Ministry of Interior. They are 'elected' by the heads of households in their village. In practice they usually inherit their positions through a lineage from the founding village family.

national amount to be legally produced — was fixed by the Forest Service each year. The national quota was not based on supply or demand data. It was based on the previous year's quota, which was lowered or raised depending on pressure to allocate more quotas to particular patrons or pressure from donors to lower the quota in the name of protecting the forests. Over the past decade, the quota has been lowered several times, despite fairly constant demand. Today the quota is around half of urban demand; since supply *is* being met, this means that the other half of current production is illegal (Bâ, 2006a; Ribot, 2006).

Each year, the nationally-set quota was divided among the 120 to 170 enterprises — co-operatives, economic interest groups (collectively-owned businesses) and corporations — all holding professional forest producer licences[5] delivered by the Forest Service. Allocation of quotas among these entities was based on their previous year's quota, with adjustments according to whether the enterprise had fully exploited its quota and had conducted voluntary forest management activities. New professional licences were also allocated in most years. The new entrants into the market were usually urban-based enterprises that had political connections to the National Union of Forestry Merchants of Senegal (UNCEFS), the Forest Service or the Environment Ministry.

After allocating quotas among enterprises, the Forest Service and Environment Ministry would hold a national meeting to open the new season. They would promulgate a ministerial order listing the quota for each enterprise and indicating the region where these quotas were to be exploited. There are two regions in which production is now legal; Tambacounda and Kolda. Shortly after this national meeting, the Regional Forest Services would call a meeting in the regional capital and 'announce' to the recipients their exact quota and the Rural Community in which they would produce their quota's worth of charcoal. The forestry agents in each region had chosen areas to produce charcoal where they knew there was sufficient standing wood. The rural councils had no say in the matter. Patrons and their workers would arrive in a village with permits in hand accompanied by local foresters to launch each production season.[6]

Progressive New Decentralization Laws of 1998

Senegal's 1996 Decentralization Law gave Rural Communities jurisdiction over forests in the territorial boundaries of the Rural Community. The rural

---

5. A 1995 law liberalizing the professions in Senegal made licensing in this sector strictly illegal, but the Forest Service continues to give licences and to exclude those without (see Ribot, 2006).
6. For details of the 1993 'participatory' forestry code — which did not change these practices — see Ribot (1995).

council was given jurisdiction over 'management of forests on the basis of a management plan approved by the competent state authority' and 'delivery of authorization prior to any cutting within the perimeter of the Rural Community' (RdS, 1996a: art. 30; see also the Forestry Code, RdS, 1998: arts. L4, L8). This general decentralization framing law gives the council jurisdiction over 'the organization of extraction of all gathered plant products and the cutting of wood' (RdS, 1996b: art.195).

Most importantly, the 1998 code (RdS, 1998) requires the Forest Service to obtain the signature of the president of the rural council *before* any commercial production can take place in their forests (art. L4). The code also gives the council the right to determine *who* will have the right to produce in these forests (arts. L8, R21). In addition, the president of the rural council plays an executive role and cannot take action prior to a meeting and deliberation of the council, whose decisions are passed by majority vote (RdS, 1996b: arts. 200, 212). In short, the new laws require the majority vote of the rural council approving production before anyone can produce in Rural Community forests.

The radical new 1998 forestry code changed everything, at least on paper. The quantity of production would be based on the biological potential of each Rural Community's forests rather than fixed by decree in Dakar and the regional capital. The enterprises to work in a given forest would be chosen by the rural council, rather than assigned by the Ministry in Dakar. If implemented, the new system would empower rural councillors to manage their forests for the benefit of the Rural Community. The law allowed a three-year transition period from the quota system to the new system based on rural council involvement, with the quota system to be eliminated by 21 February 2001 (RdS, 1998: art. R66). But February 2001 passed, and still nothing changed. Despite these progressive new laws, the Forest Service continued to allocate access to the forests via centrally-allocated licences, quotas and permits.

Given the history of tensions around charcoal production, Nambaradougou's rural council was delighted to hear of these new rights. The councils learned of the changes through an information campaign by the USAID-funded NGO Democratie et Gouvernance Locale (DGL) project. DGL translated the essence of the new laws into local languages and informed rural councils of their new rights under Senegal's decentralization laws passed in 1996. Without prompting, rural councillors across the region told us that they had learned a great deal from DGL (Faye, 2006; author interviews 2002, 2005).[7]

The visible change in practice is that the required PCR signature has become a new obstacle with which foresters and patrons have to deal in order

---

7. The DGL programme was shut down by USAID after a review considered it 'ineffective' (December 2005, personal communication with USAID staff, Dakar). We found, without expecting to, that DGL had served a positive role in civic education (see Faye, 2006).

to exploit the forests. Contrary to the 1998 law, as of 2008 the quota was still fixed and allocated in Dakar, with forestry enterprises being assigned their production sites by foresters. The only role of the rural council is for the PCR to sign off on production at the beginning of each season. If he refuses, he is pressured, threatened and bribed by foresters, patrons and the sub-prefect until he signs. The next section outlines exactly how the rural council's new rights are being attenuated by the Forest Service–patron alliance, with the help of the sub-prefect.

COERCING THE RURAL COUNCIL PRESIDENT

Under the decentralization law, the PCR helps to elaborate a production and management plan that specifies quantities and production sites and requires his signature before each season begins. But in non-project areas, no management plans are elaborated. In lieu of telling the Forest Service what they want, in these areas the Forest Service still tells rural councils where production will take place and by whom. This decision is made by the Forest Service and announced at a meeting of the Regional Council. Rather than being invited to the meeting, the meeting announcement is simply copied to the PCRs. If they do attend, PCRs' opinions are not asked and their questions are not addressed. After the regional meeting, the PCR is visited by a forester toting an administrative order that the PCR is asked to sign to open the production season for merchants to come in with their migrant labourers and cut the forests — management plans are not required. The eight PCRs interviewed by the author in 2004 to 2006 did not want to sign this order. All, however, were eventually 'persuaded' to sign.

In most cases the PCR signs the order without a deliberation of the council (which is true also in project areas; see below). There are exceptions. The council of Missirah (a project area) did meet; even here most councillors told us they were against production. But in other project areas and in the seven other non-project Rural Communities (besides Nambaradougou) in which I interviewed councillors, the councillors did not even know that a decision had been made by their PCR. This was the case in Nambaradougou. In a discussion with seven members of one rural council, including the president of the council's environment commission, one councillor said: 'No deliberation about the opening of the [charcoal] production season ever took place'. In addition, after some discussion it became evident that nobody among them even knew that the PCR had any right to sign on production decisions. One councillor just shook his head in dismay, saying 'We are not involved' (interview with seven councillors, 27 December 2005).

Although most PCRs signed without consulting their council, all initially resisted charcoal production in their areas. The actual process by which the PCRs were persuaded to sign varied from PCR to PCR, but there was a clear pattern. Each councillor refused to sign. Each was pressured to sign by the Regional Forest Service Director (the Inspecteur du Secteur de la Region) and the local Forest Brigade Chief (Chef de Brigade) in the Rural Community, the sub-prefect (district-level administrative officer), charcoal patrons and an envoy sent from the National Forestry Union in Dakar. The PCRs all felt they had no choice in the matter. This pattern was observed in a cross-sectional study of seven additional rural councils (Thiaw, 2005). The case of Nambaradougou, described below, illustrates the typical process by which PCRs are forced to approve charcoal production in their Rural Communities.

SIGNING IN NAMBARADUOUGOU: THE COERCION OF WEEX DUNX

In April 2005, Ahamadou Wuula, a forest agent from the Regional Forest Bureau in Tamba, came to Nambaraduougou to ask the PCR, Moussa Weex Dunx, to sign the annual order to open the charcoal production season in the forests of Nambaraduougou. The president of the rural council of Nambaraduougou refused to sign. This was his third year in office and he was just beginning to understand that his signature had important implications. He now knew that he was not obliged to sign the authorizations brought to him each year by the Forestry Service unless the conditions of production conformed to his — and presumably the rural council's — needs. This section presents the story of Weex Dunx and the opening of the 2006 charcoal production season in Nambaradougou from the perspective of the PCR, the sub-prefect, the Forest Brigade chief, a forester sent from the Tambacounda regional office, the National Forestry Union president and a charcoal patron.

The PCR, Moussa Weex Dunx

'There is a certain complicity with the Forest Service; it is not against us, it is for the interests of the patrons' (PCR4 in discussion at Tamba Atelier with four PCRs, 14 February 2006).

'We decide nothing. There are no benefits. We watch' (PCR1 in discussion at Tamba Atelier with four PCRs, 14 February 2006).

'The rural council is not part of the decision. They bring us the order and ask us to sign it' (PCR1 in discussion at Tamba Atelier, 14 February 2006; all four participants agreed).

'With decentralization the transfer is not transferred. The quota, the production zones, come from above' (Vice President, Rural Council of Koumpentoum, 18 December 2005).

In the early 1990s, Nambaradougou's PCR and village chiefs organized to block charcoal production in their forests. After a series of negotiations with the Forest Service and charcoal patrons, a select group of chiefs, reaping some income from charcoal production, allowed the woodcutting to continue. By and large, however, the population, many of the chiefs and the elected PCR were frustrated and unhappy (Ribot, 2000). Interviewed again in a series of interviews in Nambaradougou in 2003–06, the PCR from the early 1990s and his council members felt that they had been defeated. In April 2003, Moussa Weex Dunx's first year as PCR, Weex Dunx told me that he knew that the villagers were still mostly against charcoal production.[8]

In December 2005, Weex Dunx explained: 'During my first year [as PCR in 2003], I was just learning, so I signed. In 2003, the forester came. He doesn't come in a manner that allowed me to reflect on the issue. I did not know when I signed in 2003 that I signed a paper with this implication [that so much forest cutting would occur]'. The Nambaradougou Forestry Brigade chief, interviewed in 2003, explained that 'the new PCR got 425,000 CFA [in bribes from the patrons] his first year'.[9] But did the PCR get this much? How does the Brigade chief know the exact figure? Is it because he was involved in the transaction? Is it rumour? Or did he give this figure to make the PCR look bad? Or all of the above? Interviews with foresters and patrons across the region indicated that foresters are involved in paying off the PCRs for the charcoal patrons (ostensibly the patrons give foresters cash, which they slip to the PCR). The amount is said to vary between 100,000 and 500,000 CFA.

Weex Dunx said, 'At the beginning of 2004, I asked [at the Tambacounda Regional Council meeting at which the Forest Service "announces" the annual quota] if we could discuss exploitation [commercial use of forests] in our Rural Community'. But, it was clear from the response, recorded in the minutes of that meeting, that he had no influence on whether or not there would be production in his area. Inscribed in the minutes, Weex Dunx said at the meeting: 'We should be involved in the distribution of quotas; we should know the patrons; coming here I encountered five trucks of charcoal. We do not even know which zones are open to exploitation' (RdS, 2004: 3).

The response to Weex Dunx from the Director of the Regional Forest Service was chilling:

> I must first explain that our meeting today is not for the distribution of quotas, but rather for notifying interested parties. The distribution of quotas is done by a national commission designated by the Minister of the Environment and Protection of Nature and chaired by the director of the Forest Service. You are charged with the management of natural resources in your Rural Community, but do not forget that the state is the guarantor of these resources.

---

8. Despite most villages across the forested zones being against production, most village chiefs are for it since they are paid off by the patrons to allow it to continue in the surrounding forests. For more on the chiefs' role, see Kanté (2006); Ribot (1998, 2000); Thiaw and Ribot (2005).
9. Other figures were mentioned: 'The signature by the PCR is needed on an order to open the season. I know that the PCR signs. If I could have influence, I would not sign until they agree to have zones and organize the exploitation. The PCR signs for 100,000 CFA. I would not sign until we organize the exploitation' (interview with Nambaradougou Councillor, 23 December 2005).

> To manage the resources does not mean to refuse to let them be exploited. Go back and see your Forestry Brigade chief, who is your advisor on this matter. (RdS, 2004: 3)

The words of the Regional Director were consistent with advice from the Brigade chief in Nambaradougou a year earlier. He told us: 'Charcoal is the responsibility of the Regional Council. The PCR does not have rights over the resource. Because natural resources are for everyone, being a manager does not make one an owner or give one rights' (interview, Forestry Brigade chief, Nambaraduougou, 3 April 2003). Weex Dunx found himself confronted by a consistent wall of disempowering discourse. So in 2004, like the year before, he returned frustrated to Nambaraduougou having wasted his time with a useless trip to Tambacounda. He signed the order when it came to him.

But the following year, things were different. In the words of Weex Dunx (interview in Nambaradougou, 23 December 2005):

> In 2005 the local Forest Brigade chief [Matar Koulibaly] came and I refused to sign.[10] Koulibaly asked and pleaded for me to sign. He said to me: 'We did not make this [administrative order], but we are called in when there is a problem'. I said I would not sign unless he brought together all the actors involved in [forest] extraction in our zone: charcoal patrons, authorities in the area, the technical services and the rural council. So he gave me [the order] and I brought it home. Later, Koulibaly put me in contact with Diouf [another agent]. Diouf came and asked why I did not sign. Diouf phoned Mor Kojangue [the president of the National Forestry Union, UNCEFS, in Dakar] and Kojangue said he would send a representative from Koumpentoum [a nearby town]. Kojangue sent the regional [union] leader from Koumpentoum with 50,000 CFA. I rejected this and said this is not what I asked for.
>
> Afterwards, Kojangue called the sub-prefect. Kojangue asked me what my position was. He asked, via the sub-prefect, for me to sign. I said I would not sign. I said: 'We need to know who is here [which charcoal patrons are working in the Rural Community forests]; we don't have any contact [with these charcoal patrons]'. I asked to sit down around a table. The sub-prefect, Sasoumane Dioup, asked me to do everything to settle with Kojangue.

Weex Dunx then reflected: 'If the zone can be exploited without our decision, without us who open the season, we have nothing but a consultative position. We make no decisions'. He continued his account:

> The sub-prefect told me Kojangue was willing to send me a cellphone. The sub-prefect then made a phone call to Kojangue with me in the office. I continued to say no. The sub-prefect said: 'You must sign'. Kojangue spoke to me. The sub-prefect told me 'I am sure [Kojangue] will respect your requests'. After the conversation with Kojangue, the sub-prefect asked me to sign. He said [in a kind of veiled threat] 'Kojangue is at the national level. He is in contact with many people'.

---

10. In Nambaraduougou, the council opposed charcoal production from 1991 to 1996, but in the end they let the patrons work due to pressure from the prefect (Thiaw, 2003: 16). The following councils (elected 1996 to 2001 and 2002 to 2007) did the same (Thiaw, 2003, 2006; also Kanté, 2006).

But Weex Dunx told me that he was still not ready; he explained: 'I wanted to know how the zones are distributed. The migrant woodcutters don't have papers. We don't have the means to fight illegal cutters. We can only report them'. But, as most PCRs told us and Weex Dunx also explained, when the villagers or councillors report illegal production to the Forest Service, nobody comes to stop them or fine them. Then Weex Dunx explained: 'The Tambacounda Regional Forest Service Office [*Secteur de Tambacounda*] sent Wuula Gaggala, who came "as a brother" and [Gaggala] said: "Everyone is talking about you. I want you to stop this. This is not between us". I said: "This is not me; the council must decide". But I signed. Kojangue then called the sub-prefect and said that he would respect my demands'. Later Weex Dunx told me that the union leader Kojangue had sent him a cellphone, but had not responded to his other demands.

A few days later in Tambacounda, I asked Wuula Gaggala how he managed to get Weex Dunx to sign. Wuula Gaggala said:

> I came to Nambaraduougou. I said: 'I don't come as a charcoal patron or as a forester. I come as family'. I told him: 'Every man has his destiny. A good Muslim must facilitate things'. I asked him to sign. He said nothing. He asked his secretary to bring the papers and he signed. The whole thing was only five minutes. (Interview in Tambacounda, 25 December 2005)[11]

When I asked Weex Dunx: 'Did you have a council meeting on this?', he said that he didn't.[12] And when I asked why not, he replied, 'I know the unanimous position of the council. DGL gave us a lot of assistance and guidance on this. We know nothing should happen without our permission. The council is conscious that we can develop only with our resources.' I asked what he wanted to do with the forests. He responded, 'We want to manage and exploit the forests ourselves. We want advice from the state services. We see our forests exploited and cut 100 per cent, but we get nothing' (interview with PCR, Nambaradougou, 22 December 2005).

I then asked: 'What prevents you from exploiting your forests yourself?'. 'We need the help of the state', he replied. 'We need means. Recently we

11. There is some question as to whether Gaggala paid off Weex Dunx. Another researcher who recently conducted research in this area told me that the Forestry Brigade chief told him that the PCR had asked for 600,000 CFA plus a cellphone from Kojangue. He said that the Forestry Brigade chief had told him that the Regional Forest Service Director sent a forester from Tambacounda who explained to the PCR he could have money, but that he should not ask for it formally. When the researcher asked the PCR, he denied that he had asked for money. The PCR said that Kojangue, did, however, send him a cellphone 'to communicate with Kojangue concerning production'. The PCR showed him his cellphone and said that Kojangue had sent it (personal communication with Ahamadou Kanté, 27 December 2005).
12. I asked Weex Dunx for the minutes of any meetings he had held to discuss forest management or charcoal production with his council. He told me that there were some but he did not have the key to the council office — it was with the secretary. Others told me that the meetings had been very nasty and he had been embattled at them. One forester who worked in the area said that there were meeting minutes from 2002 and 2003 (forester interview, 25 December 2005).

had a seminar with GADEC [a local NGO in Tambacounda] and we saw protected forests. ... But', he threw up his hands, 'if we work out a plan to exploit our forests, we risk confrontation with the charcoal patrons who come with quotas'. He continued, 'We attempted to make a management plan [referring to an arrangement called Zone de Production Controlé (ZPC), a kind of simplified management arrangement that was to start there in 2004 but never materialized].[13] We tried to work it out with the Forest Service. But nothing was transferred. It is they who manage everything'. When I asked: 'What about the ZPC?', he replied: 'I brought the proposal dossier to the Forest Service office and it stopped there.[14] That's where it's stuck' (interview with PCR, Nambaradougou, 22 December 2005).

Weex Dunx said a few weeks later: 'The rural council has responsibility. What can we do when the decision makers break the law? Mor Kojangue called the sub-prefect, who said "I am in contact with the Minister: you must sign".[15] They twisted my hand. I had to sign'. He paused. 'We don't represent anyone. Even if we refuse, they exploit' (Weex Dunx, Tamba atelier, 14 February 2006).

The Sub-Prefect, Sasoumane Dioup

> PCR1: 'The sub-prefect will never make the job of elected local councillors easier. The sub-prefects threaten us'.
> PCR2: 'We live this every day' (PCRs 1 & 2, Tamba Atelier, 14 February 2006).

The sub-prefect is the representative of the central state within the Rural Community. His official role is to review and approve all council decisions to check for conformity to proper procedures and laws. This role is called 'legal control' (RdS, 1996b). It is not a decision-making role. On 21 December 2005 I interviewed sub-prefect Sasoumane Dioup. He first got involved in the charcoal production season opening in 2005 when, as he explained:

> The PCR refused to sign and the president of UNCEFS [national union president Mor Kojangue] called me. Kojangue asked me to intervene. He said: 'The PCR refused to sign'.

---

13. I suspect that he is referring to a project developed for a ZPC in this area with the assistance of DGL. When DGL was closed, the project should have continued, but it died in the office of the Forestry Brigade. The Brigade chief told me that the ZPC file was just sitting there. He said it was the responsibility of the PCR to do something. But the PCR had no idea that this file was there, nor that he had to do anything. The forester had an attitude that suggested that he would not lift a finger to assist the PCR.
14. In December 2004 the regional inspection of the Forest Service in Tambacounda called for a deliberation on ZPCs in the two Rural Communities where ZPCs were planned. This request was sent to the presidents of both Rural Councils concerned (MEPN, 2004).
15. Another researcher working in the area in 2004 and 2005 said Weex Dunx explained to him that 'when he refused to sign the authorization, "they" told him he must not, as a PDS (Democratic Party of Senegal) member, block the decisions of the government in matters of charcoal production' (personal communication, Ahamadou Kanté, June 2008).

Kojangue sent a team to see the PCR, who then called Kojangue, so Kojangue called me. ... Kojangue asked me what the problem was. So I went to see the PCR. The PCR of Nambaraduougou said: 'Each year, they prepare an order in Tamba and ask us to sign without the explanation we need'.

I asked 'What did Kojangue say to you?'. Dioup made some gestures indicating that he did not want to tell me what Kojangue said. He paused and then said: 'I went to the PCR to play my role as intermediary. The PCR said, "I will not sign before I can talk with the patrons. They exploit, and we see no benefits"'. The sub-prefect explained to me, 'The exploitation is for the nation; we need to supply Dakar with fuel.' He said, 'I told the PCR, "Don't create useless blockages. We need to supply Dakar". I explained to the PCR that he should proceed cautiously and remain within the law'.[16]
    The sub-prefect said:

> The PCR was called to the regional council for the big meeting on charcoal. But the regional council does not send any information in advance. The Regional Council needs to send the information in advance so there can be a local decision. In previous years the Regional Forest Service Director came and had the PCR sign and never left copies. The sub-prefect never got copies. Therefore the order was never approved by the sub-prefect.

He had not been involved before. He told us, 'In 2005, I saw a big document from the Forest Service' [it was the order for the opening of the season]. He paused and said in a confidential tone: 'I think everything was decided before the Regional Council meeting.[17] The discussion was only on the big questions — no details. The PCR has no decision in this. He just signs'.
    I asked the sub-prefect what he did after Kojangue called: 'What did you tell the PCR?'. He said: 'I told him "If you stay in the law, you run no risk. When you step out of your legal jurisdiction [*competence*], you can be crushed. A judge can condemn you"'. I asked him to explain what he meant. He said 'Let me give you an example of a marriage certificate. If a couple comes with all the necessary papers, I must sign; it is my job to sign! Same with the order for production. Patrons and the foresters come with papers. It is the right of the patrons to produce; it's their profession'. When I asked if this meant that it is illegal for the PCR not to sign, he nodded his head yes. This perverse interpretation of the law reduces the council and PCR to administrators, contrary to the letter and spirit of the law.

---

16. This statement needs to be understood as a veiled threat. The PCRs all told us that they feel legally vulnerable. They are constantly told that they are breaking the law when they think that they are working within their rights (Weex Dunx, Tamba atelier, 14 February 2006).
17. The quota is allocated among the patrons in Dakar. The Regional Forest Service determines the Rural Communities in which production will take place and the regional meeting is organized to announce who will get how many quotas and where they will be required to produce. Only then do negotiations begin for the signature of the PCR — exactly the opposite of what the laws say (see Bâ, 2006b; Ribot, 2006).

'What happened next', I asked. Dioup recounted: 'I brought the PCR to my office. I called Kojangue. We had a three-way conversation. The PCR agreed'. He paused and then said:

> My job is to assume that there is no scandal — neither for the PCR nor for the patrons — I don't want any problems or delays. Things have changed. I no longer exercise hierarchical power. The term *tutelle* no longer exists. Now there is only legal control. . . . The transferred natural resource powers need to be reviewed. The PCR and the rural council have no transfer of powers. The weight of the Forest Service is still dominant. On a political level, there is money generated by charcoal. The population does not understand the situation. The PCR cannot tell you the taxes that have been brought in [i.e. he does not know]. The brigade [local Forest Brigade chief] does not give the PCR monthly reports. Foresters do not inform the PCR of anything. The PCR does not know when there is overproduction of the quota. (Interview, 21 December 2005)

The Local Forestry Brigade Chief, Matar Koulibaly

> Question put to the Regional Forest Service deputy director: 'If the majority of rural council presidents do not want production in the forests of their Rural Communities, how do you choose their Rural Community as a production site?'.
> Reply: 'If the PCRs have acceptable reasons, if the local population would not like it?'. He asked this with a non-comprehending inflection. He continued: 'The resource is for the entire country. There must be technical reasons not to use it. The populations are there to manage. There is a national imperative. There are preoccupations of the state. This can't work if the people pose problems for development'.
> (Interview, assistant director of the regional forest service, Tamba, 3 December 2005)

The Nambaradougou Forestry Brigade chief oversees forestry matters for Nambaradougou and two neighbouring Rural Communities. His story was consistent with Weex Dunx's and that of the sub-prefect — with a few new nuances (interview, Nambaraduougou Forest Brigade chief, 21 December 2005). I asked him to recount what happened around the signing of the order for the opening of the charcoal season that year. Koulibaly told me, 'I got the order in Tamba and brought it here. I gave it to the PCR's secretary. The PCR then gave me a letter with requests'. Koulibaly looked for the letter, but could not find it anywhere. He continued 'It was not within my jurisdiction to respond to his letter. I told [PCR Weex Dunx] that he had to talk with the Regional Forest Service Director or to the Forest Service headquarters in Dakar — I told him this in writing'. Koulibaly searched for and found his reply. The reply, dated 22 April 2005 in response to a letter dated 18 April 2005, was short: 'The actions you have asked for before the signing of the order for the installation of exploitation entities are not within my jurisdiction; therefore, you must go to see the regional council, the Regional Forest Service Office, and the charcoal patrons'.

I asked Koulibaly what was in the letter from Weex Dunx, and he said: 'From what I remember, he asked for a meeting with the charcoal patrons and three copies of the order'. He did not remember more. He continued,

'Mor Kojangue [of the union] then called the sub-prefect. After that, the PCR decided to sign'. I asked if he knew that Wuula Gaggala had come from Regional Forest Service Office to talk with the PCR. He said 'I did not know Wuula Gaggala came to see the PCR'.

In keeping with the decentralization laws, the new role of forest service agents and officials is to only give the rural council 'technical advice' (interview 2, Chief of Tamba Regional Office, 6 December 2005). Koulibaly was supposed to do this. But he kept referring questions higher up the hierarchy although he could have given answers himself. The letter was a special matter. But according to Weex Dunx, despite having asked them, Koulibaly and the other foresters did not help him to establish a management plan or to form their own co-operatives so that they could get quotas. The higher-level authorities were also of little help, as Weex Dunx learned when he went to the regional meeting (above).

The Regional Forest Service director explained: 'The legislation says that the rural council can refuse charcoal producers. But charcoal is a national good. It is a strategic resource that is important for the government. There will be marches in Dakar if there are shortages. If we let one rural council say no, then the next year perhaps others will say no. This will cause shortages in Dakar' (interview, Regional Forestry Inspector, 4 April 2003; also see Ribot, 1999b). In another interview, a forest agent in Tambacounda explained that the PCR has no right to say no. He said: 'A PCR cannot say that he does not want production. He says no, then yes. He says yes when the patrons visit him; [patrons] use maraboutic powers [magic] or the price of cola nuts [as payoffs]. Those in the party in power follow the requests of their party'. The agent paused. He then said, as if it were self-evident that this means that people must obey: 'We are in a state!' (interview, forestry agent, Tamba, 6 December 2005).

UNCEFS President, Mor Kojangue

Kojangue told me on 22 February 2006:

> Weex Dunx wrote me a letter asking for 1) a cellphone to communicate with me, 2) money to repair the car so he could visit the forests to monitor them, and 3) money for reforestation. But I won't enter into this. If you have a programme, come and propose it as a PCR. We have finances for projects. But I will not give to the PCR without a proposal ... The sub-prefect intervened to tell Weex Dunx to sign.

He paused, 'Senegal is indivisible!' he said, as if these were definitive words, evoking the importance of 'national good'.

> The sub-prefect told [PCR Weex Dunx] he could not refuse since the [forestry] technicians have estimated the amount of charcoal to take from the Rural Community. The country needs that and he can't say no. I sent him the cellphone. I did not respond to the other requests. I

paid for it with our funds. I helped him. It was from our fund. If he has a programme from the rural council, and gives us a dossier, we will study it.

Weex Dunx had told me about the cellphone and said, with disappointment, that it was all he got; Kojangue had not honoured his requests.

Jam Yimbé, a Charcoal Patron

One of the patrons working in Nambaraduougou, Jam Yimbé, told us: 'My woodcutters are in Nambaraduougou. In Nambaraduougou there is no problem with the population. But, the forest is a bit used up. I maintain good relations with Weex Dunx, the PCR'. I asked him what he meant by 'good relations'. 'We discuss', he said with a pause, 'but I don't want to say more'. He then continued: 'With village chiefs, when I come I visit them. In the village there is water. The woodcutters cannot work without water. So I give the chief kola nuts [some money]. But if we don't agree then I go elsewhere' (interview, Patron 2, Tamba, 25 December 2005). In an earlier interview, this same patron told us: 'Mor Kojangue gave the PCR of another Rural Community 500,000 FCFA to unblock the 2005 season' (Patron 2, Tamba, 6 December 2005).

Several patrons explained that in the past, the chiefs were the only local authorities they had to negotiate with. But each patron has quotas that are earmarked for a particular Rural Community and they require the PCR's signature before they can exploit their quota. With the chiefs, the patrons can go to the next village if they do not agree to host their woodcutters. Due to quotas and assigned Rural Communities, patrons cannot go elsewhere if the PCR refuses. So, they must get the signature, one way or another, to begin their work. This has raised the stakes. In the last several years, in lieu of individual patrons negotiating with the chiefs, the National Forestry Union president, Kojangue, has been negotiating collectively for the patrons. This may be to counterbalance the new power of the PCRs — but the union president is using collective bargaining to consolidate his own power, too.

Nambaraduougou and Beyond

So, what happened in Nambaradougou? Mr Weex Dunx felt he had no choice but to sign away his new rights to manage his rural community's forests (see Faye, 2006; Kanté, 2006; Thiaw, 2005). He and the people of his Rural Community were against charcoal production, but charcoal production continued as in the past. Nambaradougou never got the management or revenue concessions Weex Dunx requested.

Despite trying to stop charcoal production in the name of the law and the local population, PCRs we interviewed across the forested regions felt powerless. They felt like 'Weex Dunxs' — scapegoats accused of corruption, abuse of power, and giving in to foresters and merchants. They had a profound sense of vulnerability in the face of the responsibilities of elected office and the liabilities of failing to carry out their mandates or crossing the many unknown boundaries of the laws to which they were subject — even though others, like the foresters and merchants, could freely break the rules. The decentralization laws empowered them to make decisions for their community, but then the merchants and foresters wrenched that power back. PCRs could not serve their communities. They held little authority.

By dint of the 1996 and 1998 decentralization laws, Weex Dunx and all the other PCRs have gained some power as a new node of access control along Senegal's charcoal commodity chain (cf. Ribot, 1998). They are all now able to reap some income in exchange for their signatures. They control forest access and the merchants and Forest Service must gain access through them. But PCRs' control is weak, since others control access to things they value such as inclusion on political lists (or slates), opportunities for commerce and work accessible through higher authorities and forest merchants, and protection from accusations and prosecution. In order to maintain access to these other things PCRs must give away the forests. So Weex Dunx gives access to the patrons and foresters who have influence over the larger political environment in which he is embedded.

The Parallel World of Project Success Stories

Each time I describe Nambaradougou and other non-project area councils to foresters, donors or project staff, they deflect attention away from my observations by mentioning project areas; they tell me how progressive practices in the projects are and that I am looking in the wrong place. But, project areas are only slightly better. In project areas, many of the new laws are being applied and a form of decentralized forest management is being implemented. Yet up to 2006 most of the residents in the project areas did not want charcoal production and very few benefited from it. Their PCRs also resisted at first, but eventually were pressured by project staff, foresters and other officials to sign onto the project and to sign the annual charcoal production order.

In project areas the Forest Service arrives backed by donors with forestry projects and insists that the Rural Community be made into a model production zone. 'Special quotas'[18] are allocated to Rural Communities in project areas (such as the Dutch PROGEDE project; see Boutinot, 2004; Boutinot

---

18. The usual national quota given to merchants is a production quota. After production they can trade it in for a 'circulation quota' which gives them direct access to markets. The 'special quota' (now being called '*contractualization*') allows production but does not automatically translate into market access.

and Diouf, 2005; Faye, 2006). Yet, until recently, just like the ordinary quotas given to patrons in the non-project zones, special quotas did not enable these Rural Communities to market their own charcoal. The special quotas only allow them to *produce* the charcoal. The Forest Service arranges contracts between the UNCEFS forestry union president and the Rural Communities to market their charcoal in Dakar. In essence, the president of UNCEFS has now locked up the project market in the form of marketing contracts with project committees. The projects have their special quotas, but they must sell to the patrons with contracts negotiated by the union leader.

Under the UNCEFS contracts, woodcutters receive a fixed 600 FCFA (US$ 1.20) per sack of charcoal while the average producer price in non-project areas was around 750 to 800 FCFA in the same year (2006).[19] For each sack of charcoal, the union leader then contributes 200 FCFA to a fund that is earmarked 70 per cent for local development and 30 per cent for forestry work. Clearly, the union leader's 'contribution' is taken from the producer price. Nevertheless, the 200 FCFA is a significant amount of income for a rural community. But it is not a fund of the rural council. While taxes would normally be the domain of the rural council — which has the right to set, collect and disburse them — the contract states that this forestry fund is managed by 'the rural council, villages near production sites, UNCEFS president, and the Forest Service'. The PCR does not have control or discretion over these funds as he would a tax. As the PCR in one of the longest-standing projects told us: 'I don't know who can draw funds or who has the checkbook' (interview, PCR, 8 December 2005). It seems that the new fund is under forest service and UNCEFS control — hardly decentralized.

The contracts make project areas into the UNCEFS leader's own supply and market-access control system, replacing the nationally-allocated quota with a Forest-Service-facilitated contract as the mechanism for maintaining oligopsony. Through 2006 a few residents of Rural Communities were able to independently sell their charcoal in Dakar, but the vast majority got a low forest-edge price and could not enter the larger market. The union president controlled project area access to markets through the new contracts while the patrons controlled market access in non-project areas through the old quota system. The project rural communities finally got a production quota, but still with highly restricted market access.

There is a notable exception. In 2006, one project unit had negotiated with the UNCEFS leader to rent trucks to villagers to bring their charcoal to Dakar. In Dakar they were able to sell to urban wholesalers and came home

---

19. Most of the Rural Communities in project areas hire the same migrant Guinean labourers that the merchants used to hire. Residents of the Rural Communities generally do not like engaging in charcoal production.

very happy, having more than quadrupled their profit.[20] So the projects have opened up some new spaces. The union leader, under great pressure from donors, threw the villagers a bone. They allowed them to market two truckloads — out of a total of 3,000 to 5,000 truckloads a year (Faye, 2003: 56–9; MEMI, 1995: 5; PROGEDE, 2002: 59). This great success amounts to less than 0.05 per cent of the market. The other 99.95 per cent remains locked up with the merchants. Villagers' market share increased in 2007 and 2008 (interviews January 2009). Forestry projects are trying to enable communities to sell and to profit, but they face steep collusive forester–patron resistance.

CONCLUSION

'"Local Communities" are just words, they are lyrics. The real power is in the hands of the authorities; [pause] government [pause], the Forest Service' (interview, meeting 2, Tamba Regional Council Vice President Kabina Kaba Diakéte, 19 December 2005).

The people of Nambaradougou do not want woodcutting. This is clear to their village chiefs and to the rural council and its president (PCR). Weex Dunx, the PCR of Nambaradougou, attempted to act in accordance with his people's desires and what he thought were the best interests of the Rural Community. In the end, however, he appears — or is portrayed by foresters, prefects and merchants — as just one more corrupt and ineffective local politician. He took a small bribe and gave away the forests. Because the Forest Service does not allow the PCR to exercise his powers, there is little chance that the elected rural council will gain legitimacy and be able to represent its people. Democracy in Nambaradougou has been deprived of its material basis. PCR Weex Dunx tried to exercise his legal powers on behalf of his population, but was stymied at every step. He gave in. It is no wonder that he — like all of the PCRs in the forested regions — felt powerless and exasperated.

'Decentralized' powers remain in the hands of a few patrons and the Forest Service. The laws give new prerogatives to the rural council. The Forest Service and its patron allies take them back. The Forest Service is breaking some laws — not those of procedural democracy, but those of power transfer. They seek to obtain the signatures of the PCR, subverting democracy while complying with its rules. By maintaining a charcoal production quota that was eliminated in 2001 by the forestry code, the Forest Service keeps the patrons happily arriving at the PCR's doorstep with production orders in hand. Upon arrival they pressure the PCR to sign the orders using

---

20. The patron's profit margin is 1,500 to 4,000 CFA per sack, depending on the season. Further, each patron handles many times more sacks than do producers, reaping enormous profits (extensive survey data, 2002–06).

arguments of national good and the moral pitfalls of depriving the patrons and their labourers of work. They spice their arguments with veiled threats of prosecution for blocking implementation of the law. When the PCR is finally worn down and signs, they reward him for his signature with a small payoff. Control over natural resources remains with the Forest Service. The authority of the rural council to grant forest rights is effectively expunged by these practices.

Senegal's legislature gave rural councils the right to determine the use of local forests in the laws establishing democratic decentralization (RdS, 1996b). The Ministry of the Interior is charged with setting up and supporting elected rural authorities. People vote and their representatives are put in office. But the line ministries — forestry, health, education — control the powers that, if transferred, could be the material basis of local democracy. Legitimacy follows power. With significant and meaningful decision-making powers, the rural councils could represent their populations. Rights to decentralized powers and the laws that outline these rights, however, do not matter when line ministries resist new laws, reigning through coercion. The ability of Rural Communities to benefit from forests is structured, not by law makers, but by line ministries who implement the law (Larson and Ribot, 2007).

Distribution of forest benefits is not determined by law or rights over forests, property rights or rights to make decisions. Rights are empty when the claims are not enforceable. Without being able to make significant decisions over material resources — forests, pastures, schools, hospitals, clinics and infrastructure — rural councils have no role. They are elected but cannot serve. Local democracy has no substance. As long as the sectoral powers remain the discretionary domain of line ministries, there is little chance for local democratic transformation in rural Senegal. Colonial forestry services were used to dominate the commercial extraction of forest resources. These resources are still colonized by line ministries. Prying the fingers of line ministries off the lucrative resources they control is a major frontier of decolonization that has not yet been crossed. The new democratic decentralization laws get us to that frontier, but not across it.

One promising path towards improvement in Nambaradougou was indicated by the action of an NGO (DGL Felo) that provided civic education to rural councils and rural populations concerning their rights to forests. Their workshops informed the current resistance that rural councils are showing towards charcoal production in their areas. There is an opportunity right now in Senegal. The laws transfer significant powers to rural councils. Now is as good a time as any to inform people of those laws and to translate them into local languages. The NGO went part of the way and significantly raised local awareness. But to exercise their new legal rights, rural councils and populations will have to make more noise. They will need to organize among themselves, use the courts and/or gain support higher up in government from the Ministry of Local Government or the Ministry of the Interior. If donors

and their project staff had the 'political will' they often accuse government
of lacking, they could support these kinds of change.

REFERENCES

Bâ, El Hadji Dialigue (2006a) 'La Réglementation de la filière du charbon de bois a l'épreuve de la decentralisation: entre discours, lois et pratiques' ('The Regulation of the Charcoal Commodity Chain Under Decentralization: Between Discourse, Law and Practice'). World Resources Institute. http://pdf.wri.org/ba_wp25.pdf (accessed 8 June 2008).

Bâ, El Hadji Dialigue (2006b) 'Le Quota est mort, vive le quota! Ou les vicissitudes de la reglementation de l'exploitation du charbon de bois au Senegal' ('The Quota is Dead, Long Live the Quota! Or the Vicissitudes of Regulating Charcoal Production in Senegal'). Working Paper for World Resources Institute, CIRAD-Foret and Conseil pour le Développement de la Recherche en Sciences Sociales en Afrique. Dakar: CODESRIA. http://pdf.wri.org/sendec_dialigue_ba.pdf (accessed 8 June 2008).

Bandiaky, Solange (2008) 'Gender Inequality in Malidino Biodiversity Reserve, Senegal: Political Parties and the "Village Approach"', *Conservation and Society* 6(1): 62–73.

Boutinot, Laurence (2004) 'Etude de la contribution du PROGEDE a la gestion decentralisée des ressources naturelles' ('Study of PROGEDE's Contribution to Decentralized Natural Resource Management'). Contrat PROGEDE-CIRAD NO. 001/04, Final Report, December 2004. Dakar: CIRAD Forêt.

Boutinot, L. and C.N. Diouf (2005) 'Quand certaines approches participatives engendrent des formes ambiguës de mobilisation de la société civile: Quelques exemples à propos de la gestion des ressources naturelles au Sénégal' ('When Certain Participatory Approaches Engender Ambiguous Forms of Civil Society Mobilization'), in A. Bertrand, A. Karsenty and P. Montagne (eds) *L'Etat et la gestion locale durable des forêts en Afrique francophone et à Madagascar* (*The State and Sustainable Local Management of Forests in Francophone Africa and Madagascar*), pp. 195–212. Paris: Harmattan Press.

Chanock, M. (1991) 'Paradigms, Policies, and Property: A Review of the Customary Law of Land Tenure', in K. Mann and R. Roberts (eds) *Law in Colonial Africa*, pp. 61–84. Portsmouth, NH: Heinemann.

Diallo, Alioune Badara (n.d./circa 1994). 'Rapport Preparatif au Seminaire sur "les Problemes Liés a l'Exploitation Forestiere et l'Applicabilité du Code Forestier" a Travers Trois Localities: Koussanar, Nambaraduougou-Koulibantan-Kolda' ('Preparatory Report for the Seminar on the "Problems Linked to Forest Exploitation and their Application to the Forestry Code" with Respect to Three Localities: Koussanar, Nambaraduougou-Koulibantan-Kolda'). Tambacounda, Senegal: Group d'Action pour le Developpement Communautaire (GADEC) (mimeo).

Faye, Mamadou (2003) 'Deuxième enquete sur les flux de combustibles ligneux' ('Second Survey of Wood Fuel Flux'). République du Sénégal: Programme de Gestion Durable et Participative des Energies Traditionnelles et de Substitution, Composante Demande (Republic of Senegal: Programme on the Sustainable and Participatory Management of Traditional Energy and of Substitution, Demand Side).

Faye, Papa (2006) 'Décentralisation, pluralisme institutionnel et démocratie locale: étude de cas de la gestion du massif forestier Missirah Kothiary' ('Decentralization, Institutional Pluralism and Management of the Forest of Missirah Kouthiary'). Working Paper for World Resources Institute, CIRAD-Foret, and Conseil pour le Développement de la Recherche en Sciences Sociales en Afrique (Council for Development and Research in Social Sciences in Africa). Dakar: CODESRIA. http://pdf.wri.org/sendec_faye.pdf (accessed 8 June 2008).

Kanté, A.M. (2006) 'Décentralisation sans représentation: le charbon de bois entre les collectivités locales et l'Etat' ('Decentralization without Representation: Charcoal between Local Government and the State'). Working Paper for World Resources Institute, CIRAD-Foret, and Conseil pour le Développement de la Recherche en Sciences Sociales en Afrique. Dakar: CODESRIA. http://pdf.wri.org/sendec_kante.pdf (accessed 8 June 2008).

Larson, A. and J.C. Ribot (2007) 'The Poverty of Forestry Policy: Double Standards on an Uneven Playing Field', *Journal of Sustainability Science* 2(2): 3–23. http://pdf.wri.org/sustainability_science_poverty_of_forestry_policy.pdf (accessed 8 June 2008).

Lund, C. (2002) 'Negotiating Property Institutions: On the Symbiosis of Property and Authority in Africa,' in K. Juul and C. Lund (eds) *Negotiating Property in Africa*, pp. 11–43. Portsmouth, NH: Heinemann.

MEMI (1995) *L'Observatoire des combustibles domestiques (The Domestic Energy Observer)*. No 5, September. Ministère de l'Energie, des Mines et de l'Industrie (MEMI), Cellule des Combustibles Domestiques. République du Sénégal (Republic of Senegal, Minister of Energy, Mines and Industry (MEMI), Domestic Energy Unit).

MEPN — Minister del'Environnement et de la Protection dela Nature (Minister of Environment and the Protection of Nature) (2004) 'Demande de délibération des conseil Ruraux de Makacoulibantang et Missirah sur les ZPC, Bordereau d'Envoi' ('Request for Deliberation of the Rural Council of Makacoulibantang and Missirah on Community Production Zones, Notification'). IREF Tambacounda, 29 December.

PROGEDE (2002) 'Enquete nationale aupres des menages sur la consommation de combustibles domestiques, rapport provisoire' ('National Household Survey on Domestic Energy Consumption, Draft Report'). Programme de Gestion Durable et Participative des Energie Traditionnelles et de Substitution, République du Sénégal (Programme on the Sustainable and Participatory Management of Traditional Energy and of Substitution, Demand Side, Republic of Senegal) (PROGEDE).

République du Sénégal (RdS) (1996a) *Loi portant transfert de competences aux regions aux communes et aux communautes rurales (Law on the Transfer of Powers to the Regions, Communes and Rural Communities)*, 22 March 1996. Dakar: Republic of Senegal.

RdS (1996b) *Loi portant code des collectivities locales (Law on the Code of Local Government)*, 22 March 1996. Dakar: République du Sénégal.

RdS (1998) 'Code forestier. Loi no. 98/03 du 08 janvier 1998 et decret no. 98/164 du 20 fevrier 1998' ('Forestry Code. Law no. 98/03 of 8 January 1998 and order no. 98/164 of 20 February 1998'). République du Sénégal, Ministere de l'environnement et de la protection de la nature, direction des Eaux, Forets, Chasse et de la Conservation des Sols (Republic of Senegal, Minister of Environment and the Protection of Nature, Headquarters of the Waters, Forests, Hunting and the Conservation of Soil).

RdS (2004) 'Compte Rendu, Reunion de Notification des Quotas de la Campagne d'Exploitation Forestiere 2004' ('Minutes, Notification Meeting for Quotas of the Forestry Exploitation Season of 2004'). République du Senegal, Ministere de l'Environnement et de la Protection de la Nature, Direction des Eaux, Forêts, Chasses et de la Conservation des Sols, Inspection Régionale de Tambacounda (Republic of Senegal, Minister of Environment and the Protection of Nature, Headquarters of the Waters, Forests, Hunting and the Conservation of Soil, Office of the Region of Tambacounda.)

Ribot, J.C. (1995) 'From Exclusion to Participation: Turning Senegal's Forestry Policy Around?', *World Development* 23(9): 1587–600.

Ribot, J.C. (1998) 'Theorizing Access: Forest Profits along Senegal's Charcoal Commodity Chain', *Development and Change* 29(2): 153–81.

Ribot, J.C. (1999a) 'Decentralization and Participation in Sahelian Forestry: Legal Instruments of Central Political-Administrative Control', *Africa* 69(1): 23–65.

Ribot, J.C. (1999b) 'A History of Fear: Imagining Deforestation in the West African Sahel', *Global Ecology and Biogeography* 8: 291–300.

Ribot, J.C. (2000) 'Forest Rebellion and Local Authority in Makacoulibantang, Eastern Senegal', in C. Zerner (ed.) *People, Plants and Justice*. New York: Columbia University Press.

Ribot, J.C. (2006) 'Analyse de la filière charbon de bois au Sénégal: recommandations' ('Analysis of the Charcoal Commodity Chain in Senegal: Recommendations'). Policy brief for the research programme 'Toward Democratic Decentralization of Forest Management in Senegal'. Dakar: WRI-CODESRIA-CIRAD.

Ribot, J.C. and R. Oyono (2005) 'The Politics of Decentralization', in B. Wisner, C. Toulmin and R. Chitiga (eds) *Toward a New Map of Africa*, pp. 205–28. London: Earthscan Press.

Ribot, Jesse C. and Nancy L. Peluso (2003) 'A Theory of Access', *Rural Sociology* 68(2): 153–81.

Thiaw, S. (2003) 'Rôles et représentativité de deux institutions locales de la gestion des forets au Sénégal: le chef de village et le conseil rural' ('Roles and Representativity of Two Local Forest Management Institutions in Senegal: Village Chiefs and Rural Councils'). Paper prepared for the workshop 'Equité, représentation et *accountability* des institutions de la GRN' ('Equity, Representation and Accountability of NRM Institutions'), Bamako (17–21 November).

Thiaw, S. (2005) 'Les conseils ruraux dans la décentralisation de la gestion des forêts au Sénégal' ('The Rural Council in Decentralization of Forests in Senegal'). Draft working paper for the Programme WRI–CODESRIA–CIRAD sur la Gestion Décentralisée et Démocratique des Ressources Forestières au Sénégal (WRI–CODESRIA–CIRAD Programme on Democratic and Decentralized Forest Management in Senegal). Dakar (mimeo).

Thiaw, Sagane (2006) 'Les Conseils ruraux et la gestion décentralisée des forêts au Sénégal: etude de cas dans les régions de Tambacounda et Kolda' ('Rural Councils and the Decentralized Management of Forests in Senegal: Case Study in the Tambacounda and Kolda Regions'). Draft final report to the Programme WRI–CODESRIA–CIRAD sur la Gestion Décentralisée et Démocratique des Ressources Forestières au Sénégal. (WRI–CODESRIA–CIRAD Programme on Democratic and Decentralized Forest Management in Senegal). Dakar (mimeo).

Thiaw, S. and J.C. Ribot (2005) 'Insiders Out: Forest Access through Village Chiefs in Senegal', in S. Evers, M. Spierenburg and H. Wells (eds) *Competing Jurisdictions: Settling Land Claims in Africa and Madagascar*, pp. 315–32. Leiden: Brill Academic Publishers.

Watts, M.J. (1993) 'Idioms of Land and Labor: Producing Politics and Rice in Senegambia', in T.J. Bassett and D.E. Crummey (eds) *Land in African Agrarian Systems*, pp. 157–221. Madison, WI: University of Wisconsin Press.

6

Recategorizing 'Public' and 'Private' Property in Ghana

Christian Lund

INTRODUCTION

Over the past decade or so, interest in African land tenure has re-emerged in international organizations with the World Bank as the most prominent actor (World Bank, 2003). In contrast to an earlier fine focus on market imperfections and the absence of private property, the ambit of concern is now broadened to include the historical evolution of property, political institutions and customary rules. These are no longer seen as inherent obstacles to growth and tenure security, but as elements to take seriously in institutional tinkering and engineering. The more comprehensive approach no doubt captures the complexity of property more adequately. However, this thinking privileges a perspective in which public authority institutions issue and enforce rules and in which rules condition behaviour.

My argument in this contribution is that this is a two way path: behaviour also validates and recognizes some rules, concepts, and institutions, and undermines others. The chapter analyses how land and resources have been assigned to one of the two 'master categories' of 'public' and 'private' in the course of political struggle in northern Ghana. Yet master categories are deceptive. As Weintraub writes: 'Attempts to use the public/private distinction as a dichotomous model to capture the overall pattern of social life in a society ... are always likely to be inherently misleading' (Weintraub, 1997: 15). It is therefore often useful to distinguish between practices that deal with concrete property objects (actual use, transfer or disputes over concrete resources) on the one hand, and practices that deal with categorical forms of property on the other (von Benda-Beckmann et al., 2006: 15).

While the categories of property may represent the concrete forms inadequately, they may indeed be invoked in concrete systems of property and influence them. Abrams (1988) reminds us of the difficulties of studying the state. He points out its double nature as an idea and an apparatus. While the former is attributed with concerns for the common good, the latter is populated with groups with more or less vested interests. In concrete situations, various manifestations of the state may be called upon. This chapter demonstrates how people refer to the more distant, abstract state in order to fend off the particular policies pursued by the more concrete incarnations of political authority.

The chapter offers a general account of conflicts and the recategorization of resources in the property system of small-scale irrigation.[1] The logics of the different stakeholders and their positioning are examined, and the ways in which different levels of public policy have provided opportunities for such changes are discussed. Thereafter, a case study allows us to examine the details of a particular controversy demonstrating the social and political powers involved in the recategorization of property. It demonstrates litigants' vain search for a powerful, legitimate institution to endorse claims as rights. First, however, some context is required.

THE CONTEXT OF LAND STRUGGLES IN THE UPPER EAST REGION OF GHANA

Land has been the object of policy in Ghana since colonial times, though with varying degrees of intensity (Berry, 2002; Firmin-Sellers, 1996), and public and private interests have competed over resources in various ways. In Northern Ghana people's struggles to establish and consolidate rights and rules have constantly been conditioned and challenged by the efforts of other stakeholders and government institutions to remake or replace them. The result is that particular resources have been negotiated into a texture of composite property relations that defies simple public–private distinctions.

Government policies for Northern Ghana, such as the Land and Native Rights Ordinance from the 1927[2] and the 1979 Constitutions, have had dramatic and far-reaching effects in the powers and interests they delivered. However, governments do not seem to have controlled the outcomes: rather, there are innumerable instances of governance in many local public spheres, with powers and interests which are difficult to harness by any particular institution. Governments in Ghana have, through time, shown a strong capacity to create opportunities for the renegotiation of land rights, but with limited influence over how opportunities were actually seized locally. The tension between the state's power to engender changes and its incapacity to direct them is not restricted to land matters or to African governance in general, but the story of small-scale irrigation in the Upper East Region provides a particularly vivid illustration of this paradox. The construction of irrigation

---

1. This chapter is based on case studies of fourteen villages and small dams in the Upper East Region from late 2001 to early 2004. Interviews were conducted with chiefs and earthpriests, groups of land owners and groups of tenants, agricultural field officers as well as their superior staff, representatives of NGOs and the Diocese Development Office in Bolgatanga, opinion leaders and local politicians, and staff from the Regional Lands Commissioner's Office. Dams and dugouts are used for watering cattle and for fishing in addition to irrigation, but this contribution focuses on the latter activity and related issues. Names of villagers and the village name of Zorobogo are pseudonyms. Parts of the chapter also appear in Lund (2008).
2. The Land and Native Rights Ordinance was amended several times between 1927 and 1931.

infrastructure increases the value of property and hence intensifies conflicts of interests, and the very operation involving public investment occasions a renegotiation of land rights in ways over which government has only partial control. Government schemes create junctures for people to reassert or to challenge the situation according to their interests.

Formal property rights in Northern Ghana[3] have changed radically on two occasions over the past century. In 1927, the Land and Native Rights Ordinance (cap. 143) declared all lands in the Northern Territories, whether occupied or unoccupied, to be native lands, and placed them under the control of the Governor, a legal situation that continued after independence. While land was legally owned by individuals and families, the general mode of operation of the state was simply to take land for the construction of public infrastructure, buildings, amenities, etc. without compensation or consultation, making it difficult to tell the difference between public land and land 'merely' vested in government. However, in 1979 land in Northern Ghana was divested from the state and thenceforth 'vested in any such person or appropriate skin [i.e. customary authority]' (Government of Ghana, 1992). In short, full ownership to land was returned to the original owners. This meant that in all instances where government had not legally acquired the land according to the State Lands Act (Act 125, 1962), land was to be returned to the owner. None of the land seized for the construction of small dams in Northern Ghana was ever properly acquired, and legally the public infrastructure established by the state was sitting on private lands.[4] The new legal situation from 1979 provided an opportunity for reassessing the past and settling old accounts.

Obviously, one of the issues at stake is what the divestiture meant to ownership. As in most places in Africa, the equivalent of ownership in a Western sense is hard to find.[5] The rights that Western law associates with ownership are rarely conferred on one single actor but are rather shared

3. Northern Ghana (or the Northern Region) was essentially the former Protectorate of the Northern Territories of the Gold Coast. In 1960, the Upper Region was carved out of the Northern Region, with Bolgatanga as its capital. In 1983 the Upper Region was subdivided into the Upper West and Upper East Regions, with the regional capitals of Wa and Bolgatanga respectively.
4. Interviews with B.S. Nyari, Regional Lands Commissioner (5 March 2002, 9 March 2004). See also Dery (1998: section 2.4).
5. Or, more accurately, 'the equivalent to the *popular notions of ownership* in a Western sense'. Popular and political ideas about property in the West are often simplified to broad categories of absolute public and private which do not withstand rigorous analytical inspection. In principle, property in the West is as composite as anywhere in the world. 'Instrumental theories and resulting policy are based on implicit or explicit assumptions about property that are empirically false for both Western and non-Western legal systems and societies. The most serious misconception lies in the area of private, individual ownership, which narrowly conceived, glosses over the many different kinds of rights and sets of obligations that can be involved both with respect to different categories of objects, and of categories of property holders' (von Benda-Beckmann et al., 2006: 11).

among several, with government, the customary authority, the owner and possibly a tenant as shareholders of rights. When this chapter mentions 'the owner', this does not imply that I confer absolute rights and obligations on him or her. It is a shorthand label for the person who has the customary freehold, that is, hereditary rights to a piece of land, rights to bequeath it to kin, and rights to transfer temporary use rights to others through either a formal lease or an unwritten agreement. Normally all such transactions are overseen and accepted by the customary institution of the earthpriest.

PRIVATE PROPERTY AND PUBLIC INFRASTRUCTURE

From the mid-1950s to the mid-1960s a series of small dams were constructed in villages throughout what is now the Upper East.[6] Population density and the resultant increasing land shortage in the area made dry season irrigation a welcome opportunity to increase productivity and offered income possibilities. During the time of construction the state was the custodian of all land. This meant that the government could place dams in locations that it considered technically suitable without much consultation with landowners. Land was virtually expropriated by government for the placement of the reservoir, the dam and other infrastructure. State control over land was simply assumed by most people, and any protest by disadvantaged landowners was brushed aside by the Ministry of Agriculture. Government agents redistributed land according to their own plans. In practice, it was considered public property.

At the time of the initial land allocation, land was officially distributed by the agricultural officer from the Irrigation Development Authority under the Ministry of Agriculture. Owners of the fields that were to be turned into irrigated plots or given up for the reservoir were allocated some three to four plots each. The remaining plots of 25 yards by 25 yards were distributed among other villagers according to the agricultural officer's estimation of who would be able to cultivate it properly. In reality, however, most of the land was allocated to relatives of the landowners. Thus the status of the plots was somewhat ambiguous; on the one hand, the landowner would consider land allocation an internal family matter, while the new beneficiaries, on the other hand, would consider the land to be theirs, granted them by government. In order to demonstrate his control over the land, the landowner would collect the money for water levies from his 'tenants' and pay it to the Irrigation Development Authority. This way, no direct relation was established between the land user and the government agency. Often the fee would be paid by the landholder to the owner in kind (generally in seeds), further obscuring the linkage between the land holding, the government agency and the monetary fee.

---

6. Since 1950 around 220 small dams have peppered the region (Andanye, 1995).

On the other hand, land users often resisted giving up their plots in the rainy season. In principle, when a plot holder had harvested his crop, the land would revert to an ordinary rain-fed field to be cropped by the landowner. But as the fertilizer used on the irrigated crops still has a residual effect on the rain-fed crops, dry-season farmers had an interest in using the small plot for rain-fed crops as well. Obviously, not all tenants were in a position to secure the year-round utilization of their plot. In general, family members of the landowner were more resistant to handing over the land in the rainy season. This led landowners in general to prefer 'strangers' over family as tenants at the later extension of the dams in the 1990s. Not only were strangers willing to pay more than landowners' own family members; they would actually pay the landowner, knowing that 'they are easy to evict from the plot' in case of default.[7]

As land was vested in government, it was the government, through the Irrigation Development Authority (IDA), that was responsible for land allocation. The general principle laid out was that allocation should take place annually. No plot holder could expect to farm the same plot year after year. However, re-allocation of plots by IDA took place only in cases where water levies were not paid, and even then only rarely.[8] Thus, at the dam sites the initial land allocation remained more or less the same; while tenants paid their water levies through the landowner they considered their rights to the plots to be permanent and irrevocable. It was considered 'government land' and the idiom of 'government land' made any individual owner's attempt to reclaim his property inconceivable. In this sense, land was seen as having passed through a period as 'public land' now to be allocated afresh to the tenants with no strings attached. The landowners, on the other hand, considered it an undue appropriation of rights by tenants to whom the owners had provided access to land on a less permanent basis. Thus, while *getting access* to a plot depended on the acceptance and choice of the landowner, the *endurance* and *growth* of the right from something temporary to something virtually permanent seemed to be secured by the fact that land was, in principle, vested in government and landowners had no practical recourse to challenge this.

The benefits of small-scale irrigation were short lived, however. Poor maintenance (and in many cases a complete lack of it) resulted in a state of disrepair evidenced by eroded dam walls, inoperational spillways and siltation of the dams. Thus in the 1980s virtually all the small dams in the Upper East Region were underperforming. Siltation of the reservoirs meant

7. Interviews with villagers in Binduri (3 November 2002; 5 November 2002; 8 November 2002); Paga Nania (12 March 2004; 15 March 2004); Baare (1 November 2002); Zanlerigu (4 November 2002; 6 November 2002; 11 November 2002). For an analysis of owner/tenant relations and the aspect of kinship in small-scale irrigation in Burkina Faso, see Saul (1993).
8. Interviews with Roy Ayariga, Regional Director of the Ministry of Agriculture (12 March 2002; 12 November 2002; 16 March 2004; 30 March 2004).

that their water retention capacity was reduced, as were the irrigable area and the cropping season as a consequence.

In 1992, the Ministry of Agriculture engaged in a Land Conservation and Smallholder Rehabilitation Project (LACOSREP) funded by the International Fund for Agricultural Development (IFAD). Some forty-four dams and dugouts throughout the Upper East Region were selected for rehabilitation. This included desilting the reservoirs, repairing and often extending the dam walls, repairing the canals, protecting the catchment area, and so forth. The philosophy was one of participation in and 'ownership' of the project. This last element turned out to be more than mere development rhetoric.

The government divestiture of land posed a problem to the Ministry of Agriculture. On the one hand, the Ministry was no longer entitled as a government agency to allocate land to producers or even to repair infrastructure on someone's property without their consent. On the other hand, the Ministry was disinclined to make huge investments merely for the owners' benefit — owners who would no doubt lease out plots with a considerable profit. Legal advice was solicited, and a new institutional arrangement was developed. Local government in the form of the District Assemblies should enter into a leasehold agreement with the landowners, thus taking over the land for a definite period of time. The District Assemblies should then, in turn, lease the land on to Water User's Associations (WUAs) registered as co-operatives with legal status to engage in contracts. In most cases, the landowners would be members of the WUA and thus lease land from themselves, as it were, but all members of the WUA would in principle enjoy equal protection of their use rights whether owners or not (Dery, 1998).

This arrangement appeared very neat to the Ministry of Agriculture and to the District Assemblies. However, there were only rather modest incentives for the landowners to relinquish their lands to the District Assembly and subsequently to the WUA. In fact, it would appear that the landowners could only be motivated if leasing of the land was a condition for the rehabilitation of the dams, reservoirs and other infrastructure. With no lease agreement, the dams would not be repaired and nobody would benefit. However, with huge funding from IFAD, the Ministry of Agriculture did not have the patience to settle the paperwork for lease contracts before physical activity could be demonstrated to the donor. Consequently, rehabilitation was initiated with the hope of rearranging the property questions along the way.[9] However, the very reason that such complicated lease arrangements were necessary was the divestiture of land since 1979: few landowners were inclined to surrender newly-acquired private rights enshrined in the Constitution to anyone. In some cases leases were prepared between the District Assembly and the earthpriest as the landowner. However, this was generally considered something of an oddity by villagers. While the earthpriest may well

9. Interview with Roy Ayariga, Regional Director of the Ministry of Agriculture (16 March 2004; 30 March 2004).

be respected as the paramount title holder, nothing seems to empower him to lease off land already occupied by someone. Such lands can be transferred only at the behest of the landowner and with the approval of the earthpriest.

The result of the repair and rehabilitation of the dams was the emergence of various tenure arrangements in the dam areas with a notable difference between the land made irrigable during the *first* land management scheme, and land which was only included in the schemes *after* the LACOSREP project. In the first areas, the following system emerged. Without a leasing agreement, landowners and their 'tenant-relatives' who had cultivated the initially-irrigated land simply took up farming the same lands as before, reviving the tension between owner and tenant as to whether the latter should pay rent for the land to the former, or only pay the water levy to the WUA. Landowners, now having ownership restored with the 1979 Constitution, had an interest in having it recognized, but tenants insisted that the land had been given to them by government when it was 'government land'. Hence, tenants saw all previous rights of ownership as expunged since the land turned over to them had once been public land. In most cases, this tension was overcome by the groups' common interest in not relinquishing any land to the newly formed WUAs and hence other farmers. Consequently, the concerned lands had been apportioned to their respective users once and had since then been held permanently; with time they had developed into hereditary property.

In the newly-developed areas the situation was different but equally muddled. In some cases, the owners of the land connected to the extension of the project — often the same landowners as in the first section — flatly refused to formally hand over full land control to the WUA. But since the WUA was promoted by the Ministry of Agriculture, some form of compromise was reached. Help with repairs and extensions depended, after all, on amiable relations with the authorities. In general, landowners would agree to hand over land and land allocation provided that they were ensured substantial plots. In this way, most of the owners were granted plots large enough for them to sublet. This time around, however, the landowners I talked to all preferred to sublet to non-kin and 'strangers', that is, people from outside the village. In practice, this was ensured by a tacit understanding with the WUA executives. The landowner would come up with a list of five to ten names for land allocation, letting the executives understand that allocation to them would be the 'price' for peacefully ceding the rest of the land for allocation among other WUA members during the dry season. The new tenants would equally be made to understand that their access to a plot hinged on the recommendation of the owner, and without it the WUA would probably have allocated the land to someone else. Moreover, water levies were to be paid through the owner, who also made sure that the farmer did not cultivate the same plot for many years, thus building up a claim. Thus, the new tenants found themselves in a rather precarious situation with weak claims to the land they tilled. The rest of the land was allocated to villagers through the WUA.

The competition between landowners and the WUA was often more formal than real. A survey shows that 44 per cent of concerned landowners were members of the WUAs, and 20 per cent were members of the executive (Nyari, 2002). Moreover, as the members of the WUAs shared an interest in tenure security with landowners, a consensus about the 'folly' of rotation of plot access soon developed in many dam sites. As land users were able to hold on to the same plot year after year over the course of a decade, landholding gradually transformed from annual to permanent rights exactly as in the early irrigation areas. The degree of control grew to encompass the right to rent out and bequeath the land: whether long-term leases and outright sales will develop remains to be seen. The WUA would, in principle, constitute a politico-legal institution involved in land allocation, but in practice, its authority was feeble due to lack of legitimacy among the leading landowners.

The development of the actual and practical property relations was ironic. In the initially-managed areas, land, although the property of landowners, was allocated to others through government intervention, and the general understanding of land as 'government land' meant that the land users managed to hold on to it. The process amounted to expropriation and reallocation of land to new landholders with permanent and transferable rights. However, the Ministry of Agriculture's idea of rotational landholding stumbled on the united interests of land users — owners and tenants alike — to build up enduring rights through permanent use of the same plot.

Land in the areas of extension, on the other hand, was supposed to be leased to local government, the District Assembly, and further to the WUA. However, most of the leases were never established and the land formally remained under the control of the owners. Nonetheless, in most places the owners relinquished some of their land to the WUA on the condition that they received reserved portions sufficiently large for them to sublet. This made it possible for the owners to secure some land for themselves, keeping formal ownership as a bargaining chip to preserve actual use rights to some of it. Here again, the mutual interests of landowners and the other villagers in building up rights through permanent use made rotational plot allocation rare. The only exceptions to this pattern were the new tenants of the landowners, who so far have failed to build up stronger rights. Thus, the weakest group — the tenants — have remained marginal although the policies had intended a relatively better deal for them. The role of the WUA became restricted to the allocation of water in the irrigation system and to the collection of water levies.

The paradox is that when land was *not* formally and legally acquired by government, government had in fact attempted to control it. Owners had little formal control over who got access to an irrigated plot on *their* land. They therefore engaged a number of strategies to compensate. After divestiture with the 1979 Constitution, a formal legal structure was set up for the leasing of land by owners through the District Assembly to the user. But landowners again managed to evade leasing their land to government and were able to allocate to themselves considerable irrigated plots and access to the public infrastructure. This conundrum of government control over private land and private control over public infrastructure can only be understood if the transactions are seen in the broader context of general government control over land before 1979 and the principle of private control endorsed after divestiture. Any policies that may have worked to the opposite effect were either drowned out or diluted. What prevailed was an interpretation of property legitimated with reference to the more distant and abstract notion of the state and the constitutional change of 1979. The property arrangement promoted by the concrete state institution — the Ministry of Agriculture — was, in contrast, sidelined.

The small dam schemes demonstrate that tenure systems transform in non-linear ways. Although government interventions have tremendous effects, seemingly trivial actions by individuals can undermine state policy as people pursue their interests with whatever institutional opportunities are available. Thus government control of land led to *de facto* expropriation before the 1979 Constitution, and land allocated to new users was not recoverable by the owners after divestiture. It had passed through the status of public property and the original claims had effectively been deleted. On the other hand, infrastructure which was to be awarded equitably to villagers was *de facto* privatized as land — crucial for accessing the benefits of the infrastructure — and remained under the control of landowners.

The dynamics of recategorization of property in small-scale irrigation are not restricted to gradual, layered negotiations within villages, however. The research uncovered numerous instances of conflicts in which political processes outside the village were significant for the outcomes. Villagers would engage with political forces of a much greater magnitude and political players in Bolga or other centres would have an important area in which to manifest themselves. The following is a case in point.

GIVING UP PRIVATE LANDS FOR THE PUBLIC GOOD

Zorobogo is a village some 20 km outside Bolgatanga. The village had a small dugout from 1960, but in 1999, the local District Assembly representative and the area's member of parliament, who was from Zorobogo itself, decided to put their weight behind the construction of a proper dam with a large capacity in the centre of their constituency. As members of National Democratic Congress (NDC), then in power, it was not very difficult to have Zorobogo's name put on the list with the Ministry of Agriculture. Thus, in 2000 pegging for the new dam was undertaken and there was great anticipation among most villagers. However, a few families soon discovered that their land was on the wrong side of the pegs and that their fields would soon be inundated by the reservoir for the dam. This marked the starting point for a series of meetings. The first meeting between the villagers and the two politicians was held in early November 2000. The result was anything but peaceful. Mr Mata, whose lands were the most affected by the plans, protested loudly. First of all, his family graves would be affected. Secondly, a small grove of mango trees would be destroyed, and finally most of the land to which he had a hereditary claim would be affected.

At first, the chief of Zorobogo offered to settle the families concerned elsewhere and to provide alternative sites for the graves, but this was flatly refused. The thought of exhuming the buried bodies and relocating the shrines was humiliating and disgraceful. Moreover, Mr Mata believed that if land were allocated to him, he would never have rights to that land which were equivalent to the rights he held to land he had inherited and which was his patrimony. At one point, however, the MP dismissed Mr Mata's objections, arguing that the *particular* interests of Mr Mata and the other concerned families would have to yield to the greater public good.[10]

Mr Mata repeatedly tried to convene another meeting by inviting the District Chief Executive — known to be of a different party than the MP and the Assembly representative, namely the New Patriotic Party (NPP) — but despite promises, no meetings were held until Mr Mata issued a press release in September 2001. Mr Mata was a teacher, and his son, John Mata, a student of political science at the University of Legon in Accra. Thus, unlike most of their fellow villagers, the Matas were men of letters. The press release displays the bitterness of the conflict in its bucolic prose:

> The supreme spiritual leaders and land owners of Zorobogo and the Mata family has been hit with a growing threat of a revolutionary iconoclasm (i.e. total destruction of our religious shrines) all in an effort to construct a dam for the development of Zorobogo and its environs. Indications are that the dam will be constructed by either fair or foul means. Meetings have been convened to discuss the matter on hand since the construction of the dam poses a serious threat to the religious and social survival of the affected people. It is worthy of note that in these meetings the supreme spiritual leaders and the Mata family remain largely unyielding to such a development. . . .

> Position of the proponents of the development as against supposedly anti-development advocates:
> They seem to be espousing a utilitarian ethos. All appeals to let the matter have a peaceful settlement seem to be a failure. Rumours are ripe in the grapevine that come the dry season some people's religious rights and land will be encroached upon for the benefit of the wider society. Meetings are now being organized behind closed doors minus the landowners, a clear violation of our rights and a sure recipe for social disagreement. There is even a boom in employment at the area since those going to help in the construction of the dam have their names written down speedily. They are poised for the construction of the dam and compensation packages are mentioned in the air, a package the Earthpriests and the Mata family disregard as a mismatch to our religion.

10.   Interviews with Mr Mata (7 November 2002; 9 November 2002); with John Mata (son of Mr Mata) (4 November 2002; 11 March 2004); with the MP (11 November 2002); and the chief and elders of Zorobogo (7 November 2002).

Position of the Earthpriests and the Mata family as regards development:
... [T]he moves by the proponents of the construction of the dam [are] entirely arbitrary and [don't] encourage peace, the very trust and fruit of development. We believe that for development to be total and beneficial to the people it must be all embracing and not selective. The purpose for which the dam is going to be constructed to our mind is even bogus and fraudulent and not worth trying.

Conclusion:
Finally, we consider the possible construction of the dam as the most inhuman event in Nabdam history and thus should not be allowed to take root and be used as a blueprint for future similar events. Consequently, we humbly appeal to the District Chief Executive (Bolgatanga), chiefs within the area and all pressure groups within and without Nabdam to intervene to help avert a seemingly simmering Palestinian intifada. Between peace, unity, development and internecine feud, we, that is the Earthpriests and the Mata family pledge our unifying support for the former.[11]

After this press release Mr Mata wrote a letter to the District Chief Executive, and a new meeting was scheduled for February 2002. On 4 February the Assembly representative, the District Chief Executive and the District Director of Agriculture gathered in a meeting at Zorobogo with the villagers. The District Chief Executive implored the village chief to find alternative sites for a possible dam. The chief and the assembly rep refused to negotiate and remained determined.

However, during the recent national elections, NDC had lost to NPP; not only was NDC the party of the District Chief Executive but the local MP from Zorobogo had also lost his seat to an NPP candidate from a different village in the electoral area. It seemed that the tide would turn in favour of Mr Mata and the other concerned families. Mr Mata was particularly encouraged when the District Chief Executive and the newly-appointed Regional Minister came to the area for a rally on 17 February, thanking the population for having voted NPP into office. The other villagers of Zorobogo were disappointed that the village no longer had its own Member of Parliament.

For a considerable time, nothing seemed to happen, and the villagers began to think that the project had been abandoned as a result of the transition of government. However, in August 2002, the District Agricultural Officer came to Zorobogo to announce that the work of the dam would resume, and a week later, the contractor known to be affiliated to NPP arrived and began to work with the grater to level the area.

Mr Mata and his son now mobilized the Zorobogo Electoral Area Student's Union, of which Mata the younger was a member. The Students' Union made

11. Press release: 'Proposed Construction of a Dam at Zorobogo and the Issues that Arise Thereupon' (21 September 2001). Many people in the region keep copies of letters, reports, newspaper clippings, petitions and minutes of meetings and I have encountered only trust and generosity as people let me make copies of their 'private archives'. In the following, such documents are referred to as 'material in private possession'. This press release is one such a document.

a petition to the District Chief Executive urging the authorities to reconsider the placement of the dam: 'We, the youth have discovered two (2) areas where we may rather suggest for the siting of the dam and these areas are [x] and [y]. We will therefore be grateful if a second look could be taken at the construction of the dam'.[12] In addition to this, Mr Mata again wrote to the authorities, this time to the Regional Security Council and in a more belligerent tone:

> We wish to remind your good offices that the battle lines are drawn between the feuding parties. Though the matter has not yet been resolved by any honest broker, there is physical evidence, demonstrably shown by the presence of a tractor to commence business. We humbly wish to re-echo our position clearly that our family dignity, family gods and future lives of the people of the area would not be compromised on the altar of some vague notion of development. Consequently, the willing and ready youth of the area and beyond are being mobilised in an unprecedented fashion for the war effort. Following this development we are respectfully calling on your good offices to intervene to avert a possible humanitarian disaster. We count on your prompt action.[13]

Neither the Students' Union nor Mr Mata received any written response; when Mr Mata approached the District Agricultural Officer he was told that the planning of public infrastructure did not depend on the political colour of the government, and that the contract with the contractor had been signed and part of the money already transferred to his account.[14] Mr Mata and the Students' Union then made a new move; they organized a public demonstration for 19 October and invited the press. The Students' Union managed to mobilize around 100 youths and other villagers, and with journalists from *Ghanaian Times* and from the local radio it made the national news. Mr Mata made a speech:

> It is worthy of note that these problems were brought to the attention of the Hon. District Chief Executive. He quickly convened a meeting of the feuding parties and stressed that minority views should not be sidelined. However, the matter was not resolved there and then. Immediately following the meeting was the Hon. Regional Minister thanksgiving rounds to the place [sic] when he intimated that there was a real problem at Zorobogo and that the feuding parties will be called at his convenience for a discussion on the matter. . . .

> [C]onstruction is steadily growing. Four trees have been levelled and farmlands, unharvested, totally destroyed. . . . We cannot reconcile government position . . . about the return of the vested land to their owners with this growing threat of land seizure. . . . Having made use of the constitutional outlet in the form of demonstration, we still humbly wish to appeal to the powers that be that they intervene to avert a looming bloodbath. . . . We are also appealing to His Excellency the Vice President through the Regional Minister to intervene and help

12. 'Construction of a Dam at Zorobogo'; Petition by Zorobogo Electoral Area Students' Union (9 September 2002). Material in private possession.
13. Letter from Mr Mata to the Regional Security Council (27 September 2002). Material in private possession.
14. Interviews with Mr Mata (9 November 2002) and John Mata (11 March 2004).

matters. This appeal is necessary because we have heard that it is his construction firm that is carrying out the construction.[15]

The speech was repeated in the press and copies were circulated to the Regional Minister, the District Chief Executive, the District Director of Agriculture, the assembly rep and the Police Commander in Bolgatanga.

When Mr Mata had first announced the public demonstration to the police they had asked the local assembly representative to oversee it and report back to them. However, the villagers in favour of the construction interpreted this as if the assembly rep had 'crossed the carpet' and now sided with Mr Mata, his clan and the District Chief Executive. As a consequence they threatened to initiate a legal process against him.

> The Zorobogo community was shocked to see our Hon Assembly Member ... leading a mob of demonstrators who are said to be kicking against the construction of a dam.... It is ... highly surprising for the Hon Member of the community who is to lead in developmental projects trying to thwart the efforts of the dam construction.... We the undersigned wish to draw your attention that for the unhonorable behaviour we will initiate the legal processes of withdrawing you as an assembly member.[16]

Following the events of the demonstration, a meeting was organized in the Regional Co-ordinating Council between the Regional Co-ordinating Director, the agricultural officers, the assembly representative, Mr Mata, the village chief and the earthpriest. It was agreed that a meeting should be organized at the village in order to look for alternative sites for the dam. That meeting was held in mid-January 2003, led by the police commander. During the meeting he asked the earthpriest whether the land concerned belonged to Mr Mata as an individual or to the earthpriest as the custodian of the land, caretaker of the shrines and the medium for the gods. The earthpriest could only confirm his own ownership, and the police commander quickly concluded the meeting by declaring that not only would public interest be served by the construction of the dam, but the man who claimed ownership and reverence for tradition and spirituality, Mr Mata, was irreverent in not respecting the earthpriest's ownership.[17]

Mr Mata and the other concerned families finally conceded at the meeting, and within a couple of days, machines had uprooted all the mango trees in what was to become the reservoir. However, Mr Mata sent yet another letter to the District Director of Agriculture threatening to obstruct the work.

---

15. 'Statement by Mr Mata and the Earthpriest during a public demonstration against the Construction of a Dam at Zorobogo' (19 October 2002). Material in private possession.
16. Letter to the assemblyman, 'Unacceptable behaviour of Hon ... an Assembly Member for Zorobogo electoral area' (1 November 2002), signed by village chief and chiefs of two neighbouring hamlets. Material in private possession.
17. Interviews with John Mata (11 March 2004) and the assembly representative (29 March 2004).

A BIG PROBLEM AT YOUR HANDS. You are informed that your intransigence at constructing a dam at Zorobogo will be met with the fiercest resistance. You are to inform the
drivers at the place to stop coming or face severe beating any time they appear.... We tried
moving there this morning but were told that the machines are broken down. You are noted
for treating our messages with disdain. Don't try doing so to this message. The frequent
breakdown of the machines is a strong clue to your secret moves.[18]

This seems to mark the end of the open confrontation at Zorobogo, because
soon after, the contractor pulled out his machines. Trees had been uprooted,
some levelling had been done, but the construction of the dam had not begun.
Mr Mata's property had largely been destroyed, but no benefits had come
to the community. Cynics in Bolga argued that the contract was awarded
to the Vice President's company but that the contractor was told to do 'a
shoddy job', so that the former NDC MP would not be able to boast about
'his' achievements for Zorobogo.[19]

The most remarkable feature of this case is probably the high-risk nature
of drawing on support from the outside. Although escalation seemed an
obvious avenue for the Matas to pursue, outside support comes at a price.
Disputes between individual members of politically opposed groups may
be transformed and the confrontation absorbed into the broader, enduring
political competition and conflict between the larger players with more
overarching agendas. The smaller conflict may become a vehicle for a large
one. In that case any settlement has further-reaching implications and the
course of conflict is strongly influenced by relations and events outside the
dispute. In a certain way, the conflict illustrates that we are not merely
talking about more or less public or private control of land. The conflict
itself may initially have been of a private nature, with the Matas venturing
into conflict with their neighbours, but it soon became a more public event,
thanks not least to Mr Mata's attempt to engage outside support. The Matas'
'forum shopping' was unsuccessful as they found no politico-legal institution
sufficiently powerful to endorse their claim, and they lost their property.
The case also gives a hint of the actual importance that the administration
attaches to the customary authorities mentioned in the Constitution and to
the divestiture of land from government. Obviously, Mr Mata's ownership
of his land was inconvenient to politics and planning, and it would appear
that the earthpriest was only invoked to twist Mr Mata out of his rights. This
harks back to the days of the colonial administration, when administrative
expediency seemed to be the overarching priority.

---

18. Handwritten letter to District Director of Agriculture from Mr Mata (17 February 2003).
     Material in private possession.
19. This version was repeated to me by a variety of sources, independent of each other, in
     and around Bolga. While this does not guarantee the veracity of the story, it shows what
     standard explanations circulate between people in Bolgatanga.

CONCLUSION

For the farmers in the villages engaged in small-scale irrigation, complying with or circumventing the law is part of a pragmatic adjustment to circumstance and opportunity. Landowners, tenants, beneficiaries of government allocation and 'stranger' farmers alike engage in a host of small-scale negotiations thus adjusting and transforming property relations and the significance of legislation. As Moore (1998: 37) notes, such activities 'are not mobilizations of collective political action, but they can undo the plans of a government as effectively as if they had been'. In villages with small dams in the Upper East Region, public and private interests have competed in various ways, and with rising land values the competition to institutionalize opposing interests appears to intensify. In practical terms, the private and public nature of the land affected by the small dam schemes has changed over the past forty years, but often out of sync with legislation. Local landowners and in particular the long-term tenants managed to invoke the state and the constitution in a somewhat abstract form to buttress their claims, while the concrete state — represented by the Ministry of Agriculture — and the WUA did not wield significant authority. Moreover, there is little to confirm any evolutionary direction in the forms of ownership. Nor is it easy to be very categorical about the public or private nature of any particular piece of landed property; a more equivocal picture has emerged. The labels private, public and government land have, most of all, served in particular strategies to legitimate different forms of command over the resource (see von Benda-Beckmann, 1995).

Before 1979, land was privately owned but controlled by — vested in — government. Government development policies of small dam construction *effectively* rendered private lands public, to the detriment of the owners, but the new beneficiaries in practice soon reprivatized public land and infrastructure for their own benefit. Government control over land was strong enough in the public eye to suspend original private landholders' rights and dispense with the procedure for public acquisition. However, in practice, landowners and in particular the new beneficiaries of the land allocation generally managed to undo plot rotation, the government's key instrument to assure the actual public ownership and control of land and infrastructure.

During the second round of building infrastructure for irrigation in the 1990s, efforts were made by the Ministry of Agriculture to do things by the book. However, the government's meticulous efforts to secure the public nature of its infrastructure were undermined by the political expediency of getting started and the general perception that land had now, since 1979, been returned to its owners. Thus the landowners managed to capture a sizable portion of the improvements, which was never the intention of government. It would appear that the landowners also found it necessary to relinquish parts of their property rights to the WUA, recategorizing their private property as public, at least temporarily. In practice, a 'contract' developed whereby some

of the private land was placed in the public realm of the WUA in exchange
for private, long-term access to the new public infrastructure. In the decades
of the 1950s to 1970s, as well as after the early 1990s, landowners seemed in
general better able to take advantage of contingencies and were effectively
able to recategorize publicly controlled land as private property.

Government policies do not go unscathed by local political negotiations,
and the categories of public and private are corrupted as a consequence. Policies and politics work through social relations, and as property is dynamic,
composite, and essentially contingent, quite unintended outcomes result.
This is not to suggest that land policies and categories do not matter. While
policies may not always deliver the outcome they propose, what they propose
seems always part of the production of the eventual outcome. Indeed, the
categories used by government do not remain secluded analytical concepts.
Rather, they become part of a dynamic production of popular distinctions,
in particular when the state operates in contradictory ways — when the abstract and remote state issues a constitution with certain possibilities, and the
concrete incarnation of government (in this case the Ministry of Agriculture)
outlines a different order of things. People take account of policies even if
effective implementation is not accomplished. Thus, the small dam policies
occasioned a renegotiation and recategorization of land rights, and the restitution of land with the 1979 Constitution provided a new context for these
operations. Despite the fact that 'the master categories' of public and private
may be wholly inadequate in accounting for the actual complexity of property
objects, social units and rights, they are not divorced from the agency of people with something at stake. Laws, rules and by-laws were referred to, as important markers, but structural powers and contingent events also fashioned
the local political struggles over the rights to and control over resources. The
consolidated behaviour of the various stakeholders, landowners, tenants,
WUA members, etc. obviously validated certain concepts of property while
others were undermined. The effective authority of the WUAs invented by
government also seems to be limited by powerful stakeholders' actions.[20]
This suggests that the actual behaviour means at least as much in the production of property as the politics intended to regulate it.

Most land tenure systems in Africa are characterized by a coexistence
of multiple rights that are often held by different persons or institutions.
Government regulation intended to replace norms seems rather to add to a
growing repertoire. This richness of norms affords considerable room for
competing arguments in a dispute, and when new government regulation is
introduced, new opportunities for rearrangement arise. The fact that government regulations in the Upper East Region were accompanied by a significant

---

20. See Laube (2007: 213–14) for a description of how village committee executives in larger
    irrigation schemes in the Upper East Region have little legitimacy and fail to execute their
    tasks when they conflict with stronger stakeholders' interests.

rise in the value of property imbued the renegotiation with a considerable degree of urgency.

REFERENCES

Abrams, P. (1988) 'Notes on the Difficulty of Studying the State', *Journal of Historical Sociology* 1(1): 58–89.
Andanye, J.E. (1995) 'Revised List of Dams and Dugouts in the Upper East Region, Ghana'. Bolgatanga: Irrigation Development Authority (mimeo).
von Benda-Beckmann, F. (1995) 'Anthropological Approaches to Property Law and Economics', *European Journal of Law and Economics* 2: 309–36.
von Benda-Beckmann, F., K. von Benda-Beckmann and M. Wiber (2006) 'The Properties of Property', in F. von Benda-Beckmann, K. von Benda-Beckmann and M. Wiber (eds) *Changing Properties of Property*, pp 1–39. New York and Oxford: Berghan Books.
Berry, S. (2002) 'Debating the Land Questions', *Comparative Studies in Society and History*, 44: 638–68.
Dery, A. (1998) 'The Legal Empowerment of Water Users' Associations'. Consultancy report. Bolgatanga: Irrigation Development Authority (mimeo).
Firmin-Sellers, K. (1996) *The Transformation of Property Rights in the Gold Coast*. Cambridge: Cambridge University Press.
Government of Ghana (1992) *Constitution of the Republic of Ghana*. Accra: Government of Ghana.
Laube, W. (2007) 'External Interventions and (De-)Institutionalisation of Local Natural Resource Regimes in Northern Ghana'. PhD Dissertation, University of Bonn, Centre for Development Research.
Lund, C. (2008) *Local Politics and the Dynamics of Property in Africa*. Cambridge and New York: Cambridge University Press.
Moore, S.F. (1998) 'Changing African Land Tenure: Reflections on the Incapacities of the State', *European Journal of Development Research* 10(2): 33–49.
Nyari, B.S. (2002) 'Colonial Land Policy in Northern Ghana: Its Shortcomings and Influences on the Current National Land Policy'. Paper presented at the National Workshop organized by Landnet Ghana, Bolgatanga (13–15 March).
Saul, M. (1993) 'Land Custom in Bare. Agnatic Cooperation and Rural Capitalism in Western Burkina', in T. Basset and D. Crummey (eds) *Land in African Agrarian Systems*, pp. 75–100. Madison, WI: University of Wisconsin Press.
Weintraub, J. (1997) 'The Theory and Politics of the Public/Private distinction', in J. Weintraub and K. Kumar (eds) *Public and Private in Thought and Practice. Perspectives on a Grand Dichotomy*, pp. 1–42. Chicago, IL, and London: University of Chicago Press.
World Bank (2003) *Land Policies for Growth and Poverty Reduction*. Washington, DC: The World Bank.

7

Land Access and Titling in Nicaragua

Rikke B. Broegaard

INTRODUCTION

Property rights to land are once again on the development agenda. In recent years important actors within the development assistance arena, such as the World Bank and US-financed Millennium Challenge Corporation (MCC) have promoted large-scale land administration programmes encompassing legal reforms, cadastral surveys and titling activities.[1] Further, the World Bank has recently developed new policy guidelines (Deininger, 2003). The legalization and titling of land rights are considered essential to obtaining land tenure security and stimulating investments in land, as well as to improving the functioning of the land market. The latter is increasingly being proposed as a way to build a more dynamic agricultural and rural sector in developing countries (Carter, 2006; Deininger, 2003).

The argument for promoting the titling of property rights is that titles increase tenure security for the land owner, as well as for potential credit institutions. This is expected to increase the value of the land itself, as well as improving access to credit (see, for example, Carter and Chamorro, 2000, on findings from Nicaragua). Furthermore, it is anticipated that increased tenure security and improved access to credit will raise the level of investment in land, as well as further increasing land value (Feder et al., 1988). In response to the improved level of information on property rights (through titles and cadastral and registry systems), land market transaction costs are said to be reduced. Finally, legal reforms associated with land administration projects often remove any restrictions related to the alienability of land, in order to make the land market more dynamic and fluid.

This chapter analyses the titling of rural land in the north-western part of Nicaragua.[2] It aims to provide insights for an improved understanding of

This research was supported by the Danish Research Council for Development Research (RUF) through a PhD grant. It also draws upon information from work financed by the Danish Consultant Trust Fund through the World Bank. The author is grateful to Christian Lund, Thomas Sikor, Helle Munk Ravnborg, Eva Broegaard and Joe Ryan for their comments. The usual disclaimers apply.

1. Millennium Challenge Corporation for Nicaragua; see www.cuentadelmilenio.org.ni (accessed 2 June 2008).
2. Property rights on the Atlantic Coast of Nicaragua are profoundly different from those in the rest of Nicaragua, due to extensive indigenous and ethnic territories that are *de jure* recognized by the government through Law 445 (see Rivas and Broegaard, 2006). The enforcement of this law, however, is another story.

inequality in the land registration process and of how differently-positioned actors are able/unable to turn land claims into property rights recognized by the state. It also illustrates how this process is conditioned by the nature of power and authority relations. Following decades of state-led land reform up to the mid-1990s, the land market in Nicaragua is increasingly becoming an important arena for accessing land. This chapter examines the importance of formal titles in land transactions, as well as the impact of land transactions on the titling status of the land (including the cadastral and registral information). Finally, it explores the different combinations of authorities that are used to endorse land rights and to settle conflicts related to land. Conceptually, the chapter contributes to the discussion about property rights to land by arguing that tenure security and the role of land titling in many developing countries cannot be understood without an understanding of legal pluralism, which ultimately allows strong actors to influence in which forum a dispute is handled.

The following section discusses the assumptions and critiques regarding land titling and tenure security from different scholarly approaches, including legal pluralism. The chapter then goes on to present the combination of qualitative and quantitative research methods used, before introducing the Nicaraguan post-war and post-land reform context. Through several land transaction histories, in which the vendor has been has pressured in different ways into selling, the chapter analyses the multiple possible providers of rights and rights recognition, as well as the 'forum shopping' that strong actors are able to perform within the system. On this basis, the chapter concludes that real-world phenomena such as inequality, power abuse, illegality and competing institutions must be taken into account in any effort to understand the dynamic setting in which land titling and land market transactions take place.

THEORY ON LAND TITLING, MARKETS AND INEQUALITY

The promotion of land titling and land administration projects is motivated by the expectation of a positive impact on the level of investment in agriculture, both through increased levels of tenure security and through improved access to credit, as well as through an increase in the value of titled land and a revitalization of the land market (Deininger, 2003; Feder et al., 1988; de Soto, 2000). The current focus on the land market as a way to redistribute land is — among other things — a reaction to past decades of state-led land reforms which have had varied results in numerous developing countries, but have almost never met expectations (Childress and Deininger, 2006). It is therefore understandable that there is a widespread call for new policy tools for influencing land distribution in order to reduce poverty and create growth in the agricultural sector, which remains important in many developing countries, both in economic and cultural terms as well as for food security.

De Soto (2004: 10) proposes that the protection of property rights expressed in property titles 'will allow a modern nation to grow and will bring peace, stability and prosperity to the world', through the revitalization of the land and credit market. The argument that property rights and titles create growth and prosperity for the poor in developing countries has also gained wide support. In a more balanced form, the proposal to use the market for resource allocation is not in itself anti-state, although it is sometimes interpreted as such by critics. Thus, a more balanced position treats the land market (including market-assisted land reform) as one of several tools to redistribute land (for example Carter, 2006), leaving an important regulative and distributive role for the state as well (see also Kay, 2006; World Bank, 2005).

Bromley (2009: 26) reminds us that: 'All legal arrangements . . . are the evolved — and evolving — manifestations of a complex pattern of scarcities, priorities, power relations, and local circumstances', and he calls for caution about the universal prescription of land titling for tenure security and pro-poor growth.[3] Concerns about the 'levelness' of the playing field, inequity and power relations, and their effects on titling and the functioning of the land market, have gained widespread acceptance. For example, more than a decade ago, prominent land tenure economists like Binswanger et al. (1995) observed that land transfers in the market can reduce equity and efficiency if economic and institutional distortions encourage the accumulation of land among large landowners. Despite this, the implications of an uneven playing field are still often not taken fully into account in economic analysis and policy recommendations, even in settings with high degrees of inequity and obvious problems related to the use and abuse of power and office (Carter and Barham, 1996; Kay, 2006; Roquas, 2002; see also Li, 2001). A World Development Report (World Bank, 2005) on inequality discusses how inequality and power abuses are often mentioned in development projects and policies, but that these are still implemented as if such projects and policies operated in an ideal world, and corruption and uneven playing fields are treated as 'system failures' or 'imperfections'. It is argued that these 'system failures' (whether market or state) should not be considered as malfunctions but rather as the very way that the system is designed to work, in favour of some, at the expense of others. To ignore this reality would either be naïve, or would give tacit approval to the status-quo operation of markets and legal systems. 'Government policies are what they are . . . because someone is making them. . . . Observed policies that fail to address inefficient inequalities are the result of political choices, implicitly or explicitly' (ibid.: 228).

---

3. De Soto has been criticized for ignoring the fact that the alienability of property rights has historically led to distress sales and increased inequality (see Bromley, 2009; Mitchell, 2007).

Titling and land administration projects often focus narrowly on the state system for recognizing rights. Unquestionably, there is an important role for the state as a provider of law and order, and at least in theory as a provider of a juridical system to ensure that agreements are kept and land transfers take place according to established rules. However, many findings from legal anthropological research stress the fact that plural authorities can be involved in the recognition of property rights (see below). Long (2001) and Nuijten (2003a, 2003b), among others, have pointed out that while rules say one thing, real life practice often differs. Bending the rules under which the land market ought to operate and challenging different practices are not uncommon, as Roquas (2002) and Coles-Coghi (1993) show in their research on land titling and land conflicts in Honduras. Furthermore, formal rules are often ambiguous, overlapping or even contradictory, thereby leaving considerable space for their interpretation, as von Benda-Beckmann (1995, 2001) and Berry (1989, 1993) show.

For property rights to be 'rights in practice' they must be recognized by someone other than the owner, that is, a group of people often represented by a leader or an authority. Without this recognition, the property rights expressed in a land title (or in some other way), have no practical meaning.[4] This 'recognition in practice' can come from a large number of groups or authorities. It can be the neighbours, the co-operative leadership, the village leader, the local police officer, lawyers, the mayor, the local or departmental judge, the state office for rural land titling, trade unions, civil servants at departmental or national level, or politicians. If accompanied by local-level enforcement, a higher-ranking authority may be able to override the decision of a lower-level authority. Often, a number of recognitions from different authorities are collected, reasoning that proof of recognition from plural sources yields stronger rights.

Property rights are produced in close connection with the production of political authority (see also Lund, 2001; Nuijten, 1998). The potential for rights' recognition to come from numerous different sources within a context of multiple political bodies competing for authority, creates a plurality of fora which could possibly recognize rights. This situation allows certain actors to 'shop around' and choose the forum or the legal framework that is most favourable for them. This has been termed 'forum shopping' (von Benda-Beckmann, 1991; Lund, 2001). Another way to describe the same mechanism is that multiple possible playing fields exist for a given land

---

4. In Nicaragua there are plenty of examples of people possessing a land title, but not having possession over the land. There seems to be no current authority that is able or willing to enforce these 'paper rights'. In these cases, it is the people in possession of the land — although without legal documents — that have been successful in establishing their land claims and having them recognized and respected, convincing the 'authorities' of their needs and rights (or of the likelihood that they will make more trouble if not granted possession of the land).

conflict or land claims, depending on which rights-recognizing fora are called upon by the parties. If one party is able to call upon a political forum that is favourable to him or her, the playing field becomes uneven, giving an advantage to the party closest to the political forum with highest authority.

Inevitably, people are in different positions when it comes to forum-shopping and seeking endorsements for their land claims. To quote Peters (2004: 270): 'processes of exclusion, deepening social divisions and class formation' are at play in competition and conflict over land, in which land reform and titling programmes are elements. She continues: 'Widespread appropriation by elites must be situated within broader processes of social inequality and class formation as well as within what commentators call new forms of governing', including corruption and local–national–global linkages (ibid.: 271). This is why it is so important to ask 'more precise questions about the type of social and political relations in which land is situated, particularly with reference to relations of inequality' (ibid.: 278).

In sum, the mainstream discourse on land titling assumes that once the poor are given the ticket (title) to the market they will take part in the game, and that it is better to be in than outside the game. The anthropological research on claims to land indicates that a wide variety of resources — not just titles — are in play during the game, and that poorer people remain disadvantaged even if invited to participate through titling. It is against this background that we now examine whether land titling in Nicaragua benefits people equitably.

LAND TITLING IN NICARAGUA

Methods

The empirical data for this chapter are drawn from fieldwork carried out between 2003 and 2006, using a combination of qualitative methods such as in-depth interviews and focus group discussions and quantitative methods such as questionnaire surveys, assisted by archival studies. Geographically, the research covers one municipality in each of three departments in the northern and western parts of Nicaragua, where a World Bank-funded land administration project (PRODEP) was started in 2003.

The questionnaire survey consisted of three individually-drawn samples of rural households, one for each of the three municipalities, carried out as a two-stage sampling. The size of the rural sample in each municipality was calculated on the estimated size of the rural population, in order to permit a desired confidence interval of 5 per cent (Krejcie and Morgan, 1970, cited in Bernard, 1994: 77). Households were selected randomly from a complete list of households in each community (sampling frame), obtained from the community leaders or the mayor's office, or elaborated with the

Table 1. Overview of the Different Samples

Case study area Fieldwork municipality in department	Villages	Rural sample		Urban sample	
		Households	Plots	Households	Plots
Estelí	21	365	429	32	47
Chinandega	21	384	466	31	42
Madríz	8	273	317	27	45
Total	50	1022	1212	90	134

help of community leaders.[5] Another sample was drawn from farmers living in each of the three municipal capitals, in order to also include larger-scale landowners in the data. These urban-based farming households were selected randomly from a list of farmers elaborated with the help of the mayor's office, rural community leaders and NGOs. Both samples focus entirely on rural land ownership. Details of the samples are presented in Table 1.

The data from the questionnaire have been analysed using SPSS. In this chapter, analysis is performed on the three samples treated as one, as the sampling process was identical and all are from small, rural, agricultural-based municipalities. In order to test the hypothesis regarding the relationships, cross-tabulations between sets of two nominal (categorical) variables were used.[6] For the in-depth interviews during the rural fieldwork, matrices with the specific research questions were prepared for each institution and/or person, based on the information obtained during the pilot visits during the preparation of the questionnaire survey. Furthermore, an interview guide for in-depth interviews was prepared. The interviews were transcribed, coded according to theme and analysed using N-vivo. All names of villages have been changed.

Land Tenure Situation in Post-War and Post-Land Reform Nicaragua

Land tenure has been especially turbulent in Nicaragua over the past three decades due to political turmoil. Land ownership in Nicaragua has traditionally been highly concentrated (de Janvry et al., 2001; Prosterman and Riedinger, 1987). Patron–client relations are still an important characteristic of Nicaraguan agriculture, and are also reflected in the hierarchical organization of almost all other parts of society. The Sandinista revolution in 1979 aimed to disrupt this hierarchy, and proclaimed a land reform to redistribute

5. The questionnaire was carried out with a total of 70 per cent of the pre-selected persons, and with 30 per cent of replacement households (also pre-selected with random numbers). Each questionnaire took an average of twenty-eight minutes, and only 10 per cent of the interviews with questionnaire formats lasted for more than forty-five minutes.
6. Three levels of significance are used: 99.9 per cent ($\ast\ast\ast$), 99 per cent ($\ast\ast$) and 95 per cent ($\ast$).

land much more equally. Idle land, indebted farms and the land holdings of the former dictator, Somoza, and his close associates, were confiscated (CIERA, 1984; Dorner, 1992; Stanfield et al., 1994), and vast amounts of land were converted into agricultural co-operatives and given collectively to the beneficiaries of the land reform (Maldidier and Marchetti, 1996).

After the Sandinista government was defeated in the elections of 1990, a new era of land reform was launched as part of the peace treaty signed to end the Contra war. Former soldiers and counter-revolutionary forces were promised land. This land reform often involved land that was already allocated to — and maybe even titled in the name of — beneficiaries of the Sandinista land reform. The legitimacy and legality of the property rights of those benefiting from the Sandinista land reform were challenged after the change of government. The new government also tried to accommodate thousands of land claims by former owners whose lands had been confiscated or expropriated by the former Sandinista government. This led to overlapping land claims, tenure insecurity and conflicts. Many of these conflicts became violent. Both eras of state-led land reform were highly politicized and produced neither the expected nor the desired redistribution of land in the long run. Some land was redistributed to politicians and other powerful persons, while much of the land given to agricultural co-operatives was subsequently sold. According to recent agricultural statistics in Nicaragua (CENAGRO, 2001), land is (once again) highly concentrated, with just 9 per cent of the farms controlling 56 per cent of the existing farmland. At the other extreme, 61 per cent of the (smallest) farms command only 9 per cent of the land area.[7]

The complex legal framework for the formal regulation of property rights that resulted from the changes of government has introduced both real (legal) and perceived tenure insecurity (described in detail in Broegaard, 2005a). Recently, it has been estimated that more than half of the households in Nicaragua have untitled or unregistered land, and overlapping titles are still a problem (Lavadenz, personal communication; see also Baumeister and Fernandez, 2005). More than a decade ago, Stanfield (1995) estimated that about 40 per cent of all households in Nicaragua were in a situation of property conflict or potential conflict. Many landholdings are still under contradictory laws and regulations due to inherent ambiguities and overlaps in the existing legislation. Conflicts and competing land claims are only settled slowly in the overburdened court system (Merlet and Pommier, 2000). Thus, as of mid-2001, 83 per cent of the cases of rural farms under court

---

7. While the analysis of the agricultural censuses by Baumeister and Fernandez (2005) does not reflect the process of concentration of land, due to large time gaps (from 1971 to 2001), it does show a process of redistribution and growth in the farms owning between 50 and 500 *manzanas* (1 *manzana* = 0.7 hectare). The recent growth of cattle and milk production in Nicaragua is also partly a reflection of the ongoing reconcentration of land (see for example EIU, 2005: 25).

review after the 1990 change of government were still pending or on appeal (EIU, 2001).

The present land tenure situation in Nicaragua is characterized by farms that lack formal land tenure documents. Ironically, there is at the same time a problem with land that has multiple documents, such as land that has been titled by the land reform more than once in the name of different owners, or titled land inscribed in the property registry, but for overlapping areas.[8]

The poorest producers have historically been most affected by insecurity of land tenure (Deininger et al., 2003). As a result, land titling and updating of the property registry and cadastral system are often recommended as the cure for land tenure insecurity, land conflicts and lack of investments, which could benefit the poor (see for example de Janvry and Sadoulet, 2000). The importance that some donors have placed on titles as a way to improve land investment and land markets can be appreciated by the following quote: 'The extreme low coverage of property titles in Nicaragua limits the ability of the poor to use one of their largest assets, and to improve land and housing markets. Lack of titling also reduces incentives to invest' (World Bank, 2003: 40, with reference to both rural and urban households).

Given the prevalence of this approach, it is not surprising that the World Bank has set the legalization of property rights as a top priority in Nicaragua. It has funded a five-year US$ 38 million (loan-financed) pilot land administration project, PRODEP (after its Spanish abbreviation). The aim of PRODEP is to secure property rights, activate the land market and stimulate investments as a way to integrate Nicaragua's agriculture into the world market (World Bank, 2002). The project focuses on cadastral surveys, titling and legal reforms in three prioritized departments in the northern and western parts of the country, where the fieldwork for this chapter was also carried out. The MCC is investing a further US$ 26 million in strengthening property rights in neighbouring departments.[9]

Nicaragua is ranked as the poorest country in Central America,[10] with almost half of the population (46 per cent) estimated to live below the poverty line (World Bank, 2003). This widespread poverty is further aggravated by

---

8. The Nicaraguan property register and cadastre have only been vaguely connected until a recent legal reform. This has allowed for inscription of more *manzanas* in the property registry than physically exist, due to transposed (overlapping) titles. It is estimated that roughly 20 per cent of the territory has updated cadastral information (Broegaard and Mendoza, 2004: 10). While cadastral maps were produced in the 1970s for most of the so-called 'Pacific' region of Nicaragua, virtually no updates were undertaken at the national level until PRODEP started to pay for the update. Cadastral searches require something close to detective work. Fortunately, the personnel at the departmental cadastral office have often worked there for a long time and can — if they want to — contribute a lot of information. However, this renders the system quite untransparent and also biases access to information, as good contacts with (and bribing of) staff may be needed.
9. See the website: www.cuentadelmilenio.org.ni
10. The gross national income was calculated to be US$ 810 per capita in 2004 (EIU, 2005).

the fact that the country's economic resources are unevenly distributed.[11] About a third of the rural population above ten years of age is illiterate (World Bank, 2003: 10). A recent corruption perception index gives Nicaragua a score of 2.6 on a scale from zero (highly corrupt) to ten (no corruption) (Transparency International, 2005).

FINDINGS AND ANALYSIS

The titling status of land in Nicaragua depends greatly on the way the land was acquired, as well as the economic wealth of the current owner, as discussed below. Land can basically be acquired through land market purchase, inheritance (or pre-inheritance), and land reform.[12] There are several broad categories of titles, which include individual titles (whether privately requested public deeds or individual land reform titles), collective land reform titles, informal titles (here defined as a wide variety of different pieces of paper that attempt to document recognized property rights, as well as more formal documents issued in the name of someone different — and not even related — to the current owner). Finally, there are some pieces of land that have no title at all.

Benefits of Titling in Reformed Areas

Land rights given by the Nicaraguan state are frequently challenged, especially when the government that gave those rights is no longer in power, as was the case with plots that had been involved in the land reform at the time of the fieldwork.[13] A statistically significant relationship is found between the mode of land acquisition and the frequency of land conflicts (see Table 2). The data show that lands that were never affected by the land reform experience fewer conflicts, whereas the reformed areas experience conflicts much more frequently, despite land reform areas being titled and registered (often as collective titles) more often than non-reformed areas. Thus, the land transaction history must be taken into account when analysing how titles influence land tenure security, conflicts and land sales.

That said, for the landholdings that have been affected by land reform, the data show that inscription in the property registry tends to lead to reduced land conflicts, although this tendency is not statistically significant. However, when turning to the private farms that have never been affected by land

11. The top 10 per cent of income-earners account for 35 per cent of total consumption, while the lowest 10 per cent account for under 2.5 per cent (World Bank, 2003).
12. Only on the expanding agricultural frontier can farmers still obtain rights through clearing and first occupancy; however, this often happens at the expense of indigenous groups.
13. This was before Daniel Ortega and the Sandinista party won the presidency again, in November 2006.

Table 2. Percentage of Farms in Reformed/Non-reformed Areas According to Land Conflict, Rural Sample

Land tenure history	Reformed areas (directly obtained through land reform, inherited or bought from beneficiary)	Land not affected by land reform	All plots
Rural sample*** Number of farms	*393*	*434*	*827*
Have experienced land conflict during the past ten years	20	9	14
Have not experienced land conflict during the past ten years	80	91	86

Note:
***Correlation between land reform affectation and land conflict significant at 0.001 level (Pearson's chi-square test).

reform, the statistical analysis shows that inscribing a private farm in the property register alone does not reduce land conflicts, even though land titling theory would predict otherwise (for example, Feder et al., 1988). This is also in line with findings by Alston et al. (1999) and Jansen and Roquas (1998), who report frequent and violent conflicts exist from their case study areas, even when land is titled.[14]

The *collective* character of the land-reform property right produces insecurity of tenure in the Nicaraguan setting. The fact of having obtained the land through an administrative procedure from a nation state, which is often not considered to be a legitimate authority, partly due to Nicaragua's recent past of dictatorship and revolution, and partly due to the general perception in the poorer parts of the population that the government does not protect their rights, further aggravates the insecure tenure situation as it is perceived by these beneficiaries of the land reform. The state is not the sole provider of legitimate rights and tenure security, and furthermore it often fails to provide such rights to the poorer parts of the population. Therefore it is not surprising that many land reform beneficiaries perceive their land tenure situation as being insecure because they depend on a collective land title, even when that title is legally sound and inscribed in the property registry (Broegaard, 2005b: 65ff).

Inequity in Land Market Transactions, Titling and Registration

Although it is repeatedly argued that land titles and the formalization of land rights are important for improving the way that the land market functions, the sustainability of such titling activities is rarely discussed, nor are the effects of inequality. Interestingly, the data from the study show that a large

14. See also Benjaminsen and Sjaastad (2003) on titling and conflicts in Africa.

percentage of cases of land transactions taking place via the land market are *not* followed up, either by updating formal land titles, or by inscribing such documents in the property registry (chi-square, rural sample ***, urban sample **, table not shown). For farmland obtained through the market, less than half is inscribed in the public registry in the name of the current owner, and a similar proportion is inscribed in the name of somebody else, frequently the previous owner.[15] These findings show that land market transactions actually undermine the land titling and registration activities promoted by donors and the state through projects such as PRODEP.

There are several reasons why many land market transactions are not followed up with titling and inscription in the property registry. One explanation is that the process of inscribing land is too expensive and cumbersome for many people (Broegaard, 2005b; MAGFOR, 2002). Those who are most affected by this situation are those who are least familiar with the legal system. This is especially true for poorer farmers with the smallest land areas, because many of the costs related to inscription are fixed costs, irrespective of the size of the land. The fact that the existing setup is unfavourable to small-scale farmers is also reflected in the statistically significant relationship between size of farm and its inscription in the property registry, especially in the rural sample. Not surprisingly, the largest farms are those that are most frequently inscribed (see Table 3). Nevertheless, it is remarkable that less than two-thirds of the biggest farms are inscribed in the property registry in the name of the current owner.

Another explanation is that experience tells (poor) farmers that the formal, legal system does not work to their advantage, and as such, does not necessarily provide them with a higher degree of tenure security (even if they manage economically to enter it in the first place). This is related to the different resources (both economical and in terms of connections and 'favours') that are needed to manoeuvre within the legal system. Thus, while many small-scale farmers dream of having a title for their land, they frequently have to look beyond the state for alternative sources of recognition of their land rights. In the fieldwork data, this was most frequently encountered among the poorest small farmers who had never been involved in the land reform.[16]

Plural Sources of Recognition of Property Rights

There is a third explanation for the observed low percentage of land rights being inscribed in the property registry after land market transactions. This is related to the state not being the only provider of recognition of land rights.

---

15. Other cases are inscribed in the name of a relative.
16. Geographically, these examples mainly came from the western part of the fieldwork municipality in the department of Estelí and fieldwork municipality in the department of Madríz.

Table 3. Percentage of Farms Inscribed in the Property Registry by Size of Farm (ranges)

Inscription status in the property registry	Range of area of farms, *mzs*					
	≤1	1.01–5	5.01–10	10.01–50	>50	All ranges
Rural sample*** Number of farms	*161*	*186*	*234*	*190*	*54*	*825*
Document registered in name of current owner	28	45	54	55	63	48
Document registered, but not in name of current owner	50	39	32	32	33	37
Document not inscribed	22	17	14	13	4	15
Urban sample** Number of farms		*35*	*16*	*44*	*29*	*124*
Document registered in name of current owner		49	56	59	83	61
Document not registered, or registered in name of other than the current owner[a]		51	44	41	29	39

Notes:

***Correlation between size of farm and inscription status significant at 0.001 level (Pearson's chi-square test), rural sample.

**Correlation between size of farm and inscription status significant at 0.05 level (Pearson's chi-square test), urban sample.

[a]Categories of not inscribed and inscribed in name of other are merged here, as there are only nine observations of inscriptions in the name of somebody other than the current owner in the entire urban sample. Likewise for categories of area, where there were only four observations of farms at or below one *manzana* in the entire sample.

There are other entities, such as the local farmer community, the agricultural co-operative directive, the mayor or a high-ranking civil servant, that can also be a source of recognition that land rights are considered legitimate at the local level.

Some owners who have accessed their land through the land market or through inheritance feel such a high degree of tenure security that they see no sense of urgency about elaborating and/or inscribing formal land titles. In these cases, the elaboration of a simple sales agreement, certified by a lawyer, or the use of local witnesses to the land market transaction, may provide a locally legitimate proof of transaction and thus of property rights. This may be related to the high level of legitimacy associated with market-based land transactions, as suggested Bastiansen et al. (2006). The qualitative field data show that bought land is often considered to have greater legitimacy than land rights obtained from the state through land reform (see also Gengenback, 1998, quoted in Peters, 2004: 293).

Many interviews with private small-scale farmers (who did not receive land through the land reform) reveal a perception of nothing good coming from the state. In their view, there are many reasons to be sceptical and suspicious about the state. In general, this group of farmers does not view their lack of a land title as being a problem. Rather, they fear that intrusion of the Nicaraguan state into land titling in their peasant society will actually cause problems. As a result, they reject the idea of being subordinated to control by the state and its entities: there are even some who say that they may not want to have their land measured and titled for free under the PRODEP programme, because this would also force them to pay taxes and — even worse — it would subject them to supervision or control by the state (see also Bastiansen et al., 2006).

The Dynamics of Titling: Abuses of Office

At virtually every level of government one can find 'officials' or civil servants who take advantage of their office in order to form alliances with wealthy and powerful actors in exchange for favours and political and monetary rewards (such as granting land rights, giving a positive judgement in a court case or letting titles be inscribed in irregular ways in the property registry). While lower-level officials such as village committees or municipal or departmental level officials can, and often do, play an important role in mitigating land conflicts and power abuses, some are actually involved in land conflicts themselves. Generally, these officials are wealthier and better-connected than their constituency. Throughout the fieldwork, cases of land conflicts and abuses of office were encountered in the interviews, both in the rural and the urban settings.

The history of land grabbing described below offers one such example of how relations to higher-ranking officials and politicians determine land rights outcomes. While this case should not be considered as typical or representative, it nevertheless is a good example of the gross abuses of influence that occur. It thus also illustrates the kind of expectations that small-scale farmers may have when they enter a property conflict — or decide *not* to enter.

During his period in office, the former mayor of the fieldwork municipality in Chinandega department bought a large tract of land in the municipality. According to people in the neighbouring village, he fenced in much more land than he bought and took advantage of the fact that the farm was adjacent to so-called 'national lands' (land owned by the state as not previously registered as belonging to a private owner) in a nearby estuary, which had never been measured and thus was not included in the national cadastre system. Thereafter, he had the land measured by a topographer and then made a formal land title.[17] Using his contacts and position as a mayor, he succeeded in having the title accepted in the cadastral record and subsequently inscribed in the property registry. As the national land had never been measured, it

---

17. *'Título Supletorio'*, a supplementary land title based on possessionary rights, is commonly used to register land not previously included in the property registry or that was inscribed as a reformed area, for example.

was hard to prove after the inscription of the title that the land in question was really part of the 'national lands'. As one local lawyer said about the case: 'Those with most economic resources are those who can move the border [of the farm].'

For decades, members of a neighbouring land reform co-operative had used the estuary wetland as pastureland for their animals in the dry season. However, once he had successfully fenced, titled and inscribed the national wetland area that was formerly a *de facto* communal area, the mayor restricted the co-operatives' traditional practice of pasturing the animals. The co-operative then started a legal case against the mayor for usurpation of public property, but the local court chose to support the mayor because he was able to present an inscribed title. The fact that he was an influential mayor and politically well-connected probably did not hurt his case. Subsequently, the mayor filed a legal counter-case against the co-operative farmers for fence destruction and trespassing on private property.

The co-operative farmers visited the Office for Rural Land Titling (OTR) to ask the departmental officials to make a legal case on behalf of the State of Nicaragua regarding the usurpation of public property. OTR at the departmental level responded that they did not have the money to do this. Meanwhile, several of the co-operative members were sentenced to six months in prison. The mayor from a neighbouring municipality supported the co-operative and they agreed to visit the capital and further pursue the case. However, the first mayor — in the middle of his time in office — switched allegiance to the Constitutional Liberal Party, to which the President of the Republic belonged at the time. When the mayor had been seen several times with the President, the opponents gave up the case against the mayor, commenting that 'it would have been like fighting a monster'.[18]

This example of abuse of office illustrates the highly personalized face of the State of Nicaragua, in which the rights of the powerful triumph over others. The result of the land conflict came to illustrate the relative power of the mayor (and his allies) *vis-à-vis* the local farmers. The legal system or the state do not work neutrally, with civil servants following pre-established rules. Rather, local 'kings' exchange favours with other individuals, by bending, reinterpreting, challenging or simply ignoring formally-established rules. As a result, land tenure security is not just about *rights*, but very much about *relations*.

The Dynamics of Titling: Influencing the Slope of the Playing Field

Another case from the same municipality concerns a non-formalized donation of land from a co-operative. Although a piece of land was given *de*

---

18. The former President was subsequently jailed for money laundering and other alleged crimes.

facto to the co-operative by the land reform, it exceeded the area described in the land title. 'Excess area' is very common in land reform co-operatives. This case not only exemplifies the lack of enforcement of rights, but also illustrates how wealthy and well-connected people are able to go forum-shopping by overriding the departmental-level officials and going right to central-level officials in order to get support for their contention.

In the 1980s, a (men's) co-operative with collective land reform title verbally donated an 'excess area' of land to a women's collective. In 2000, when the men's co-operative sold its land collectively they gave the land reform title to the buyer. However, when the buyer had taken possession of his new farm he ignored the verbal agreement between the co-operative and the women's collective and subsequently established a legal case against the women for trespassing on private property and for cattle-theft (which is close to the worst crime one can be accused of in a cattle-ranging society). He also dug up the fence separating the women's area from the former co-operative area. Although titles had never been issued in favour of the women, the women went to the Departmental delegate of the OTR, who had records of the land donation from the co-operative to the women's collective. The OTR official appeared, accompanied by the police and a team of topographers to delimit the bought area from the area of the women's collective. Weight was given to the original agreement between the co-operative and the women's collective, as well as to the existence of land improvements such as fruit trees planted on the women's land. However, as soon as the OTR officials and the police officers left, the buyer invaded the women's land again. Soon after, he presented a letter signed by the National Director of OTR (who belonged to the same political party as the wealthy buyer) ordering that he should not be molested again. He then closed an access road to land situated behind the former co-operative land and put in armed guards to make sure that nobody crossed his land. The women's collective filed a legal claim against him for taking over their land; the women obtained a court sentence in their favour, but the sentence was never enforced. Given that they could not bear the constant pressure from their neighbour, nor did they have money for another court case or to demand enforcement of the first sentence, they were obliged to abandon their land (see also Broegaard, 2005b).

Another case of 'forum shopping' happened in a village in the fieldwork municipality in Estelí department, where the majority of the members of a former agricultural co-operative, whose land had been divided into indi-vidual plots like most other co-operatives, had sold their plots to a single buyer. Only one of the former beneficiaries of the land reform still had his land intact and this plot was now situated like an island in the sea of the land of the new landowner. Being the owner of the vast majority of the former co-operative's land, this new landowner had received the origi-nal collective land title from the former co-operative directive, as this was the only formal document that existed for the land. While this is not the correct legal procedure, it is nevertheless very common. With the title in hand, the new landowner had a stronger legal basis, as well as a firmer economic position, *vis-à-vis* the only remaining land reform beneficiary. The new owner used his land mainly for grazing cattle, but refused to fence it in order to prevent the cattle from eating the crops of the (smaller) neighbour. This made life difficult for the small-scale farmer, who depended on his own crops to provide him with food.

While preparing his one *manzana* of land, the land reform beneficiary burned plant residues, which is illegal according to the most recent environmental act in the municipality, but is very common practice nevertheless. On top of this offence, the fire got out of hand and burned some of the land of the rich neighbour. The rich neighbour had no interest in reaching an agreement on compensation for the damage through the village council, as is the norm in the area for a small incident like this, but instead went straight to the local court and filed a legal claim against the land reform beneficiary. The judge failed to notify the small-scale farmer about this claim until after the judgement was issued. While failing to notify one party is not correct legal procedure, it is also common. Not surprisingly, the judgement was made in favour of the new landowner, as no objections were presented. Conveniently, the demand for 4,000 C$, or exactly the local value (at that time) of one *manzana* of land in that area, was supported by the judge. The money was ordered to be paid within a period of two weeks, which was not possible for the land reform beneficiary unless he sold his entire one-*manzana* plot of land.

These cases from the two municipalities illustrate how powerful actors are able to move land conflicts from one forum, or playing field, to another (in this case from OTR at the departmental level to OTR central level, and from the village council to the local court). This ensures that the strongest party can mould the system to work to his advantage, by creating a situation in which the slope of the non-level playing field is shifted in his favour. These cases also show how the high degree of inequality of economic resources and access to legal advice combine to influence the outcome of land conflicts. In some cases counter-claims are not even presented, or cases are not brought to court, because of the unlevel slope of the playing field.

CONCLUSIONS: DIFFERENTIAL EFFECTS OF LAND TITLING AND REGISTRATION IN NICARAGUA

Institutional and legal frameworks in Nicaragua are either contradictory or open to the highest-paying party. In most cases legal ambiguity favours the wealthy in Nicaragua. Although there is nothing new about the finding that land titling and land market transactions take place in real-world settings of inequality and abuse of office, this reality is not sufficiently reflected in the prevailing land administration programmes and discourses about the 'mysteries of capitalism', which provide important arguments for promoting such programmes. The donors and government focus on titling and legal reforms (but not on access to legal advice), despite the fact that its pro-poor label does not overcome the inequality that influences the way that both the market and the formal titling system work in favour of the already most prosperous. The lack of benefits and high costs of titling and registration, as well as the lack of trust in the state, affect the poor more negatively than they affect the rich.

Many landholdings in Nicaragua are handled in extra-legal ways, for example, when being sold or inherited. If this practice is not changed, it will undermine the large-scale, loan-financed investments made in land titling and administration projects such as PRODEP. The generalized practice of not formalizing and inscribing documents in land market transaction cases and not updating documents in cases of inheritance and division is related to the high cost of titling and updating registry information, as well as the lack of direct incentives to do so. It is also related to the low level of trust placed in state authorities, as well as to the existence of plural providers of land rights recognition.

The custom of handing land conflicts extra-legally and not using the legal-formal system for land registration is a response to the way the state works. Small-scale farmers often try to avoid contact with the formal legal system, not only to cut costs but also to avoid the control of the state entities. Other authorities, such as village councils, co-operative leaders and lawyers may recognize the property rights of the rural poor, but while they create a situation of perceived tenure security, they do not prevent the abuse of position. For the land reform beneficiaries, their contact with the state through land reform has been positive. However, with every change of government, their relation to the state also becomes increasingly ambiguous.

The land transaction case histories presented in this chapter illustrate abuses of public office and inequality. Many highly-positioned civil servants, including judges and mayors, use their position to force through land transactions or land-grabbing in favour of themselves or other powerful players. This weaves a web of illicit favours and debts involving higher-level officials and influential actors. Wealthy private landowners, as well as members of co-operative directives, were often found to use their privileged position in terms of economic wealth and/or information to buy land cheaply. The case studies also show that there are multiple providers of recognition of rights, and that strong actors are able to choose the body of authority that gives them the most advantageous outcome in a land dispute. Obviously, they choose a playing field where the slope is tilted to their advantage.

The results from the fieldwork in Nicaragua show that in practice, the functioning of the legal system often depends on the resources the actors are able to draw upon, more than on their formal titling status. This in itself not only reflects the unequal possibilities, but also creates even more unequal conditions, with the risk of this process continuing *ad infinitum*. There is ample evidence to show that the assumptions about investments in titling and the more fluid functioning of the land market as benefiting the poor do not hold true in contexts of inequality, power abuse, illegality and 'forum shopping'.

REFERENCES

Alston, L.J., G.D. Libecap and B. Mueller (1999) *Titles, Conflicts and Land Use: The Development of Property Rights and Land Reform on the Brazilian Amazon Frontier.* Ann Arbor, MI: University of Michigan Press.

Bastiaensen, J., B. D'Excelle and C. Farmerée (2006) 'Political Arenas around Access to Land: A Diagnosis of Property Rights Practices in the Nicaraguan Interior'. Antwerp: Institute of Development Policy and Management, University of Antwerp and Nitlapán.

Baumeister, E. and E. Fernandez (2005) 'Análisis de la tenencia de la tierra en Nicaragua a partir del censo agropecuario 2001' ('Analysis of Land Tenure in Nicaragua based on the Agrarian Census 2001'). Managua: FAO, INEC and MAG.

von Benda-Beckmann, F. (1995) 'Anthropological Approaches to Property Law and Economics', *European Journal of Law and Economics* 2: 309–36.

von Benda-Beckmann, F. (2001) 'Legal Pluralism and Social Justice in Economic and Political Development', *IDS Bulletin* 32(1): 46–56.

von Benda-Beckman, K. (1991) 'Forum Shopping and Shopping Forums: Dispute Processing in a Minagkabau Village in West Sumatra', *Journal of Legal Pluralism* 19: 117–62.

Benjaminsen, T.A. and E. Sjaastad (2003) 'Mathieu versus de Soto: A Comment', *Forum for Development Studies* 30(1): 89–92.

Bernard, H.R. (1994) *Research Methods in Anthropology: Quantitative and Qualitative Approaches.* Thousand Oaks, CA, and London: Sage Publications.

Berry, S. (1989) 'Social Institutions, and Access to Resources', *Africa* 59(1): 41–55.

Berry, S. (1993) *No Condition is Permanent: The Social Dynamics of Agrarian Change in Sub-Saharan Africa.* Madison, WI: University of Wisconsin Press.

Binswanger, H., K. Deininger and G. Feder (1995) 'Power, Distortions, Revolt and Reform in Agricultural Land Relations', in J. Behrmann and T.N. Srinivasan (eds) *Handbook of Development Economics*, Vol. III, pp. 2659–72. Amsterdam: Elsevier.

Broegaard, R.J. (2005a) 'Land Tenure Insecurity and Inequality: A Case Study from Nicaragua', *Development and Change* 36(5): 845–64.

Broegaard, R.J. (2005b) 'Inseguridad de tenencia y conflictos de propiedad en Nicaragua' ('Land Tenure, Insecurity and Property Conflicts in Nicaragua'). 157 Report I. WB UPI No. 0000246858, Purchase Order No 7590565. Financed by the Danish Consultant Trust Fund. Managua: World Bank.

Broegaard, R.J. and F. Mendoza (2004) 'Capacidad municipal en servicios de regularización de tierra en Nicaragua' ('Municipal Capacity Related to Land Regularization Services in Nicaragua'). 66 Report III. WB UPI No. 0000246858, Purchase Order No 7590565. Financed by the Danish Consultant Trust Fund. Managua: World Bank.

Bromley, D.W. (2009) 'Formalizing Property Rights in the Developing World: The Wrong Prescription for the Wrong Malady', *Land Use Policy* 26(1): 20–27.

Carter, M.R. (2006) 'Land Markets and Pro-Poor Growth: From Neo-Structural Scepticism to Policy Innovation'. Keynote address to the International Conference on Land, Poverty, Social Justice and Development, ISS, The Hague (9–14 January).

Carter, M.R. and B.L. Barham (1996) 'Level Playing Fields and Laissez Faire: Postliberal Development Strategy in Inegalitarian Agrarian Economies', *World Development* 24(7): 1133–49.

Carter, M.R. and J.S. Chamorro (2000) 'Estudio de las Dinamicas de la Economia Rural. Impacto de Proyectos de Legalización de la Propiedad en Nicaragua' ('Study of the

Dynamics of the Rural Economy: The Impact of Property Legalization Projects in Nicaragua'). Department of Agricultural and Applied Economics. Madison, WI: University of Wisconsin.

CENAGRO (2001) http://www.inec.gob.ni/cenagro/portaltabulados.htm (Accessed 26 June 2008).

CIERA (1984) *Nicaragua, . . . Y Por Eso Defendemos la Frontera: Historia Agraria de la Segovias Occidentales* (*Nicaragua . . . And This is Why We Defend the Border: Agrarian History of the Western Segovias*). Managua: CIERA.

Childress, M. and K. Deininger (2006) 'Land Policies for Growth and Poverty Reduction: Recent Experiences with Policies to Improve Land Access and Land Distribution'. Keynote Address to the International Conference on Land, Poverty, Social Justice and Development, ISS, The Hague (9–14 January).

Coles-Coghi, A. (1993) *Agricultural Land Rights and Title Security in Honduras*. Madison, WI: University of Wisconsin.

Deininger, K. (2003) *Land Policies for Growth and Poverty Reduction*. Oxford: World Bank and Oxford University Press.

Deininger, K., E. Zegarra and I. Lavadenz (2003) 'Determinants and Impacts of Rural Land Market Activity: Evidence from Nicaragua', *World Development* 31(8): 1385–404.

Dorner, P. (1992) *Latin American Land Reforms in Theory and Practice: A Retrospective Analysis*. Madison, WI: University of Wisconsin.

EIU, The Economist Intelligence Unit (2001) *Country Profile. Nicaragua 2001*. London: The Economist Intelligence Unit Limited.

EIU, The Economist Intelligence Unit (2005) *Country Profile. Nicaragua 2005*. London: The Economist Intelligence Unit Limited.

Feder, G., T. Onchan, Y. Chalamwong and C. Hongladarom (1988) *Land Policies and Farm Productivity in Thailand*. Baltimore, MD, and London: The Johns Hopkins University Press.

Gengenbach, Heidi (1998) '"I'll Bury You in the Border!": Women's Land Struggles in Post-War Facazisse (Magude District), Mozambique', *Journal of Southern African Studies* 24(1): 7–36.

Jansen, K. and E. Roquas (1998) 'Modernizing Insecurity: The Land Titling Project in Honduras', *Development and Change* 29(1): 81–106.

de Janvry, A. and E. Sadoulet (2000) *Property Rights and Land Conflicts in Nicaragua: A Synthesis*. Berkeley, CA: University of California.

de Janvry, A., G. Gordillo, J.-P. Platteau and E. Sadoulet (2001) 'Access to Land and Land Policy Reforms', in A. de Janvry, G. Gordillo, J.-P. Platteau and E. Sadoulet (eds) *Access to Land, Rural Poverty, and Public Action*, pp. 1–26. Oxford: Oxford University Press.

Kay, Cristóbal (2006) 'Survey Article: Rural Poverty and Development Strategies in Latin America', *Journal of Agrarian Change* 6(4): 455–508.

Krejcie, R.V. and D.W. Morgan (1970) 'Determining Sample Size for Research Activities', *Educational and Psychological Measurements* 30: 607–10.

Li, T.M. (2001) 'Agrarian Differentiation and the Limits of Natural Resource Management in Upland Southeast Asia', *IDS Bulletin* 32(4): 88–94.

Long, N. (2001) *Development Sociology: Actor Perspectives*. London and New York: Routledge.

Lund, C. (2001) 'Seeking Certainty and Aggravating Ambiguity: On Property, Paper and Authority in Niger', *IDS Bulletin* 32(4): 47–53.

Maldidier, C. and P.S. Marchetti (1996) *El Campesino-Finquero y el potencial económico del campesinado nicaragüense*. (*The Campesino Farm-owner and the Economic Potential of the Nicaraguan Farmers*). Managua: Nitlapán-UCA.

Merlet, M. and D. Pommier (2000) 'Estudios Sobre la Tenencia de la Tierra' ('Study of Land Tenure)'. Study No OPA-001-2000 carried out for Office for Rural Titling (OTR) and the World Bank. Managua: IRAM.

Ministerio Agropecuario y Forestal (MAGFOR) (2002) 'Estudio sobre Costos y Tiempos de

Legalización de Propiedades Rurales en Algunos Municipios de Nicaragua' ('Study of Costs and Times of Legalization of Rural Properties in Selected Municipalities in Nicaragua'). Managua: MAGFOR.

Mitchell, T. (2007) 'The Properties of Markets', in D. MacKenzie, F. Muniesa and L. Siu (eds) *Do Economists Make Markets? On the Performativity of Economics*, pp. 244–75. Princeton, NJ: Princeton University Press.

Nuijten, M. (1998) *In the Name of the Land: Organization, Transnationalism and the Culture of the State in a Mexican Ejido*. Wageningen: Agricultural University Wageningen.

Nuijten, M. (2003a) *Power, Community and the State. The Political Anthropology of Organisation in Mexico*. London: Pluto Press.

Nuijten, M. (2003b) 'Illegal Practices and the Re-Enchantment of Governmental Techniques: Land and the Law in Mexico', *Journal of Legal Pluralism* 48: 163–83.

Peters, P. (2004) 'Inequality and Social Conflict over Land in Africa', *Journal of Agrarian Change* 4(3): 269–314.

Prosterman, R.L. and J.M. Riedinger (1987) *Land Reform and Democratic Development*. Baltimore, MD: The Johns Hopkins University Press.

Rivas, A. and R. Broegaard (2006) *Demarcación Territorial de la Propiedad Comunal en la Costa Caribe de Nicaragua* (*Territorial Demarcation of Communal Property on the Caribbean Coast of Nicaragua*). Managua: CIDCA-UCA.

Roquas, E. (2002) *Stacked Law: Land, Property and Conflict in Honduras*. Amsterdam: Rosenberg Publishers.

de Soto, H. (2000) *The Mystery of Capital: Why Capitalism Triumphs in the West and Fails Everywhere Else*. New York: Basic Books.

de Soto, H. (2004) 'The Mystery of Capital: The Role of Property Rights in Creating Wealth and Alleviating Poverty'. CGIAR Sir John Crawford Memorial Lecture, Mexico DF (27 October).

Stanfield, D.J. (1995) *Insecurity of Land Tenure in Nicaragua*. Madison, WI: Land Tenure Center, University of Wisconsin.

Stanfield, D., M. Molina and R. Guevara (1994) *An Analysis of the Current Situation Regarding Land Tenure in Nicaragua*. Mt. Horeb, WI: Terra Institute; Madison, WI: The Land Tenure Center, University of Wisconsin.

Transparency International (2005) www.transparency.org/policy_and_research/surveys_indices/cpi/2005 (accessed 05 December 2007).

World Bank (2002) 'Project Appraisal Document, PRODEP'. Washington, DC: The World Bank.

World Bank (2003) *Nicaragua Poverty Assessment: Raising Welfare and Reducing Vulnerability*. Washington, DC: The World Bank.

World Bank (2004) World Development Indicators 2004, http://ddp-ext.worldbank.org/ext/ (accessed 15 June 2006).

World Bank (2005) *World Development Report 2006: Equity and Development*. New York: The World Bank; Oxford: Oxford University Press.

8

Negotiating Post-Socialist Property *and* State: Struggles over Forests in Albania and Romania

Thomas Sikor, Johannes Stahl and Stefan Dorondel

INTRODUCTION

Central and Eastern Europe has experienced a massive transformation of property rights over the past two decades. Property reforms belonged to the key projects undertaken by post-socialist states (Stark and Bruszt, 1998). In rural areas, they brought about radical changes in property rights to agricultural land and forest. Yet property reforms were not only state projects but also projects undertaken by millions of rural people asserting various kinds of claims to rural resources (Verdery, 1996). People's abilities to get their claims recognized as property in the form of land titles or other documents varied, however, depending on the economic, political and cultural resources available to them (Hann, 2003).

As important as these legal processes were, the processes of 'making' property extended far beyond the implementation of property reforms. After many people had acquired statutory rights to land, they wanted to exercise these rights in practice. Yet exercising rights was not an easy undertaking in agriculture, as many did not know the exact location of their land, did not have access to the necessary machinery, credit and inputs, or did not find attractive outlets for their products (Hann, 1993; Verdery, 2003). One of the reasons why they could not translate their formal ownership into 'effective ownership' (Verdery, 2003) was the practices of powerful actors. After land reform was over, some of these powerful actors pursued their interest in agricultural profits by other means. Using the terms of Ribot and Peluso (2003), they sought to gain access to agricultural land no longer by way of property but through other access mechanisms, such as control over product markets (Giordano and Kostova, 2002) and highly speculative productive ventures based on short-term leases of agricultural land (Verdery, 2003).

In this contribution, we seek to set out these practices and processes 'making' post-socialist property in relation to processes constituting authority. Following Sikor and Lund (this volume), we suggest that it is useful to examine linkages between the processes shaping access and property on the one hand and those forming power and authority on the other. We are particularly interested in exploring how negotiations over access and property intersect with the formation of state power and authority. Post-socialist

This research was funded by the Emmy Noether-Programm of Deutsche Forschungsgemein-schaft. We thank Christian Lund and To Xuan Phuc for their insightful comments.

property negotiations appear to be intimately interwoven with the 'state of the post-socialist state' (Sturgeon and Sikor, 2004). This is because post-socialist states assume a primary role in implementing property reforms (Stark and Bruszt, 1998), and because control over property titles is among the most important political resources available to state actors in Central and Eastern Europe (Kurtz and Barnes, 2002). The authority enjoyed by post-socialist states, therefore, has some bearing on negotiations over property. *Vice versa*, struggles over property are a key influence in the quest for authority by post-socialist states (Verdery, 2002).

Such an inquiry into the foundations of post-socialist states appears appropriate considering the momentous changes experienced by them as part of the broader political economic transformations since 1989. As suggested by Grzymala-Busse and Luong (2002), Central and Eastern European states experienced a process of reconstitution as the relationships among the multiple actors making up the state, and thereby their practices, changed. Decision-making powers moved from the executive to the legislative branches at the national level and from the national to the local levels of the state. They also followed increasingly rule-based procedures, in contrast to the personalized style of the early 1990s. Yet the challenges faced by post-socialist states went beyond changes in their operational structures and styles. Post-socialist states have struggled to reassert their authority against competition from other politico-legal institutions that offer personal security, promote development and sanction property. The latter have included a wide array of institutions, such as local customary arrangements (de Waal, 2004), local-level associations (Sikor, 2005), Mafia-style networks (Verdery, 1996), religious groups (Hayden, 2002) and broadly-recognized moral values (Humphrey, 1995; Verdery, 1999).

Thus we refer to the state in two senses in this chapter. We look at the state as an abstract social institution in the sense of what Abrams (1988) calls the 'idea of the state'. Understood this way, post-socialist states have encountered competition from other politico-legal institutions for authority over property. States have not been the sole institutions conferring property rights, enforcing them and resolving disputes over property, as in classical spheres of state jurisdiction. In addition, we examine the practices of concrete state actors. We are particularly interested in the actions of local state officials, including local governments, the local representatives of central government agencies and various kinds of local commissions. Their actions regarding property may be very different from what central organs expect them to be, as illustrated by the influence that local land commissions have exerted on the conduct of land reform (Kaneff, 1996; Verdery, 1996). Local governments, in particular, may take advantage of decentralization and the dissolution of centralized party structures to employ the newly-acquired powers for their own purposes (Verdery, 2002; Mungiu-Pippidi, 2005).

In the context of forestry, we surmise that struggles over forests provide a particular opportunity to examine the simultaneous constitution of post-socialist property and authority (cf. Verdery, 2004b). Just as in agriculture, property reforms in forestry have been key state projects (Staddon, 2000). The implementation of the property reforms, therefore, has direct implications for the reconstitution of state authority, as forests have become the most valuable resource in many rural areas (Staddon, 2001a). Yet in contrast to agriculture, state authority is also at stake in forestry in other significant ways. Environmental concerns continue to motivate a strong involvement of the state in forestry, even where ownership is considered 'private' (Staddon, 2001b). In addition, the reconfiguration of state authority in the forestry sector takes place against a particular historical background. Prior to nationalization, many forests were under either *de facto* or officially-sanctioned customary authority such as co-operatives (Cellarius, 2004) and village councils of elders (de Waal, 2004).

This contribution proceeds as follows. We begin with a comparison of national politics in Albania and Romania to explore contestations over authority at the national level. We then examine practices and processes constituting property and authority regarding forest in four local case studies, two each from Albania and Romania.[1] We conclude with a comparison of local negotiations over property and authority among the four sites and between the two countries, linking local struggles over forests with national politics.

NATIONAL POLITICS IN ALBANIA AND ROMANIA

Turbulent Extrication from Socialism in Albania

> *S'ka shteti, s'ka ligji!* (There is no state, there is no law!)
> (Albanian saying after 1990)

Major instances of violence accompanied Albania's extrication from socialism. In the aftermath of the collapse of the social regime in 1991, the country experienced an orgiastic wave of vandalism (Vickers and Pettifer, 1997). Albanians took to the streets, indiscriminately destroying any kind of physical structure associated with the socialist state: the buildings of agricultural co-operatives, schools and most of the rail and rural telephone systems. In 1997, people across the country once again went on the rampage, ransacking banks, town halls, courthouses, land registries, police stations and even military barracks (de Waal, 1998). The lawlessness came to a head when military depots were looted and arms stolen, including some 600,000

---

1. The case studies draw on ethnographic fieldwork conducted in 2004. Stefan Dorondel (in Romania) and Johannes Stahl (in Albania) spent between two and four months at each site collecting information primarily through semi-structured household interviews, informal conversations and direct observation. Unless otherwise specified, direct quotations originate from this fieldwork.

Kalashnikov AK-47s. Armed bands of people controlled roads, villages and towns for months, causing nothing less than a temporary collapse of the state (Biberaj, 1998). This situation compelled the European Union to send in an international intervention force to support new elections.

The violence and open unrest in 1991 and 1997 reflected the lack of legitimacy of the Albanian state in the eyes of the general population. In 1991, people vented their frustrations with a socialist regime that had isolated them from the rest of the world and made their country the poorest in Europe (Vickers and Pettifer, 1997). In 1997, many again took to the streets as they felt betrayed by political leaders perceived to engage in personal feuds, to use violence and to enrich themselves in office (Saltmarshe, 2001). In particular, political leaders were thought to be implicated in the collapse of pyramid investment schemes, which wiped out about 60 per cent of Albania's private savings (Abdul-Hamid, 2003). Many people also resented the state for not being able to guarantee their personal security. They felt that it had done little to stop the cross-border trafficking of people, arms and drugs by Mafia-style gangs, which openly challenged state monopoly over the means of law enforcement (Saltmarshe, 2001).

As the authority attributed to the state was low, many Albanians turned to customary arrangements in the conduct of their daily lives. Commonly referred to as *Kanun*, these customary regulations reach back centuries in Albania, being transmitted orally from generation to generation. Their influence declined under socialism but made a strong comeback after its demise. The regulations apply to many aspects of personal life and economic production such as inheritance rights, the prosecution of killings and other personal offences (Lastarria-Cornhiel and Wheeler, 1998). Their influence is particularly salient in northern Albania (de Waal, 2004), but they also govern social relations in squatter settlements in the capital, Tirana (Voell, 2003).

However, the causes of the rapid decline in the authority of the state went far beyond people's frustrations with the political leadership and their turn to customary arrangements. Many people simply left Albania. Starting in 1991, large numbers of Albanians left their country in search of jobs and a better life in neighbouring countries, particularly Greece and Italy. The prospects of migration continued to be seductive, as by 2002 around a quarter of the population continued to live below the national poverty line (Nicholson, 2003). Poverty was especially prevalent in rural areas, as reflected not only in low income levels but also in a more general sense of exclusion (de Soto et al., 2002). By 2001, more than a sixth of all Albanians lived abroad, their remittances accounting for almost a quarter of the country's GDP (Nicholson, 2003). The Albanian state no longer assumed significance in their transnational strategies, as they oriented their lives towards the countries in which they or their close relatives now lived and worked (Rapper and Sintes, 2006; Stahl and Sikor, forthcoming). Migration, therefore, posed as significant a challenge to the authority of the Albanian state as the people's frustrations with the political leadership, open violence and customary arrangements.

Property was a major field in which contestations over authority took place. Property reforms were a cornerstone of the legislation enacted by Albania's governments throughout the 1990s (de Waal, 2004). Agricultural reforms mandated the distribution of all collective farmland to the current agricultural labour force in equal shares. In forestry, the government legislated the restitution of forests to historical owners. This meant in practice that the state retained ownership of over 92 per cent of the country's forests, as this had been under state ownership at the time of collectivization in 1944 (de Waal, 2004: 33). In addition, the Albanian government instituted strict regulations to enforce the state ownership of forests, creating a police-like body of forest guards to enforce forest regulations. Nevertheless, the reforms were repeatedly challenged by people asserting competing claims to land. In agriculture, many rural villages opted for restitution of agricultural land to its historical owners despite the national policy of distribution (Kodderitzsch, 1999). The demands for restitution culminated in a law in 2004 that granted historical owners rights to compensation. Control over property, therefore, appeared to be just as contested as broader authority relations in Albania. State legislation and customary regulations, in particular, offered competing authorizations for property claims.

Negotiating a 'Law-Governed State' in Romania

> *Să se aplice legea!* (The law must be enforced!)
> (Romanian saying commonly heard in the early 2000s)

Romania's 'revolution' of 1989 involved a far less radical change in political regime than the term suggests. After the execution of the previous dictator, Ceausescu, and his wife, the National Salvation Front, which included many high-ranking politicians from the previous regime, took over (Hollis, 1999). The Front won the elections in 1991 under the leadership of Ion Iliescu, a former socialist party secretary. Illiescu also managed to win the 1992 elections, now as the head of the successor to the Communist Party. Moreover, Romania did not experience the violence and collapse of public order that accompanied Albania's extrication from socialism. There was some sense of public disorder when miners marched into Bucharest in 1990 and 1991. Nevertheless, their actions were much smaller in scale and not directed against the state as an institution (Gledhill, 2005). Rather, some high-level politicians had called the miners in as a political weapon against students and other demonstrators, resorting to the kind of personalized exercise of state authority which characterized the Ceausescu regime.

National politics remained highly personalized during the first half of the 1990s (Pop-Eleches, 1999). The new constitution granted the president powers far in excess of those known in other presidential systems and allowed governments to make abundant use of emergency ordinances (Hollis, 1999). Political leaders were quick in shifting their stance on political issues and forming new alliances, showing little inclination to adhere to more durable political programmes (Pop-Eleches, 1999). They engaged in dubious and illegal manoeuvres, protected by the far-ranging immunity given to parliamentarians (Hollis, 1999). This led to general dissatisfaction with political leaders over the 1990s, causing massive shifts in electoral majorities in the 1996 and 2000 elections (Pop-Eleches, 2001; Tismaneanu and Kligman, 2001).

Local politicians and officials did not fare any better in the general perception of the Romanian population. Many mayors and other local decision makers wielded powers that went much beyond those granted in the Law on Local Government Autonomy in 1991 (Verdery, 1996). Many ignored higher-level regulations, relied on local networks involving previous socialist cadres and channelled locally-raised revenues into their own and their allies' coffers (Mungiu-Pippidi, 2005; Verdery, 2002). In some cases, their actions took the form of local 'parasitism, barely controlled anarchy, and scavenging on the part of virtually everyone' (Verdery, 2003: 113).

Nevertheless, disorganized national politics and local nepotism did not seriously damage the authority the state enjoyed as an institution in the eyes of the Romanian population (Pop-Eleches, 2001; Tismaneanu and Kligman, 2001). In contrast to Albania, the Romanian state remained the sole politico-legal institution possessing authority. There were no politico-legal institutions that offered viable alternatives to the state. Customary arrangements, for instance, did not take on a role as significant as those in Albania (cf. Cartwright, 2000). Mafia-like networks, which had sprung up in the 1990s, did not form separate institutions which could contest the authority of the Romanian state, as they often penetrated state institutions. On the contrary, local power abuses and Mafia-like structures often worked to consolidate the authority of the Romanian state, understood as a set of abstract laws and procedures set apart from local officials' predatory practices (Verdery, 1996). People blamed individual politicians or the political leadership in power at any particular time, but did not question the idea of the state as the primary institution of authority.[2]

What was at stake, however, was the exercise of state authority. There was a wide range of political models available, ranging from the highly-personalized exercise of state authority under Ceausescu to the law-governed exercise built on a system of rules and procedures. The former gained visibility in the authoritarian leadership promoted by the ultranationalist leader Tudor, who won an astounding percentage of votes in the 1990 presidential elections (Hollis, 1999). The latter found increasing support under the Constantinescu government in the second half of the 1990s (Tismaneanu, 1997). The government instituted a series of reforms which sought to reduce the possibility of politicians and officials influencing the distribution of state

---

2. Another relevant factor was that Romanians did not enjoy the migration opportunities available to Albanians.

services to their own advantage (Pop, 2006). The move to a 'law-governed state' was associated with Romania's application for membership of the European Union. It eventually won accession in 2007, even though the process took the country somewhat longer than others in Central and Eastern Europe.

Property rights assumed a key role in the struggle between the personalized and the law-governed exercise of state authority (Verdery, 2003). The restitution of agricultural land and forests to their historical owners was one of the first legislative projects undertaken by the National Salvation Front in 1990 (Cartwright, 2001; Strimbu et al., 2005). Moreover, in an effort to achieve the broad support of the rural population, the government restricted the maximum areas of agricultural land and forest that individual owners could receive in the process. Ten years later, the Constantinescu government expanded the ceilings for the size of agricultural land and forest and mandated the restitution of collective and communal forests next to individually-owned forests. As a consequence, the share of Romanian forest in private ownership increased to 21 per cent in 2004 (National Forest Department, 2007).

The implementation of restitution played out the struggle between personalized and law-governed forms of exercising state authority. The initial reform provided considerable leverage to local land commissions, giving local power holders ample opportunity to influence the process and its outcomes (Verdery, 1996, 1999, 2002). Yet over time, the central government imposed increasingly stringent rules on the management of private and communal forests. For example, the Forestry Code (Law 26/1996) imposed tight controls on forest owners, individual or communal, to be executed by Romania's National Forest Department. The Code also provided the legal foundations for a body of armed forest guards with policy-like powers, widely known as *armata verde* (green army) in Romania.

Thus, Albania and Romania divested themselves of socialism and moved into post-socialism along different paths. Albania experienced a serious crisis of state authority, as reflected in two major outbreaks of violence and the widespread emergence of customary arrangements. The Romanian state also faced a problem of legitimacy, but it was far from the radical challenge to authority encountered by the Albanian state.[3] In Romania, contestations over authority centred on the struggle between personalized and law-governed exercise of state authority. Control over property was a central arena in which these contestations took place in both countries, yet their governments pursued different strategies to assert control. Albanian governments sought to retain forests under state ownership, while Romania's governments restored a fifth of the country's forests to private actors.

---

3. Romania also experienced outbreaks of violence, but these were much smaller and did not challenge the state in the sense of a politico-legal institution (Gledhill, 2005).

LOCAL FOREST POLITICS

This section uses the four local case studies to examine the processes constituting property and authority regarding forest on the ground as these are conditioned by and feed back into national-level politics. We begin with the two cases from Albania.

Kodra (Albania): The Emergence of Customary Property and Authority

Kodra is a thriving village located close to the road connecting Tirana with the town of Korça.[4] The village's population has remained stable at around 1,000 since 1990, unlike many other villages in rural Albania that have experienced significant out-migration. People have stayed in Kodra because farming, and off-farm jobs in nearby Pogradec, afford them a secure livelihood basis. As for forest, Kodra's surroundings include some blocks of chestnut forest (*Castanea sativa*), chestnuts having long been prized as a specialty throughout Albania. Prior to collectivization, households from the village used to consider these forests their own. The socialist regime expropriated them, however, putting the forest under the control of the Directorate General of Forests in 1966.

Kodra was not left untouched by the general turmoil taking hold of Albania at the breakdown of the socialist regime in 1991. As elsewhere in Albania, some villagers from Kodra set out to destroy major assets held by the agricultural co-operative and state organs. Alone and in small groups, they sneaked out at night to dismantle the irrigation system and loot the animal shelters. They also cut down most of the fruit trees that villagers had planted under the co-operative and sold the valuable wood, through middlemen, to Greece. They also cut down significant portions of the chestnut forests, which remained in state ownership and were managed by the District Forest Service.

These actions were not merely attempts by individual villagers in Kodra to gain access to co-operative and state assets. Neither were they random acts of violence caused by villagers' frustration with the socialist regime. Rather, the actions also reflected the conscious desire to unmake socialist property. As villagers explain today, some people engaged in these acts of destruction to eliminate the possibility that the socialist regime would recover and assert control over agriculture and forestry once again. By cutting down 'communist trees' and destroying co-operative buildings, they wanted to erase key objects of value upon which the state's claims to rural resources had rested. If these pillars no longer existed, they thought, there would be no way for the state to regain control over production.

---

4. Kodra is a pseudonym, as are the other village and personal names used in this chapter.

Yet there was also another type of reaction to the situation: villagers undertook individual and collective efforts to save some assets that they thought might be of value in the coming years. Some villagers decided to patrol patches of chestnut forest and/or camp out in them at night as a way to keep loggers away. They targeted the patches of forest that they or their parents had owned prior to collectivization. They felt that they continued to possess rights to the forest, and that now was the time to assert their rights before the forest was cut down by other people. Villagers also engaged in collective efforts to assert their claims to chestnut forests. In 1991, the village council pressed claims on a block of chestnut forest against the neighbouring village of Arrat in reaction to logging activities undertaken by people from the latter village. The council argued that Kodra should receive exclusive rights to the chestnut forest because it had been used only by families from Kodra prior to collectivization. The village council eventually succeeded in its efforts, but not before the loggers from Arrat had cut down most of the trees.

In this way, Kodra's villagers engaged in significant property-making efforts following the demise of the socialist regime. They were not satisfied with gaining access to the chestnut forests surrounding their village; they also sought to legitimize their claims with reference to historical rights. In 1992, Kodra's people asserted control over three more patches of chestnut forest located in the immediate vicinity of the village. They proclaimed that the forests were no longer in state ownership but now belonged to Kodra. Kodra had a right to the forests because villagers had possessed proprietary rights to them prior to collectivization. The villagers did not seek any endorsement from the state of their specific claims. The District Forest Service, in turn, did not initiate any action either in support of or in opposition to Kodra's claims. Asked about the event, a forest officer explained in 2004 that the Service was 'too busy' protecting forest in other areas.

The villagers based their claims on the legitimacy attributed to historical rights. Historical rights were also the defining criterion that the village used to allocate parcels of chestnut forest to individual households. As the village elders still remembered the old borders, they had little problem pointing out what household was entitled to which parcel of forest on the basis of historical patterns. It was also no problem that, after more than thirty years of collectivization, many original families who claimed rights to chestnut parcels had grown into extended families (*fis*). In such cases the extended families divided the parcels among all member households in an egalitarian manner. As a result, households received an average of 0.3 ha, the largest parcels measuring 1 ha. About 40 per cent of all households did not receive any chestnut trees in the process, as they could not claim historical rights. This inequality did not diminish the general acceptance of restitution, however, as virtually all villagers recognized the legitimacy of historical claims.

These insights, we suggest, show that Kodra's villagers made a significant effort to unmake socialist property and develop new property relations in 1991 and 1992. The new property relations were customary in the sense that they emerged from villagers' practices and reflected their notions of which kinds of claims were legitimate and which were not. Kodra's property relations *vis-à-vis* chestnut forest therefore resembled the customary property relations regarding agricultural land in Albania's northern mountains described by de Waal (2004). The property relations stood in contrast to the legislation and regulations of the Albanian state, in particular the state's claims of forest ownership, control over forest access by way of the concession system, and mandate to oversee the restitution process.

As a consequence, we find that property making in Kodra was intimately connected with the reconfiguration of authority relations. As forest property became defined in customary ways, authority shifted from the state towards custom. The state was no longer a significant institution authorizing claims to forest as property. It was replaced by custom as the primary institution endorsing forest claims as legitimate. Custom possessed sufficient authority to back up villagers' property rights against competing claims. In this way, authority relations regarding forest in Kodra reflected and simultaneously contributed to the emergence of custom witnessed across Albania as discussed above.[5]

Bagëtia (Albania): At the Frontiers of Property, State and Custom

Compared to Kodra, Bagëtia is located near much richer forest resources, as it is adjacent to immense old-growth oak and beech forests in the Qafë Panje and Guri Nikes Forest Sector. During socialism, the Forest Sector was intensively used, managed and controlled by Albania's General Directorate of Forests. Many villagers from Bagëtia and surrounding villages worked there as woodcutters and guards or in the timber yards. Qafë Panje also supplied the co-operatives of Bagëtia and other villages with firewood and timber. Yet today, the gravel road connecting the village to the lowlands has become impassable. Bagëtia's population has drastically dropped over the same period, from 350 in 1991 to 99 in 2004. Many people have left permanently, seeking employment in Greece. The remaining villagers live on remittances, seasonal labour migration, state assistance and livestock production.

Like their peers in Kodra, the villagers of Bagëtia claimed property rights to the forests surrounding their village in the early 1990s. They asserted that they should be the only ones entitled to exploit the forests, as they

---

5. We emphasize that this finding refers to authority with regard to forest property and does not apply to general authority relations in Kodra. As we discuss elsewhere (Stahl and Sikor, forthcoming), the sanctioning offered by custom for claims to agricultural land was weaker.

had possessed proprietary rights to these prior to collectivization. They marked their claims by spraying warnings on trees and rocks all over the claimed territory, such as 'Property of Bagëtia' (*Prona e Bagëties!*) or 'Don't touch Bagëtia's forest!' (*Mos prek pyllin e Bagëties!*). As in Kodra, their claims were ignored by the District Forest Service. The Service continued to issue concessions to traders from the lowlands for the exploitation of the forest.

Starting with the general turmoil of 1997, an ever-growing number of people from the entire region became involved in logging the forests. Every summer, when the dirt roads dried up, large numbers of woodcutters went up the mountain to cut timber and firewood. By 2004, there were many individual woodcutters from Bagëtia and other villages who cut down trees with their own chainsaws and transported the logs using horses or mules out to the roads. There were also logging crews consisting of four to six young men. Both kinds of loggers sold to wood traders without concessions, who typically owned a single truck and distributed the wood to households in the lowlands. Finally, there were six logging companies that had obtained concessions from the District Forest Service in a tendering process.

Individual woodcutters and concessionaires not only sought to gain access to the forests of Qafë Panje and Guri Nikes but also asserted the legitimacy of their claims. The woodcutters argued that they had problems making ends meet and relied on the income gained from woodcutting for their subsistence. Or, as an elderly man yelled at a forest guard who asked him to stop extracting wood: 'Do you think we came here for fun? We came here because we have to eat!'. Everybody, woodcutters reasoned, should have the right to ensure a secure livelihood. In contrast, the concessionaires based their claims on the fact that they had followed the legal stipulations for forest exploitation. They had participated in the tendering process and placed the highest bid. Yet they also took out higher volumes of wood than permitted by the Service on a habitual basis.

The Service turned a blind eye to the common practice of the concessionaires of violating the conditions of their licences; nor did it make any serious effort to stop the activities of individual woodcutters. In the latter case, the subsistence argument carried some weight with forest officials. The director of the District Forest Service, for example, admitted frankly: 'In the past the Directorate has been a bit lax with loggers around Bagëtia because we know that they are poor and need the forest as a livelihood source'. On the ground, woodcutters did not have to fear detection. If they were approached by a forest guard, they could settle the issue with a small bribe.

In contrast, the Forest Service did make serious efforts to stop unlicensed wood trade, or 'organized contraband' in forest officers' language. For instance, on one day in August 2004, the Service initiated a concerted action involving all nine forest guards and the director, fining illegal loggers in Qafë Panje and confiscating a huge volume of wood. This action was part of a broader campaign to deter unlicensed wood trade. Although lack of staff and vehicles limited the means available to the Service, it at least tried to heighten the perceived risk of detection. 'Fear guards the graveyard', the director of the Service explained.

Nevertheless, keeping unlicensed traders out of the forest was no easy feat and was sometimes even dangerous. In one case, in 2004, a forest guard was physically attacked when he tried to fine an unlicensed trader. The trader simply jumped out of his truck and pushed the guard into the ditch next to the road. In another case, a high-ranking forest officer caught a young trader driving a truck full of firewood without the necessary paperwork. The case was crystal clear according to the law, yet never resulted in any fine, as a mutual friend resolved the matter over large quantities of *raki* (locally distilled liquor).

Thus, the forests of Qafë Panje and Guri Nikes represented a frontier, not only in the sense of a rush on economic riches but also in the sense of the ongoing formation of property relations. Many actors enjoyed access to the forests, and the majority of them asserted their property rights. The rights claimed by the concessionaires on the basis of forest regulations existed side by side with the customary rights declared by woodcutters and villagers. At the same time, the latter adhered to different notions of customary rights: rights of subsistence equally shared by rural Albanians versus the historical rights held by local residents. In addition, while many actors enjoyed access and/or use rights, it was virtually impossible for any of them to exclude competing claims.

The forests were also at the frontiers of state and custom because authority relations had not gravitated towards a clear centre. The District Forest Service possessed neither the capacity (in terms of staff and vehicles) nor the legitimacy to make woodcutters and traders comply with state regulations. Custom, in turn, did not take the form of an institution that is clearly recognizable and generally considered legitimate, as in Kodra. Custom instead offered people a very ambiguous point of reference for making claims on forests, legitimizing historical rights as well as more broadly-shared subsistence rights. Authority relations in the forests around Bagëtia, therefore, appeared highly diffuse, similar to what de Waal (2004) describes regarding agricultural land in the plains near Tirana. In this way, authority over forest in Bagëtia reflected the kinds of processes underlying national-level challenges to the Albanian state discussed above.

Dragomireşti (Romania): Unravelling Property but not the State

Dragomireşti is a commune of worker-peasants in Arges County, Romania. Many people from Dragomireşti used to work in the nearby Dacia car plant. The commune's population of 2,850 remained relatively stable after 1991, when people dismantled the agricultural collective and took up subsistence farming to complement their salaries, pensions and social assistance payments. The large forests surrounding the commune gained special significance as the timber represented assets of significant value. Before their nationalization under socialism, the locals or their parents had owned a large share of these forests in the form of individual and collective holdings.

After the demise of socialism, the villagers received a significant portion of the forests surrounding Dragomireşti. In 1993, the State Forest Department restored a patch of 172 ha to the villagers, in accordance with Law 18. Initially, this restituted forest was used collectively, as the mayor's office was reluctant to divide it amongst individuals. Forest use was monitored by a forest guard paid by the mayor's office, according to the regulations issued by the State Forest Department. But in 1997, in response to a request by the majority of villagers, the mayor's office divided the forest patch up into individual holdings and dismissed the forest guard. Villagers had not been pleased with the perceived limits imposed on their newly-acquired ownership rights to forest. 'It is my forest', many argued; 'why does the state regulate how the forest should be used when the forest belongs to *me*?'. A few years later, in 2002, the people's forest holdings increased by another 428 ha as Law 1/2000 expanded the ceiling on forests eligible for restitution.

However, one particular group missed out on forest restitution completely: ethnic Rudari, an ethnic group often considered to be a sub-group of the Roma. Although they had lived in the area and worked in its forests for many generations, the small group of Rudari living in Dragomireşti received neither forest nor agricultural land in the post-socialist land reform. According to the law, they were not entitled to benefit from restitution because they had not owned any land or forest prior to collectivization. At the same time, it was the same Rudari who took to the forests starting in 2003. They no longer restricted their exploitation of the forest to firewood and underbrush as in the 1990s but went for valuable timber. The logging involved simple woodcutters, some with horse carts for the transport of the wood out of the forest, and a few more powerful men with trucks. The latter transported the wood on commission for wholesalers or sold it directly to buyers in southern Romania.

The logging also involved a few ethnic Romanian patrons, who possessed at least as much power over the Rudari woodcutters as the Rudari big men. These included the staff of the mayor's office, the local police and the forest guards employed by the State Forest Department to protect the forests remaining in state ownership. For obvious reasons, the guards were particularly feared by the Rudari, who considered them to be 'worse than dogs' (*pădurarii sunt mai răi ca câinii*). Similarly, the local policemen were an object of constant concern, as the Rudari depended on them turning a blind eye to the illegal wood trade and protecting them from prosecution by other police units. The staff in the mayor's office, in turn, wielded significant power over them by disbursing the social assistance payments, allowing them to use communal land, and deciding whether or not to report the trucks owned by Rudari patrons to the tax authorities.

The Romanian patrons used their power to exact favours from the Rudari. A forest guard received free wood supplies from Rudari for his private wood-processing business. The policemen regularly received bribes for their protection services. More importantly, the forest guards used their power to direct the Rudari to specific private forest holdings where they could cut timber and incur low risk of detection by the owner. The Rudari logging, in turn, allowed the staff in the mayor's office, the forest guards and village policemen to advise forest owners to sell their timber to them at a low price 'because the Rudari will cut it anyway'. They also helped forest owners to arrange deals with companies, receiving a small payment from the owner and a large commission from the company for the brokerage.

How did forest owners react to the logging? Many blamed it on the Rudari. Mobilizing long-held ethnic stereotypes, they were convinced that the Rudari could not do anything else but encroach on forest owned by others. Many even declared that the Rudari 'should be killed since they are not good for anything else but stealing our forest'. Nevertheless, some villagers undertook actions against the predatory practices of local state officials, turning to other entities of the state in search of support. For instance, a forest owner sued the local bookkeeper in 2004, after the bookkeeper had tipped off some Rudari about the pending sale of timber to an outside company. The Rudari had logged over the forest before the owner could initiate any action against them. In another instance two years later, a newspaper reported that the county police had caught a policeman as he exacted bribes from Rudari woodcutters in return for his 'protection'.

These observations tell us that the villagers of Dragomireşti devoted considerable attention to their newly-acquired property rights to forest in the 1990s. To them, property meant not only the right to exploit an important economic asset but also a departure from the restrictions on their productive activities and personal lives imposed by the socialist regime. The language of private ownership was highly seductive to them, as it promised unlimited freedom in the pursuit of assets. Yet the actions of the Rudari and Romanian patrons unravelled their property rights. Despite having ownership rights, many villagers did not derive significant economic benefit from them. Much of the value contained in Dragomireşti's forest accrued to the logging companies that purchased timber cheaply, the Romanian patrons receiving favours and commissions, and the Rudari big men.

Nevertheless, we also note that the unravelling of property rights to forest in Dragomireşti did not diminish the authority that the Romanian state — understood as a politico-legal institution — enjoyed in villagers' minds. From their perspective, both the formation of property relations in the 1990s and their unravelling in the early 2000s served to reconstitute the authority of the post-socialist state on a new basis. This basis rested on the positive notions villagers attached to private ownership and the need for the state to enforce ownership rights. In this way, the predatory practices of local officials actually served to enhance the legitimacy of the Romanian state in the eyes of the local population, as Verdery (1996: 213–5) notes in her discussion of land reform. This legitimacy accrued to the state as a politico-legal institution — or idea (Abrams 1988) — set apart from the concrete practices of its agents. It also referred to a state that exercises its authority by way of abstract rules and procedures, distinguishing such a law-governed exercise clearly from local officials' attempts to personalize it. In this way, local struggles over forests in Dragomireşti played out the contestations over the exercise of state authority discussed above.

Dragova (Romania): Manipulating Property, Transforming the State

Dragova is a commune of three villages and 1,100 people in the mountainous part of Arges County, Romania. Its residents used to own a large part of the surrounding rich forests individually, communally and as a collective, before nationalization. Agricultural production was never collectivized in the commune, which was quite common in villages concentrating on animal husbandry. Animal husbandry, trade and some tourism provided relatively high incomes under socialism. After 1990, tourism gradually became the dominant source of income.

The people from Dragova received larger forestland holdings in the restitution process than their peers in Dragomireşti. In the village located in the commune centre alone, 145 households received 1 ha of forest each in 1993 in accordance with Law 18, and another 277 ha in 2003 as a consequence of Law 1/2000. In addition, they gained joint ownership over a forest of 300 ha on the basis of a forest that they had collectively owned before 1948. Together with people from the other two villages in Dragova commune they gained the rights to a communal forest of 70 ha, to be managed by the mayor's office. Furthermore, a number of households acquired 500 ha in 2005 as part of a forest they had collectively owned with families from neighbouring communes in the past.

The villagers set out to exercise their newly-acquired statutory rights. Some took to the forest themselves, using chainsaws to cut logs and horses to transport the logs to the road. Many, however, contracted a local logging company for the harvest. The company had begun operations in 1993, the same year in which villagers received their first forest parcels. It started out as a small venture, building on the skills and networks its owners had acquired as managers in the local tourism co-operative under socialism. Later, when operations increased in volume, the company purchased trucks, using them to transport the logs to their own furniture factory or to sell them directly to buyers abroad.

The company benefited from close relations with the mayor's office, as it was formally owned by the wife of the man who became the local mayor in 1996. The mayor made sure to provide his wife with an advantage at timber auctions of the communal forest wood, so that her company's bids were always successful at the auctions. The mayor also pushed a decision through the commune council to increase the volume extracted from the communal forest as a way of financing the upgrading of the local road. Furthermore, thanks to his position he was always informed about the actions of the regional and national branches of the Ministry of Agriculture and Forestry, which helped his wife's company to engage in illegal logging and employment practices without risk of detection.

The mayor also used his position as head of the local land commission to influence the second round of forest restitution in 2003 to his wife's advantage, in several ways. First, the mayor arranged for the restitution of rich, accessible forest to some villagers, requesting them to sell at least half of the standing timber to his wife's company at low cost. Second, he used persuasion, force and trickery to get the local land commission to allocate forest to some villagers, even though they could not claim any historical rights. Again, he made sure that the beneficiaries would return the favour by selling at least half of their standing timber to his wife's company at a low price. Third, the mayor manipulated the restitution of the collective forest to the group of households from the commune. He wielded his influence on the land commission to shrink the area of forest restored to the families. The difference between the claimed and actually restituted area offered the mayor the necessary manoeuvring space to arrange for the allocation of forest parcels to villagers without historical rights, once again exacting preferential sales to his wife's company in exchange.

The mayor expended significant economic and political resources to ensure his re-election in 2004. He arranged for the allocation of some forest to people from his own village in Dragova commune, although they could not assert any historical rights. This move won him critical votes in the upcoming election. In addition, he sought to portray himself as a local benefactor and powerful broker between Dragova and the outside world, investing some of the profits from his wife's logging business. He distributed free basic food items to old people. He invited the President of the Romanian Parliament to visit the commune. He promised to get funds from the European Union to improve the road connecting Dragova with surrounding villages. He also promised villagers that he would protect them against attempts by adjacent Piatra Craiului National Park to restrict their forest rights. His outside contacts left a strong impression on the local population, as noted by a middle-aged man: 'All the people from this village know that he is well-known in central government as well.'

The actions of the mayor and his wife thus influenced property relations in two ways. First, as in Dragomireşti, they unravelled property as a key influence in the distribution of forest values. The benefits derived from ownership titles were diminished because the mayor and his wife controlled the timber business, including the logging, transport, trade, and some processing. Second, the mayor manipulated the restitution process in favour of his wife's company. His manipulation not only increased the volume of timber available for extraction but also ensured the company made high profits from it. People in Dragova saw the connection between the mayor's practices and the declining value of their rights very clearly. In contrast to Dragomireşti, there were no Rudari to serve as scapegoats for logging in Dragova. The obvious villains were the mayor and his wife.

The mayor reacted to this problem by moving towards a personalized style in the way he managed communal affairs. In addition, he sought to 'capture' not only the local state (cf. Mungiu-Pippidi, 2005) but also the state understood as a politico-legal institution. In contrast to the local officials in Dragomireşti, the mayor spent much effort enhancing his legitimacy in local people's eyes. As part of this, he made sure to enlist the support of higher state organs, not allowing any cleavages between himself and other state actors. These manoeuvres made local people believe that 'if you fight him you fight the state'. That 'state', therefore, took on a very different meaning for villagers in Dragova in comparison with their peers in Dragomireşti. Just as in the other village, state practices reflected the struggle between personalized and law-governed forms of exercising state authority discussed in the section on Romanian politics above. Yet unlike the other village, the mayor's practices and the villagers' reactions strengthened the influence of personalized exercise in Dragova.

CONCLUSIONS

The four cases indicate the broader social dynamics affecting forests in post-socialist Central and Eastern Europe. There is nothing short of a mad scramble for access to forests, as forests represent one of the few valuable assets remaining in rural areas. Various kinds of actors engage in a rush on the forest as they fear that they will lose out if they let others make the first move. For this reason, they attempt to gain, maintain and control access to forests in different ways. Many actors focus their energy on property by either asserting their own claims or influencing the recognition of other claims. Some actors display little concern with property and instead concentrate on gaining access to forests in other ways. Some participate in, or control, timber logging, transport and trade, while others take advantage of their state positions to get a share of forest benefits. As these actors negotiate access and property regarding forest they constantly make and unmake property relations.

These cases show that negotiations over access and property regarding forest are intimately linked with contestations over authority at the local and national levels. More broadly, property constitutes a primary field in which post-socialist states — understood both as social institutions and sets of concrete practices undertaken by multiple state actors — have sought to reassert authority and move its exercise to new foundations. Nevertheless, property reforms and the emphasis they give to statutory property rights and the law-governed exercise of state authority have been contested by competing claims of property and authority regarding forest. Underlying these contestations are two distinct dynamics. On the one hand, state actors exercise authority by way of different practices, thus offering support to different sets of claims on forests. As illustrated by the manoeuvres of Dragova's mayor, local state actors are clever at drawing on personalized traits to circumvent laws and procedures about property. On the other hand, post-socialist states face competition by other politico-legal institutions such as customary arrangements. State and custom offer local actors competing authorizations for claims on forests. Custom itself, like the state, emerges as a somewhat ambiguous institution that supports multiple and often competing claims on forests.

As a result, we find significant variations in the specific processes establishing, modifying and diminishing property and authority. On the one hand, there is the frontier-like situation in Bagëtia, where various kinds of actors assert use rights to forests on the basis of multiple politico-legal institutions. In this situation authority relations have not gravitated towards a discernible centre. On the other hand, there are situations like those in Kodra and Dragomireşti, where people reference a relatively clear set of property rights to the rules and procedures of a single politico-legal institution. The authorized property rights take the form of statutory or customary rights, which in turn legitimize the state or custom as the primary politico-legal institution holding authority. There are also constellations of property and authority like those in Dragova, where authority may gravitate to a clear centre but is exercised in a personalized manner.

Despite the local variations, we detect systematic differences in property and authority regarding forest between the Albanian and Romanian cases. Statutory rights carry much more weight in Romania, as indicated by the Romanian government's concern to implement forestry reforms and local people's preoccupation with their statutory rights. The attention to statutory rights corresponds with the central role that the Romanian state assumes in authority relations. The central position of the Romanian state, in turn, may afford its local agents special leverage not only in property rights but also in access to forest by other means at a level unknown in Albania. In Albania, customary rights assume a surprising significance regarding forests, not only in our cases but also nationwide. This significance sets Albania apart from Romania, where local practices may be different from statutory law and regulations but do not form systematic bodies of customary rights (cf. Cartwright, 2000). Custom, in its varied incarnations, therefore, competes with the state over authority, challenging the state as the primary institution sanctioning property rights regarding forest and thereby setting struggles over forests in Albania apart from those taking place in Romania.

These insights on forests suggest the presence of larger differences in the dynamics of property and state between the two countries. Albania experienced a serious crisis of state authority in the 1990s. Although the government conferred ownership on forests to the state, the Directorate General of Forests and Pastures has not been able to enforce it. In addition, the Directorate ignores villagers' demands for it to recognize their customary property rights. Both factors weaken the authority of the Albanian state further as local people identify the state with the actions of its local agents. Weak state authority and ineffective state ownership reinforce each other, facilitating the emergence of custom as an alternative politico-legal institution contesting the authority of the state.

The connections between national politics and forest dynamics look different in Romania. National politics are characterized by contestations between personalized and law-governed forms of exercising state authority that are played out in local struggles over access and property regarding forest. Local state agents have implemented forest restitution, helping to establish the authority of the state in a new arena from the local people's perspective. Yet they have also manipulated restitution to their own advantage and created new avenues of access to forest for themselves, taking advantage of their positions in the local state. Their predatory practices feed into the national-level contestations over the exercise of state authority. On the one hand, they strengthen law-governed elements in the exercise of authority as long as people separate the state as a politico-legal institution from the practices undertaken by its local agents (Verdery, 1996). On the other, they foment personalized forms of exercising state authority if local people equate the state as a politico-legal institution with the predatory practices of local officials (Verdery, 2002).

Given this variation between local cases and between the two countries, what is post-socialist about the dynamics of property and authority examined in this contribution? One special element is that the reconstitutions of property and state have not only been radical in nature but have also reinforced each other. Of course, post-socialist property negotiations occur on massive scales unknown in other contexts (Verdery, 1999). Nonetheless, it is the *simultaneous* nature of negotiations over property *and* authority that has thrown property and authority relations up in the air (cf. Sturgeon and Sikor, 2004). The simultaneity facilitates local negotiations over property's extraordinary influence in emergent authority relations; it also creates special openings for contestations over authority to affect property relations. They challenge the very notions of statutory property rights and the state as social institutions, not just the distribution of property rights among social actors and the positions of specific state actors. In this way, they provide exceptional manoeuvring space to those social actors who command advantageous economic, political and cultural resources, giving them extraordinary leverage on emergent property and authority relations.

Nonetheless, we do not want to say that these dynamics of property and authority are unique to post-socialist settings. After all, people in the post-socialist countryside seem to share a fundamental experience with their peers in other settings characterized by radical reconstitutions of property and authority relations (see, for example, Berry, this volume). The promotion of private ownership turns out not to provide the expected miracle basis for a prosperous future. Expectations ran high in Central and Eastern Europe in the early 1990s. Many people thought that the move to ownership would help them to achieve important goals, such as economic efficiency, social equity and a western-style democracy. These expectations rested on two myths: first, that ownership clarifies and enhances the share of resource value derived by owners; and second, that ownership emerges through a state that sanctions it by way of legal acts and derives part of its authority from that. The massive decline in the resource value accruing to post-socialist owners has dispelled the first myth over the past decade (Sikor, 2006; Verdery, 2004a). The insights presented in this chapter dispel the second myth. The state is not the sole institution sanctioning property rights, nor do property relations necessarily strengthen state authority. The relationship between property and state cannot be taken for granted, but requires empirical investigation.

REFERENCES

Abdul-Hamid, Y. (2003) 'A Fair Deal for Albanian Farmers'. Oxfam Briefing Paper No 45. London: Oxfam.

Abrams, P. (1988) 'Notes on the Difficulty of Studying the State', *Journal of Historical Sociology* 1(1): 58–89.

Biberaj, E. (1998) *Albania in Transition: The Rocky Road to Democracy*. Boulder, CO: Westview Press.

Cartwright, A.L. (2000) 'State Law and the Recognition of Property in Rural Romania'. MPI Working Paper No 10. Halle: Max Planck Institute for Social Anthropology.

Cartwright, A.L. (2001) *The Return of the Peasant: Land Reform in Post-Communist Romania*. Aldershot: Ashgate.

Cellarius, B.A. (2004) '"Without Co-ops There Would Be No Forests!": Historical Memory and the Restitution of Forests in Post-socialist Bulgaria', *Conservation and Society* 2(1): 51–74.

Giordano, C. and D. Kostova (2002) 'The Social Production of Mistrust', in C.M. Hann (ed.) *Post-socialism: Ideals, Ideologies and Practices in Eurasia*, pp. 74–91. London and New York: Routledge.

Gledhill, J. (2005) 'States of Contention: State-Led Political Violence in Post-Socialist Romania', *East European Politics and Societies* 19(1): 76–104.

Grzymala-Busse, A. and P.J. Luong (2002) 'Reconceptualizing the State: Lessons from Post-Communism', *Politics & Society* 30(4): 529–54.

Hann, C.M. (1993) 'From Production to Property: Decollectivization and the Family-Land Relationship in Contemporary Hungary', *Man* 28(2): 299–320.

Hann, C.M. (2003) *The Post-Socialist Agrarian Question: Property Relations and the Rural Condition*. London and New Brunswick, NJ: LIT Verlag.

Hayden, R.M. (2002) 'Intolerant Sovereignties and "Multi-kulti" Protectorates: Competition over Religious Sites and (In)Tolerance in the Balkans', in C.M. Hann (ed.) *Post-socialism: Ideals, Ideologies and Practices in Eurasia*, pp. 159–79. London: Routledge.

Hollis, W. (1999) *Democratic Consolidation in Eastern Europe: The Influence of the Communist Legacy in Hungary, the Czech Republic, and Romania*. Boulder, CO: Eastern European Monographs.

Humphrey, C. (1995) 'The Politics of Privatization in Provincial Russia: Popular Opinions amid the Dilemmas of the Early 1990s', *Cambridge Anthropology* 18(1): 40–61.

Kaneff, D. (1996) 'Responses to "Democratic" Land Reforms in a Bulgarian Village', in R. Abrahams (ed.) *After Socialism: Land Reform and Social Change in Eastern Europe*, pp. 85–114. Oxford: Berghahn.

Kodderitzsch, S. (1999) 'Reforms in Albanian Agriculture'. Technical Paper No 431. Washington, DC: The World Bank.

Kurtz, M.J. and A. Barnes (2002) 'The Political Foundations of Post-Communist Regimes', *Comparative Political Studies* 35(5): 524–53.

Lastarria-Cornhiel, S. and R. Wheeler (1998) 'Gender, Ethnicity, and Landed Property in Albania'. Albanian Working Paper No 18. Madison, WI: University of Wisconsin, Land Tenure Center.

Mungiu-Pippidi, A. (2005) 'Reinventing the Peasants: Local State Capture in Post-Communist Europe', in S. Dorondel and S. Serban (eds) *Between East and West: Studies in Anthropology and Social History*, pp. 308–26. Bucharest: Editura Institutului Cultural Român.

National Forest Department (2007) 'Statistical Data on Romania's Forest Sector'. www.rosilva. ro. (accessed 22 March 2007).

Nicholson, B. (2003) 'Migrants as Agents of Development: Albanian Return Migrants and Micro-enterprise', *International Conference on Migrant Remittances* 1(1): 94–110.

Pop, L. (2006) *Democratising Capitalism? The Political Economy of Post-Communist Transformations in Romania, 1989–2001.* Manchester and New York: Manchester University Press.

Pop-Eleches, G. (1999) 'Separated at Birth or Separated by Birth? The Communist Successor Parties in Romania and Hungary', *East European Politics and Societies* 13(1): 117–46.

Pop-Eleches, G. (2001) 'Romania's Politics of Dejection', *Journal of Democracy* 12(3): 156–69.

Rapper, G. de and P. Sintes (2006) 'Composer Avec le Risque: La Frontiere Sud de l'Albane Entre Politique des Etats et Solidarites Locales' ('Accommodating Risk: Albania's Southern Border between State Policy and Local Solidarities'), *Revue d'Etudes Comparatives Est-Ouest* 37: 244–71.

Ribot, J. and N. Peluso (2003) 'A Theory of Access', *Rural Sociology* 68(2): 153–81.

Saltmarshe, D. (2001) *Identity in a Post-Communist Balkan State: An Albanian Village Study.* Aldershot: Ashgate.

Sikor, T. (2005) 'Rural Property and Agri-environmental Legislation in Central and Eastern Europe', *Sociologia Ruralis* 45(3): 187–201.

Sikor, T. (2006) 'Land as Asset, Land as Liability: Property Politics in Rural Central and Eastern Europe', in F. von Benda-Beckmann, K. von Benda-Beckmann and M. Wiber (eds) *Changing Properties of Property*, pp. 106–25. New York: Berghahn.

de Soto, H., P. Gordon, I. Gedeshi and Y. Sinoimeri (2002) 'Poverty in Albania: A Qualitative Assessment'. Technical Paper No 520. Washington, DC: The World Bank.

Staddon, C. (2000) 'Restitution of Forest Property in Post-Communist Bulgaria', *Natural Resources Forum* 24: 237–46.

Staddon, C. (2001a) 'Restructuring the Bulgarian Wood-Processing Sector: Linkages Between Resource Exploitation, Capital Accumulation, and Redevelopment in a Postcommunist Locality', *Environment and Planning A* 33: 607–28.

Staddon, C. (2001b) 'Local Forest Dependence in Postcommunist Bulgaria: A Case Study', *GeoJournal* 55(2-4): 517–28.

Stahl, J. and T. Sikor (forthcoming) 'Rural Property in an Age of Transnational Migration: Ethnic Divisions in Southeastern Albania', *Anthropologica*.

Stark, D. and L. Bruszt (1998) *Post-Socialist Pathways: Transforming Politics and Property in East Central Europe.* Cambridge: Cambridge University Press.

Strimbu, B.M., G.M. Hickey and V.G. Strimbu (2005) 'Forest Conditions and Management under Rapid Legislation Change in Romania', *The Forestry Chronicle* 81(3): 350–8.

Sturgeon, J. and T. Sikor (2004) 'Post-Socialist Property in Asia and Europe: Variations on "Fuzziness"', *Conservation and Society* 2(1): 1–17.

Tismaneanu, V. (1997) 'Romanian Exceptionalism? Democracy, Ethnocracy and Uncertain Pluralism in Post-Ceausescu Romania', in K. Dawisha and B. Parott (eds) *Politics, Power, and the Struggle for Democracy in South-East Europe*, pp. 403–51. Cambridge: Cambridge University Press.

Tismaneanu, V. and G. Kligman (2001) 'Romania's First Postcommunist Decade: From Iliescu to Iliescu', *East European Constitutional Review* 10(1) (Internet publication). http://www1. law.nyu.edu/eecr/vol10num1/features/romaniafirstpostcomdecade.html

Verdery, V. (1996) *What Was Socialism? And What Comes Next?* Princeton, NJ: Princeton University Press.

Verdery, K. (1999) 'Fuzzy Property: Rights, Power, and Identity in Transylvania's Decollectivization', in M. Burawoy and K. Verdery (eds) *Uncertain Transition: Ethnographies of Change in the Post-socialist World*, pp. 53–81. Lanham, MD: Rowman & Littlefield.

Verdery, K. (2002) 'Seeing like a Mayor: Or, How Local Officials Obstructed Romanian Land Restitution', *Ethnography* 3(1): 5–33.

Verdery, K. (2003) *The Vanishing Hectare: Property and Value in Post-Socialist Transylvania.* Ithaca, NY: Cornell University Press.

Verdery, K. (2004a) 'The Obligations of Ownership: Restoring Rights to Land in Postsocialist Transylvania', in K. Verdery and C. Humphrey (eds) *Property in Question. Value Transformation in the Global Economy*, pp. 139–59. Oxford and New York: Berg.

Verdery, K. (2004b). 'The Property Regime of Socialism', *Conservation and Society* 2(1): 189–98.

Vickers, M. and J. Pettifer (1997) *Albania: From Anarchy to a Balkan Identity.* London: Hurst & Company.

Voell, S. (2003) 'The Kanun in the City: Albanian Customary Law as a Habitus and its Persistence in the Suburb of Tirana, Bathore', *Anthropos* 98: 85–101.

de Waal, C. (1998) 'From Laissez-Faire to Anarchy in Post-Communist Albania', *Cambridge Anthropology* 20(3): 21–44.

de Waal, C. (2004) 'Post-socialist Property Rights and Wrongs in Albania: An Ethnography of Agrarian Change', *Conservation and Society* 2(1): 19–50.

9

Property and Authority in a Migrant Society: Balinese Irrigators in Sulawesi, Indonesia

Dik Roth

INTRODUCTION

In recent years the role of property rights to natural resources in processes of rural transformation has enjoyed rapidly growing scientific and policy attention. This is primarily evidenced by the booming literature on common property. Studies on common property have directed attention to local definitions of rights and responsibilities, and to the importance of local resource management practices and institutions. This has yielded a more empirically based understanding of resource use and management, in which local resource users are no longer by definition the perpetrators of the 'tragedy of the commons'. This in turn opened up new options for institutional solutions to management problems.

However, according to critics, this new focus also has its price. Mosse (1997) has criticized both the mainstream approach based on rational choice theory and institutional economics (for example, Ostrom, 1992) and approaches based on 'moral economy' thinking (stressing the importance of social norms and traditions in collective action) for oversimplifying complex realities. Both overemphasize local autonomy, neglecting the state; both are a-historical and biased to economic thinking; and both reduce institutions to socially homogeneous entities. According to Johnson (2004), the normative focus in common property studies on sustainable management, rational choice, and incentives and institutions for collective action is not conducive to a deeper social and historical understanding of property rights. Agrawal (2003: 257) suggests that common property theorists have, 'in their preoccupation with sustainable management and successful institutions', paid too little attention to the role of coercion and enforcement, of power relationships, conflict and competing institutions.

Property can itself be analysed as a social institution (Bruns et al., 2005; Meinzen-Dick and Pradhan, 2001). This brings us to the way institutions are often dealt with in common property literature. The literature inspired by institutional economics is also rule-focused, normative, and driven by instrumental ambitions of 'crafting institutions' (Ostrom, 1992) for efficient management (Agrawal and Gibson, 1999; Mosse, 1997). Complex property relationships, competing claims, and legitimizing legal systems are often presented as unambiguous and uncontested. Policy recipes recommend 'getting the rules in place' by using the neo-institutionalist toolkit of creating the right incentives and reducing transaction costs. However, rather than a stable and uncontested core of institutions, the 'rules of the game' or 'rules in use' often referred to (for example, Ostrom and Schlager, 1996) can be the very focus of contestation.[1]

Alternative approaches — often based in social anthropological research rather than institutional economics — focus on the social and cultural 'glue' of institutions rather than on rules, instrumentalities and economic rationality. For their functioning, institutions need the socially, culturally and morally binding forces and qualities of specific societal contexts (Jentoft, 2004). This surplus value is often taken to be the core characteristic that distinguishes institutions from organizations. This brings us close to approaches to property rights that stress the importance of taking into account their socially and otherwise 'embedded' character (Hann, 1998; McCay, 2002; McCay and Jentoft, 1998). Thus, McCay (2002) stresses that property is not only about valuable goods but also about meaning, identity, power and competing rights and claims. Hann (1998: 5) approaches property as 'directing attention to a vast field of cultural as well as social relations, to the symbolic as well as the material contexts within which things are recognized and personal as well as collective identities made'. It is important to stress that 'embeddedness' does not presuppose the stability, unity and homogeneity so often taken for granted in community-based approaches (Agrawal and Gibson, 1999). Embeddedness may be a source of coherence as well as of competition and conflict. Assuming too much 'glue' and too little contestation and conflict here would make such approaches liable to Agrawal and Gibson's (1999) and Mosse's (1997) critique of idealizing approaches to common property, community and collective action.

Vandergeest and Peluso (1995) have directed our attention to the role of the state and state strategies of territorialization. In local settings of resource use and management such strategies, aimed at greater control over people and resources, may create conflicts of authority, legitimacy and power between different enforcing institutions (ibid.). We have to deal, then, not only with the management instrumentalities of 'getting the institutions right' but with resource management as a field of tensions between the abstract or disembedded space of state territorialization in the domain of natural resources, and resources as embedded in local society, lived and experienced by local resource users.

Empirical research on property rights in relation to such processes of institutional competition over legitimate authority is badly needed. It should start from a contextualized understanding of how institutions are embedded in society. This includes the role of religious and cultural notions and practices as the 'glue' of such institutions (see Hotimsky et al., 2006), but also of competition and conflicts over power, authority and legitimacy within and between institutional/organizational arrangements. Second, these need

1. More refined approaches to institutions and institutional design take into account factors like the plurality of sources of legitimacy (e.g. Bruns et al., 2005), the socio-cultural embeddedness of property rights (e.g. Schlager, 2006), and the importance of attention to ontological and methodological aspects (Hotimsky et al., 2006).

to be related to the specific ways in which property rights to resources are established, defined and redefined in the dynamic resource use context being researched.

This chapter focuses on the relations between property rights and competition for legitimacy between different (state and non-state) sources of power and authority in a migrant society of Balinese cultivators of irrigated rice in Luwu District, South Sulawesi, Indonesia (see Figure 1).[2] Increased mobility and inter-regional migration by various population groups play an important role in property transformations. These processes may give property rights and their transformations specific and plural characteristics of ethno-religious identity, norms and values, and knowledge and experience. The increasing diversity of population groups in a region like Luwu creates legally and institutionally plural ways of dealing with property. Focusing on property in a migrant society allows for research on the 'reinvention' of property and on the role of 'mobile' values, norms and rule systems in this process (see also von Benda-Beckmann et al., 2005).

The chapter analyses a history of plural definitions of property rights, of ways of dealing institutionally with management, and socially organizing around property. These are explored in a setting of government intervention and regulation of irrigation management which has public, private and common property characteristics (see Meinzen-Dick, 2000). As these domains are complex and overlapping, there tends to be little clarity and much disagreement about 'the rules', the bundles of rights and responsibilities. Property rights are claimed, negotiated, defined and contested by social actors at various levels of organization (Zwarteveen et al., 2005: 257). In this case it is not so much access and claims to resources *per se* that are contested, but rather the legitimacy of state and non-state sources of authority. Which bodies of rules are seen as legitimate? Which rights and responsibilities apply to which case? Who has legitimate decision-making power? In-depth analysis of these issues requires a perspective that starts from a broad conception of law taking into account the plural character of legal regulation and its close relationship to the social, political and cultural dimensions of life; that approaches property rights in land, water and irrigation infrastructure as 'bundles' of rights and responsibilities ('goods' and 'bads' of property; see Verdery and Humphrey, 2004); and that takes into account the 'layered' character of property relationships (von Benda-Beckmann et al., 2006).[3]

---

2. This chapter is based on research carried out in 1996–97, shortly before the (1998) political changes in Indonesia that led to the fall of Soeharto's 'New Order' regime, and during another short period in 1999. Names of individuals have been changed.
3. In other publications I have dealt with the relationships between technical, normative and organizational dimensions of irrigation management (Roth, 2005), and with aspects of 'order' and 'disjuncture' pertaining to interventions for irrigation development (Roth, 2006).

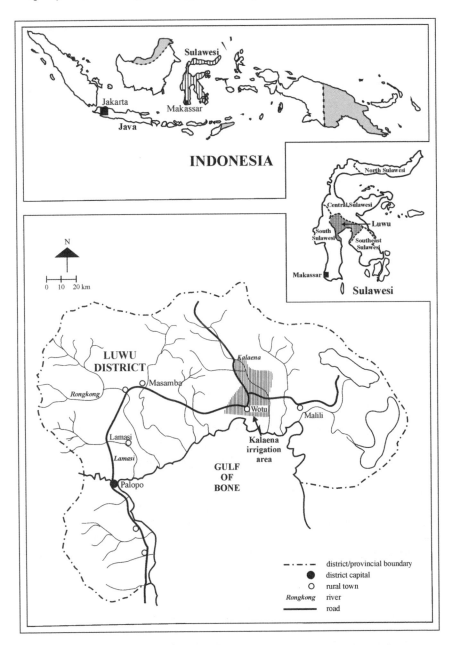

Figure 1. Indonesia, Sulawesi, Luwu and the Kalaena Irrigation Area

The following section describes the context of the case study and discusses how state-allocated resources are given meaning by Balinese migrants. This is followed by a more specific discussion of the rights and responsibilities attached to state-allocated land, water and irrigation infrastructure. Here, I focus on the relationships developing between the Balinese irrigators' association, *subak*, reinvented in a migrant setting, and the state-introduced water users' associations (WUAs) of the tertiary irrigation units (TUs), including the property rights dimension and consequences for local management practices. The subsequent section illustrates the contested character of both WUA and *subak* by focusing on the role of Balinese identity in an ethnically mixed tertiary irrigation unit and on the diverging interpretations of legitimate *subak* authority in Balinese society. Finally, a brief conclusion relates the insights from the case study to the main theme of transformations of property rights.

FROM STATE-ALLOCATED RESOURCES TO 'EMBEDDED PROPERTY'

The Setting: Luwu District, South Sulawesi

Luwu is a large district in South Sulawesi Province.[4] The North Luwu Plain is particularly suitable for irrigation development. From the 1930s, Luwu became a destination for the Dutch 'colonization' programme through which farmers from Java were resettled.[5] The main objectives of the programme were poverty alleviation and the reduction of population density in Java and Bali, the economic development of the archipelago, and greater colonial control over both population and resources. The programme aimed at creating rural settlements based on irrigated agriculture, using Javanese and Balinese farmers' experience. In northern Luwu, the Dutch combined resettlement of Javanese with the construction of irrigation systems.

After independence, the Indonesian transmigration programme continued this policy. From the 1960s to the 1990s (when the programme stopped with the demise of the 'New Order' regime of former president Soeharto), thousands of farmer families from Java and Bali were resettled in Luwu.[6]

---

4. Recently Luwu was split up into the districts of Luwu, North Luwu, and East Luwu. As this is not relevant to the topics discussed here, I continue using 'Luwu'.
5. Dutch resettlement of Balinese took place on other islands. Note that 'colonization' means pioneer settlement here, not colonial rule (although it was, of course, crucially based on colonial conceptions of political order, economic development, and resource exploitation).
6. State-sponsored transmigration resettled Javanese and Balinese farmers on major islands like Sumatra, Kalimantan and Sulawesi, which were characterized by a relatively low population density and extensive forms of agriculture like shifting cultivation, and which were inhabited by a variety of ethnic groups. The programme has rightly been criticized for its negative ecological, economic, social, political and human rights effects (especially on ethnic minorities).

In the twentieth century the population of Luwu increased rapidly under the influence of colonial resettlement, transmigration and regional migration. Regional migrants, attracted by Luwu's resource potential, often engaged in smallholder agriculture. Until the 1990s there was a strong focus on irrigated rice cultivation; since the 1990s, the booming cocoa sector has become increasingly attractive.

Kertoraharjo village forms the northern part of the former transmigration settlement Kertoraharjo I. It is located in the command area of the Kalaena irrigation system. In 1972–73, 500 hundred families — 350 from Bali and 150 from Java — were resettled here by the government. Each family received 2 ha of (forest-covered) land to be developed into home yards (0.25 ha), irrigated fields (1 ha) and rain-fed fields (0.75 ha). In later years two administrative villages emerged from the former settlement: in the late 1990s, Kertoraharjo had a fully Balinese population of some 1,300 people, while Margomulyo has a mixed Javanese and Balinese population. As the Javanese often sell land to the offspring of Balinese settlers, the number of Balinese households in this village is increasing. From the early 1980s, when the expanding irrigation canals reached the settlement, Kertoraharjo became a relatively thriving village. Almost all agricultural land is irrigated and yields two rice harvests a year. In addition, many Balinese have expanded, or sometimes shifted completely, into cocoa cultivation on land bought primarily from Javanese transmigrants and the local population around the Balinese settlement.

Thus, from a transmigrant settlement, Kertoraharjo gradually became a blueprint Indonesian administrative village (*desa*). However, Balinese migration also entailed a recreation and reinvention of Balinese culture, identity, social organization and institutions for local governance. An elaborate domain of Balinese customary arrangements was gradually established. The most important Balinese village institutions in Kertoraharjo are customary villages and temple groups. The customary village (*desa adat*) covers all Balinese people living in the two administrative villages that emerged from the initial mixed Javanese–Balinese settlement. Balinese inhabitants of the (mainly Javanese) *administrative* village of Margomulyo therefore belong to the *customary* village of Kertoraharjo. In daily life the customary rather than administrative village tends to be their main point of reference.

Customary villages are ritual communities united through the village temple; they have religious, administrative, social and legal functions. Paraphrasing Guermonprez (1990: 62), Warren (1993: 20) stresses that 'the fundamental conception of village territory as sacred space in which the land belongs ultimately to the gods who are ancestors and "real social partners" is central to the meaning of *desa* in Balinese cosmology, irrespective of structural variations'.

Water Users' Associations and Balinese Irrigators' Associations

From the 1970s, water users were organized into water users' associations (WUAs),[7] which were responsible for operation and maintenance of the irrigation system at the level of so-called 'tertiary units' (TUs), blocks of land irrigated from a tertiary canal.[8] The establishment of WUAs in most Public Works irrigation systems was made obligatory in a 1984 Presidential Decree. This resulted in a form of 'co-management' in which operation and maintenance of the main system (weir, primary and secondary canals, and tertiary gate) remained the responsibility of the irrigation agency of Public Works, while that of the TUs was transferred to WUAs. The heads of administrative villages became responsible for WUA affairs. Since TUs may cover irrigated fields belonging to one or more administrative villages, WUA membership often also cuts across village boundaries.

At the same time, there is the customary Balinese irrigators' association, the *subak*, which enjoys a relatively high degree of autonomy from the customary village leadership.[9] The forested land allocated to the Balinese settlers had to be ritually transformed into irrigated fields. These fields have to be maintained physically and in a ritual–ceremonial sense, to maintain the balance between gods, human beings and resources. Other 'stakeholders' are involved — spirits that, if not treated with care, may threaten people and crops. Clearing forest, therefore, must be accompanied by ceremonies, rituals and offerings (Charras, 1982). As in the village, the gods are also 'real social partners' (Guermonprez, 1990: 62) in the irrigated fields.

Once land becomes productive, this relationship continues. The rice cultivation cycle, from field preparation to post-harvest offerings, forms a highly ordered chain of interrelated activities. Gods subsist on the essence of rice and the existence of rice (the substance) in the human world is due to them. This essence originates from the body of the rice goddess Devi Sri, and should be returned to her after the harvest to allow the cycle to continue. Rice cultivation is susceptible to the transgression of ceremonial rules, ritual pollution and disturbance of the relationship between humans and the rice goddess; the cultivation cycle is therefore accompanied by a ritual–ceremonial cycle. In the words of Howe (1991: 454): 'Rice production is a cooperative endeavor between gods and people'.

---

7. In Indonesia these are called P3A (*Perkumpulan Petani Pemakai Air*).
8. In the Indonesian context, TUs can cover an area between around 50 and 150 ha, depending on local conditions. TUs are defined by a set of formal principles for design and use (e.g. subdivision into quaternary units irrigated by quaternary canals, separate canal functions for irrigation and drainage, rotational water distribution) as well as for internal organization (a WUA board with various functionaries, prescribed administrative procedures, etc.).
9. Therefore the subak was also referred to as the 'wet village', in contrast to the 'dry village' (Geertz, 1972).

LAND, WATER AND INFRASTRUCTURE: BETWEEN *SUBAK* AND WUA

Property Rights to Land, Water and Infrastructure

The creation, definition and development of property rights to land, water and irrigation infrastructure are crucial in the management of irrigated land. The situation appears straightforward, with the state as primary actor in land allocation, settlement and irrigation development. Current rights to land were defined and allocated by the state in the framework of transmigration.[10] Between the 1960s and 1990s, when transmigration was a spearhead of the 'New Order' regime, the state appropriated extensive areas of land throughout the country that had previously been held under local customary tenure, and reallocated it to transmigrants under an individual ownership title. This has also been the case with transmigration in Kalaena.

As to water, the picture seems equally simple. The Kalaena irrigation system, in which the Balinese own and cultivate land, was planned, designed and built by a state agency. It has a blueprint set-up of state-devised technology, organizational arrangements and regulations. Water rights are state-provided and tied to landownership in the command area. As noted, system management takes the form of 'co-management'; the irrigation agency operates and maintains the main system, while responsibility for the TUs has been transferred to WUAs. This came down to a devolution of management responsibilities, under a superficial ideology of 'community participation' and the creation of 'sense of ownership' (*rasa milik*). Through the WUAs, the state agency has delegated to the farmers a limited bundle of (operational) water rights and managerial responsibilities. Establishment of WUAs — and farmers' membership of them — are compulsory. Administrative responsibility for the WUAs rests with the leadership of the administrative village to which the WUA belongs.

Water rights (in the narrow sense of a right to a share of the resource; Pradhan and Meinzen-Dick, 2003), defined in terms of crop water requirements per area irrigated, are allocated by the state agency responsible for main system operation.[11] Formally, determination of water requirements takes place in a management-intensive process of bottom-up field data gathering, involving regular contacts between WUA representatives and the agency. Water distribution by the agency takes place at the level of the TU (at the tertiary off-take). Inside the TU, the WUA (through its 'water master') is responsible for rotational water distribution to the 'quaternary' units into which TUs are subdivided.

---

10. As in other parts of Indonesia, transmigration in Luwu has caused conflicts between local populations and settlers. In Kalaena such conflicts have only occurred on a small scale.
11. The 'main system' refers to the weir, primary and secondary canals (in contrast to the tertiary canals and TUs).

All irrigation infrastructure is state-owned. Farmers organized in a WUA have the right to use the TU infrastructure and the duty to contribute to cleaning and maintenance. Use of tertiary water division structures is narrowly circumscribed. Farmers are not allowed to operate or bring about changes to the tertiary gate. Operation of the tertiary systems by changing the gate settings of water division boxes is formally the task of the TU water master. Farmers are formally not allowed to change tertiary infrastructure (division structures, canals, drains). Their role is mainly limited to maintenance and small repairs.

Subak and WUA: Competing Claims of Authority

The establishment of *subak* gave state-allocated resources a specifically Balinese meaning. In Bali, the *subak* has many functions related to irrigated agriculture in the broadest sense. These include construction, repairs, operation and maintenance, agricultural planning and pest control, conflict resolution, the organization of rituals and ceremonies, temple construction and maintenance, maintenance of religious purity, collection of tax and fines, creation and enforcement of *subak* regulations and sanctions. A *subak* typically includes a complex which covers anything from tens of hectares to hundreds of hectares of (mainly) irrigated rice fields (*sawah*). Physical boundaries (rivers, ravines), hydrology (a water source shared by a group of farmers), and socio-political factors co-determine the *subak* area, which often crosscuts village boundaries. *Subak* may be subdivided into smaller units or be part of larger complexes (Birkelbach, 1973; Geertz, 1980; Jha, 2002; Lansing, 1991; Spiertz, 2000; Sutawan, 1987).

The head of the *subak* (*klian subak* or *pekaseh*) is assisted by other functionaries.[12] Membership entails a bundle of rights and duties with regard to water, ritual, agricultural planning, organization and management. Important responsibilities and obligations are labour contributions, water use in accordance with allocated shares, following planting and cropping schedules, guarding against pollution (in a religious sense) of the irrigated fields, attending meetings, and contributions in money or kind. Technology for water division is based on fixed proportional division of continuous flows through wooden, stone or concrete overflow weirs. An advantage of this method is that the water flow is divided in a direction parallel to the current.[13] Water division through these structures is relatively transparent and easily controllable by farmers (Horst, 1996; Sutawan, 1987).

---

12. The term *pekaseh* is also used to describe the higher level, encompassing various *subak* and their heads.
13. In contrast to division structures of Public Works systems, where water is divided in a direction perpendicular to the flow direction. Acceptance of this latter method by Balinese farmers is low (Horst, 1996; Sutawan, 1987).

In Kertoraharjo, *subak* establishment and development was determined by the specific conditions of settlement and irrigation development outside Bali. Although much of the land was still forested and agriculture rain-fed, the first settler groups established a *subak* upon arrival. After some years, when all Balinese settlers had arrived and developed their land, the initial village *subak* was split up into four separate ones, defined more or less spatially by the boundaries of the areas of land allocated to these groups. The organizations are still primarily known by names that refer to the settler groups initially forming their membership: *subak* 150KK, *subak* 100KK, *subak* 50KK, and *subak* 50KK Tampaksiring.[14] Each was headed by a *klian*, assisted by other functionaries. Together, the four *subak* formed a *pekaseh*, headed by a functionary with that name. *Subak* regulations taken from Bali were adapted to the local situation.

In their development, the *subak* in Kertoraharjo potentially showed the same wide variety of functions already known from Bali, covering ritual, agricultural practices and decision making, and irrigation. Contrary to those in Bali, *subak* in Kertoraharjo were not defined by hydrological or physical boundaries. The pattern of land allocation to settler groups rather than water flows determined *subak* membership and approximate boundaries. This definition of the *subak* in terms of land allocation by the state became an important 'resource' in later conflicts about the scope of legitimate *subak* authority (see below).

Irrigation water of the expanding system reached Kertoraharjo around 1983, with important consequences for the *subak*. Management arrangements in the form of WUAs were delivered as one package with the TU infrastructure. Layout and construction of the TUs were fully based on irrigation-technical criteria, and did not take into account pre-existing social organizational, settler group or ethnic boundaries. The TU boundaries (based on design criteria) cut across the pre-existing *subak* which, based on earlier land allocation, had never been directly linked to irrigation. This boundary cross-cutting, and the compulsory nature of WUA establishment, made the *subak* lose relevance as organizations for irrigation management. However, the WUAs, with their sometimes ethnically heterogeneous farmer population, could not fulfil the *subak* functions of organizing Balinese rituals and offerings.

Thus, upon establishment of TUs and WUAs, the broad *subak* domain of agronomic-agricultural, irrigation-managerial, and religious-ritual activities of irrigated agriculture was torn apart. This separation arose from diverging perceptions of irrigated agriculture between the government–administrative world and the life world of Balinese. The bureaucratic understanding of 'management' as a separate category of activities includes routine operation

---

14. KK (*Kepala Keluarga* — 'household head') refers to the number of initial Balinese settler families (350). The second group of fifty households (from Tampaksiring) is often referred to as 'Tampaksiring', to distinguish it from the first group of fifty.

and maintenance tasks (canal cleaning, repairs), but excludes agronomic and religious–ritual dimensions of irrigated agriculture. While the former is mainly the responsibility of the Agricultural Service, the latter is classified as belonging to the domain of religion. Neither of the two is associated with irrigation management.

Balinese have different perceptions of irrigated agriculture. Rather than using 'management' (*manajemen*), Kertoraharjo farmers tend to use '*per-subakan*' to refer to the broad domain of irrigated agriculture as covered by the Balinese *subak* — system management and agricultural planning as well as the religious–ritual cycle associated with rice agriculture. However, 'irrigation management' in the narrow sense of operation and maintenance of the tertiary unit became the responsibility of the WUAs. Agricultural planning belongs to the government domain as well, with an important role for the Agricultural Service and the district Irrigation Committee. Hence, the *subak*, as organizations, were forced to retreat to the religious–ritual domain and refrain from interference with management as sectorally defined by government agencies.

In the first years after the establishment of WUAs and the forced separation of religious–ritual and 'management' functions, when the system was already fully functioning and farmers were adapting to the new TUs and WUAs, the *subak* continued to play an important role in irrigated agriculture. The Balinese had accepted government management regulations, but farmers' accounts show that they had great difficulty in making WUAs function without using important elements of *subak*. In this period *subak*-derived elements emerged in the WUA domain. The Balinese created an organizational structure in which the *pekaseh* became 'WUA coordinator' of all WUAs in Kertoraharjo. Later, a conflict with the (then Javanese) village head forced the *pekaseh* to retreat from the WUA domain, reasserting the formal functional separation between *subak* and WUA. Since then, the TUs and WUAs are said to have seriously deteriorated (Roth, 2005).

The four *subak* and the *pekaseh* have developed regulations which are restricted to those issues the *subak* are formally allowed to deal with: they organize rice rituals, are the guardians of ritual purity, collect tax, determine the schedule of the agricultural season, and provide cash loans to members. As formal organizations, they are no longer involved in 'water management issues' of the WUA domain. Nevertheless, they remain important institutionally in regularizing patterns of behaviour between individuals and groups (see Leach et al., 1999; Meinzen-Dick and Pradhan, 2001). In the TUs and WUAs with a Balinese farmer population, the influence of *subak* on the legal, organizational and technical dimensions of irrigation continues. In some places, farmers have taken full control of water division technology and replaced the Public Works division boxes — which farmers are formally only allowed to operate and not to change — with Balinese division structures. It is often around such technology, where small groups of farmers are active in maintaining and improving the system, that Balinese organizational arrangements and regulations develop as well. Wherever the Balinese have organized around water management, *subak*-derived arrangements and practices have become the institutional 'glue' that keeps the state-imposed WUAs together (Roth, 2005).

Subak as Guardians of Purity: Determining Cropping Season and Transplanting

The rice transplanting ritual forms the main point of interaction between *subak* and government policy. It also influences Balinese agricultural practices.[15] For Balinese, determining a suitable transplanting date is crucial in agricultural planning. The beginning of transplanting is marked by a ritual and accompanied by strict regulations on timing and on agricultural labour. Transplanting before the ritual is regarded as a polluting act that disturbs the harmonious relationship between nature, people and gods. While farmers are allowed to start transplanting after the ritual, other labour is forbidden on that day. Rules are strictly maintained and enforced by 'spies' in the fields. Transgressors are fined by the *subak*, and must finance a cleansing ritual.

The *pekaseh* is not free to determine the transplanting date. He must take into account complicating factors and competing interests. The same goes for farmers and their agricultural activities. First, there is the government schedule for system opening and closure, and government indications for stages of the agricultural season (ploughing, transplanting, harvesting). Agencies and administrators try to increase cropping discipline among farmers: district policy is based on the latest advice from provincial research centres about crop resistance against pests and diseases, expected seasonal influences and rainfall. These government agencies co-operate in shifting forward the beginning of the dry season cropping period to as early a date as possible. For this, their most powerful instrument is choosing an early opening date for the irrigation systems, while strictly adhering to the planned closure date.

The district Irrigation Committee determines the opening and closing schedule of irrigation systems. These dates, a schedule for agricultural activities, and instructions on rice varieties and inputs are passed down hierarchically to the subdistrict and administrative village through so-called *tudang sipulung* meetings.[16] After the subdistrict meeting, ideally a village-level meeting is held. For Balinese, the agricultural season is so closely

---

15. This is where *subak* becomes most clearly visible as a normative and legal order. Other ritual is either left to the individual farmer, depending on the growth stage of the crop or the harvest moment, or taken care of by the *subak*.

16. This is a Bugis term meaning something like 'sit and discuss together'; the Bugis are a major ethnic group in South Sulawesi. The term refers to a Bugis tradition of collective decision making on rice cropping. It is a good example of the use of an 'indigenous' term appropriated by state agencies as an instrument of top-down control, veiled in participatory rhetoric (see Acciaioli, 1997).

related to ritual obligations that this meeting is crucial. In Kertoraharjo it provides a forum for discussion and decision making on how to match the government schedule with Balinese preferences for a day for starting land preparation, receiving the first irrigation water, and especially transplanting, based on the Balinese calendar.

Other factors — crucial for farmers — also play a role. These include crop conditions and expected planting behaviour in neighbouring villages, from which Balinese farmers do not want to deviate too far, and availability of tractors and labour power (for land preparation, extracting and bundling, and transplanting) during peak periods. Irrigated agriculture depends to a large extent on wage labour at all stages except harvesting. Appointments with tractor owners and transplanting groups have to be made weeks in advance. Land preparation schedules, especially the last stage of levelling, must be attuned to transplanting.

The transplanting ritual on the village customary land is organized by the *pekaseh*. He instructs a Hindu priest specializing in rice ritual to enact this ritual on the morning of the date determined in the village meeting. After praying for a good harvest and absence of pests and diseases, a bundle of stalks is ritually cleansed with holy water from the irrigation temple, and planted out by the priest. In the core *subak* areas — the irrigated fields initially defined as *subak* areas — transgressions of the rules for the beginning of transplanting seldom occur. In the following case a *subak* member transplanted his rice before the day of the ritual. The farmer was convicted and had to pay a cleansing ritual, executed on his field by the *subak* priest. In the words of the farmer:

> I had my rice transplanted one day before the transplanting ritual. The problem was that the definitive date chosen by the *pekaseh* had been announced very late. . . . When it was finally announced, I had already contracted a transplanting group that I could not cancel without getting into serious trouble with finding new labour power at short notice. My rice stalks had already been extracted and bundled . . . ready for transplanting. So under these circumstances I was forced to steal one day. The transplanting group arrived and transplanted my rice before [the official opening of transplanting season]. Late announcement of the transplanting date is a problem for farmers. It makes finding a transplanting group very difficult. If it is a late date, it makes it impossible for us to follow the government schedule (source: field notes)

The Balinese often stress that these *subak* regulations only apply to Balinese farmers. However, I witnessed a case of a Javanese farmer (a Muslim) who started working his land located near the field hut of the (Balinese) water master of the TU. Immediately the water master forbade him to transgress Balinese *subak* rules. The water master told me that he had been ordered by the chairman of the WUA (also a Balinese) to guard the fields against transgressions of *subak* regulations forbidding agricultural labour on this day (source: field notes). This example shows that the formal separation of functions and spheres of influence between the WUA and the *subak* is not always clear in agricultural and management practices on the ground. Such formal distinctions need not correspond to actors' understandings of the domains of human activity on which they have been imposed. In this case, a WUA chairman was enforcing *subak* rules upon a non-Balinese farmer.

CONTESTED BOUNDARIES OF WUA AND SUBAK

Dividing a Tertiary Unit: A WUA for Balinese Only

The TU known as PS3 covers about 90 ha of irrigated fields. It cuts across village and ethnic boundaries. The upstream (head) part belongs to Patengko village with a migrant population from Tana Toraja[17] in highland South Sulawesi, while the middle and tail end belong to Kertoraharjo. As a consequence of the history of land allocation, land tenure in the Balinese part of the TU is relatively egalitarian. Land ownership still reflects the state allocation pattern of 1-ha plots of irrigable land (*sawah*; see above). Most land in Patengko used to be owned by a small number of initial Toraja settlers. Gradually, they sold land to Toraja and Balinese farmers or had it worked in sharecropping arrangements. One trend in land tenure is clear: land ownership shows a 'Balinization' of the Patengko part of this TU. About eighteen Balinese farmers own land here bought from Toraja farmers, and this Balinese take-over of land is continuing.[18] There is a marked difference in cropping schedule between Balinese and Toraja. Most Toraja cultivate and harvest one to two months later than their Balinese neighbours. The Balinese, who have no control over the head end of the TU, see this as an advantage: spreading the high water demand of land preparation over a longer period may prevent conflicts about water.

Many parts of the infrastructure did not function well when the system began to be used. The original tertiary canal is still in use, but all five water division boxes in the TU have lost their function of rotational water distribution. Many quaternary canals from the boxes have disappeared. On several locations in the Patengko part of the unit, water is taken directly from the tertiary canal by opening the tertiary embankment or boring (usually invisible) holes in the canal embankment, a practice of water appropriation common among Toraja farmers but strongly disapproved of by the Balinese. The water thus appropriated flows directly into an irrigated field and is further distributed on a field-to-field basis. In the Toraja part of the TU, there is much water loss through leakages from tertiary canal and degraded boxes. All quaternary canals have disappeared, as have many drains.

Where the tertiary canal enters Balinese village territory, Balinese farmers have constructed a proportional division structure (*temuku*) using bricks and cement. This guarantees water allocation to the Balinese with land

---

17. Toraja are mainly Christians.
18. At the time of the research the TU had fifty-eight Balinese and thirty-four Toraja landowners.

in Patengko, and an equitable share for the middle and tail ends. Further downstream, Balinese have constructed another division structure to replace a Public Works division box which never functioned because of its low position. It divides the water supply proportionally into three, the larger portion of which enters the tertiary canal, while two smaller shares enter smaller canals from which groups of eleven farmers each take water. Farmers taking water from these small canals have been very active in improving access to water, making culverts, and maintaining a farm road. Many farmers place a small wooden division structure[19] in the canals to divert the water proportionally into their field. A relatively controlled and transparent water distribution exists in this part of the TU. Thus, all kinds of irrigation-technical adaptations to the degraded TU infrastructure have come into being here.

In terms of the organizational arrangements, the WUA has an all-Balinese board consisting of a chairman, vice-chairman, secretary, treasurer, and water master. At a lower level of organization, four Balinese farmers function as group leaders of four 'quaternary unit' subgroups of the WUA. This formal structure and the relationship between quaternary infrastructure and formal organization have never existed in practice. The small groups have primarily developed where Balinese farmers have constructed new division structures to replace degraded ones, thus changing the boundaries of quaternary irrigation units as well as arrangements for their management.

As a consequence of the tensions between the two groups about water appropriation and collective labour, the Toraja farmers have been excluded from the WUA. Although the TU has physically remained one irrigation unit, organizationally the Balinese have separated off and formed their own WUA without Toraja farmers. The fifty-eight farmers registered in the WUA administration are all Balinese. They belong to four smaller farmers' groups, three of which are located on Kertoraharjo land while the fourth consists of Balinese farmers who have bought land in the Patengko part of PS3. The thirty-four Toraja farmers are not organized in such groups, and not registered with or represented in the WUA. The Balinese chairman of the WUA states that the organization now exclusively represents Balinese farmers.

During a meeting of the Balinese section of the TU — part of an initiative by the Balinese administrative village head (responsible for WUA affairs) to bring new life into the badly functioning WUAs — new rules were formulated to strengthen its performance. The regulations, drafted by the WUA chairman, were presented to the members and accepted unanimously. The regulations, later to be extended with rules concerning water allocation and distribution, cover collective labour (rules and fines for absence), labour compensation for those unable to work, in proportion to land ownership,[20]

---

19. These are also called *temuku*, like the concrete ones built in some places; see above.
20. In the latter, a 'standard' area is determined (in this case 1 ha), for which owners must perform collective labour. Owners of more land should pay per hectare per season for land above the standard, while farmers owning less receive compensation.

cattle and fowl (fines on damage to canals and crops), and purity of the irrigated fields (fines on sexual intercourse in the irrigated fields; the need for a cleansing ritual). Reference to religious–ritual purity, rules on labour compensation and other rules in the new regulations have given the TU a strongly Balinese identity. The Balinese have turned the WUA into a fully Balinese organization to which *subak* regulations are increasingly applied.

The Contested *Subak*: Multiple Definitions of Legitimate *Subak* Authority

Initially, land allocation had determined *subak* membership (see above). Although different from the situation in Bali, this definition, emerging under the specific migrant conditions in Kertoraharjo, was clear enough at the outset. However, it no longer suffices for defining and demarcating *subak* authority in certain domains of *subak* activitiy. The active role of Balinese as buyers of land and their increasing land ownership in other villages influence the *subak* and make the initial definition of its membership problematic. These ambiguities and different interpretations have now become a destabilizing factor.

A key issue is the status of land bought by Balinese outside areas initially defined as *subak* areas. Are its owners subject to *subak* taxes and contributions, rights and responsibilities? The status of this land is unclear, the issue not covered by *subak* regulation. This problem of boundaries of authority — not this time between *subak* and WUAs but between land under *subak* control and land outside its control — haunts the Kertoraharjo *subak*. Two elements make this problem particularly sensitive: payment of *subak* tax proportional to irrigated land owned, and the regulations on transplanting. According to strict interpretations, *subak* ritual must be performed for all Balinese and their irrigated fields, irrespective of location of the land. If Balinese own irrigated fields in surrounding villages, according to this interpretation they are subject to *subak* regulations.

However, this interpretation is not shared by all. For irrigated areas initially under *subak* control the picture is more or less clear. Balinese transmigrants started off with an equal area of (mostly irrigated) land: 1.75 ha.[21] In the meantime, some have sold (part of) their land while others have bought additional land from Balinese in the *subak* areas. Such changes are taken into account in determining the seasonal member contributions, paid in proportion to area owned in one of the initial areas.[22]

---

21. The official allocation pattern was 1 ha of *sawah*, 0.75 ha of *lading* (rainfed land). Most of the latter turned out to be irrigable in Kertoraharjo. Apart from this, settlers received 0.25 ha of houseplot; see also above.
22. Though the status of such land bought by Balinese is widely acknowledged, there is no general agreement. Some farmers do not agree that taxation should cover land acquired through purchase.

Other cases are more difficult. Farmers owning land located partly within and partly outside the initial areas tend to pay for the former only, and usually do not respect the *subak* transplanting schedule for the latter areas. There are also farmers who own irrigated fields outside the initial *subak* areas only. Most are not *subak* members, do not pay tax, and do not respect the transplanting date. The status of land bought by Balinese from Javanese farmers in neighbouring Margomulyo is also unclear. Some farmers pay for this land, while others do not. Farmers take widely diverging positions on the issue, as the examples and quotations below clearly demonstrate. The first, Wayan Gatra, once openly refused to pay *subak* tax for his land located outside the initial *subak* areas. Irritated by the unwillingness of fellow villagers to pay tax for such land, he decided to stop paying:

> *Subak* ceremonies are held for all Balinese who work irrigated fields. I held the opinion that either everybody should take his responsibility and pay the full tax, or that it should be collected on the basis of irrigated area in the transmigration areas only. But nothing in between, me paying my tax and others not taking their responsibility. That is why I refused to pay. In the end, I remained a *subak* member... though I have sold my land in the *subak* areas a long time ago and bought irrigated land in another village. *Subak* ceremonies are organized for all Balinese rice farmers, including those outside the *subak* areas. So we have to be members.... The best solution would be to decide that all irrigated land owned by Balinese from the customary village of Kertoraharjo must pay *subak* tax (source: field notes)

This farmer pleads for taking customary village membership as the key criterion. Others would even leave tax collection to the customary village, limiting the relative autonomy of *pekaseh* and *subak*.

The following farmer defies *subak* authority by refusing to pay tax for land bought from another Balinese, located in one of the initial *subak* areas:

> Many years ago Pan Budarsana bought an irrigated field from a Balinese transmigrant who returned to Bali. Since then Budarsana refuses to pay tax and observe *subak* decisions on transplanting. For his other land, acquired by transmigration, he pays the amount due. Budarsana avoids the subject and does not want to comment. According to other farmers, the case is clear: Budarsana bought his land from a transmigrant who had received it by government allocation. Therefore, it is *subak* land. There is quite general agreement among farmers that he should pay. Budarsana, however, maintains that he acquired the land not by state allocation but by purchase from a transmigrant. According to him, even though the land is located in a *subak* area, it is not subject to its regulations. Since many years this case threatens *subak* unity. If Budarsana is fined by the *subak*, he simply does not pay. Budarsana continues to turn up for *subak* meetings, where he is tolerated. The *subak* uses no further sanctions to enforce its regulations (source: field notes).

The following farmer, Made Suarna, owns land outside the *subak* areas only. He uses his status as a 'spontaneous transmigrant' (not state-sponsored) as an argument for not joining *subak*.

> Made Suarna owns two irrigated fields, both outside the original *subak* areas. He is not a *subak* member, does not pay tax and only partly follows the planting schedule. On one irrigated field in Purwosari he does not follow the *subak* schedule; under the influence of

his neighbours, he says. The mostly Javanese-owned fields in this village are usually planted before the Balinese transplanting ritual. On his other land he follows the *subak* schedule, because there are other Balinese landowners nearby who do so as well. Suarna: 'In Bali it is a great advantage to be a member of the *subak*; it regulates everything: water, offerings, holy water. Here, if your irrigated field is located outside the *subak* areas, you get information from hearsay only. I should actually be a member, but I am not because the farmers around me are all Muslims. Let us not unnecessarily show off our religion. I do my own small offerings and that is it' (source: field notes).

What keeps Suarna from becoming a member, and what is the difference between his situation and that of others like Wayan Gatra in the first case? According to Suarna:

Wayan Gatra is a transmigrant. He sold his transmigration land and bought new land in another village. Though his current land is located outside the initial *subak* areas, he has been a member from the beginning and should remain so. I came as a spontaneous transmigrant and did not get government land. Therefore, I am not a *subak* member. *Subak* is for owners of irrigated fields in the *subak* areas or for those who were members but transferred their land to another location. I happen not to own any irrigated fields there, and I never did. Once the *subak* leaders tried to force people like me to become members, but their proposal was voted down. If we join *subak*, the consequence is that we also have to execute the [ritual for welcoming the water], bring offerings and respect the transplanting date. That will probably not be accepted by non-Balinese who own irrigated fields there (source: field notes).

Sometimes, conflicts occur about temporary use of the land of *subak* members by other farmers, especially non-Balinese. The following account comes from Ngurah:

Sarin tahun [*subak* tax] means 'the proceeds of a year's labour'. Payment for land outside the *subak* area would not be a problem to me. Whenever there are proceeds we must pay. But we have to be consistent with regard to its meaning. The following happened to me some time ago. I own three irrigated fields in Margomulyo, totaling 2.25 hectare. Some time ago I pawned one of these fields to a Javanese farmer, so 1.5 hectare was left for cultivation by myself. As I did not harvest from the pawned field, I did not pay tax for it. I ended up having a conflict with the *subak*. The chairman demanded payment for a *sawah* I do not work. He demanded payment for 2.25 hectare while I only owed him tax for 1.50 hectare. I told him that he should realize the meaning of *sarin tahun*. If a farmer with another religion uses the land, what can we do about it? . . . If the land user is a Balinese, tax payment is settled by an agreement between the owner and the temporary user. But if the user is a Javanese, that is not possible: I do not want to pay because I have no proceeds, and he does not want to pay either because he is not a Balinese and does not recognize *subak* (source: field notes).

Some Balinese stress that the unity of the Balinese Hindu community is at stake. Taking location of land rather than religious affiliation as a criterion for membership and contributions would severely jeopardize the unity and authority of the community. Other considerations related to processes of economic differentiation, particularly, also play a role. Should differences in land ownership be expressed in a proportional differentiation of member duties? Should tax, additional contributions in kind, or labour contributions (for example, for temple maintenance) *all* be collected and demanded on the basis of irrigated area owned? Another problem concerns the specific position of land outside the initial *subak* areas. There is a dilemma here, between following *subak* regulations or adapting to the people in the area where the land is located. Should a minority of Balinese farmers among a non-Balinese majority be forced to follow *subak* regulations or be left free to adapt to the agricultural practices of farmers of different origin and ethno-religious identity around them? Many Balinese stress that individual farmers can and must make their personal field offerings, but should refrain from 'showing off' by expanding *subak* ritual to areas with a non-Balinese farmer majority.

Subak legitimacy is uncontested only in those areas that were initially under *subak* control, but often ignored elsewhere. Balinese farmers owning irrigated land outside these areas only have a completely different relationship to *subak* than farmers who own land within the area. The former are mainly spontaneous settlers without initial access to transmigration land, and offspring of transmigrants, dependent on inheritance and land purchases. Their different relationship to *subak* makes such landowners vulnerable to accusations of 'free riding': *subak* members finance the necessary rice ritual, and fulfil labour and other requirements. The same goes for farmers who have sold land in the initial areas and bought new land in other areas.[23]

CONCLUSION

Debates about property rights, common property and institutions for resource management have often under-emphasized the role of competing claims and legitimizing institutions, and of disjunctures, tensions or conflict between state and non-state authorities. Studies about rural property transformations should pay more attention to the relationships between state agencies and their strategies of territorialization in the domain of resource governance, on the one hand, and local resource users and their specific perceptions of property rights, resource governance and authority, on the other. The case study presented here of the competition for legitimate authority between state and non-state arrangements in the domain of local irrigation management against the backdrop of complex property rights to land, water and infrastructure clearly illustrates this point.

Property rights to state-allocated resources are given meaning in the life world of Balinese migrants in a new socio-cultural and agro-ecological environment. Transmigration and settlement were products of, and structured by, increasing state control over natural resources, definitions of property rights, and arrangements for management and governance. Gradually, however, new structuring forces have emerged locally, accompanied by new

---

23. Sometimes such farmers were accused of shirking *subak* responsibilities. Usually other considerations prevail: land quality, access to water, or distance between the irrigated field and the home.

values, norms, definitions of rights and responsibilities, and regulatory ar-rangements; specifically Balinese but also the product of 're-invention' of Balinese society. This process of giving meaning to a state-defined space and associated governance and managerial arrangements is crucial in the settlement history of these migrants.

This re-embedding also brought to the surface differential interpretations of the scope of the bundles of rights and responsibilities pertaining to re-sources, of irrigation management, of the boundaries between the state-defined and the Balinese domain, and of the legitimacy of *subak* authority under conditions of expanding Balinese land ownership. Even in a setting where property rights to the resources *per se* are relatively 'clear', such dif-ferential interpretations and related sources of legitimacy give the domain of irrigated agriculture and irrigation management an ambivalent, institution-ally and legally complex character.

The TU/WUA structure introduced with the irrigation system involves specific bundles of rights and responsibilities, and forms of management. The Balinese have at their disposal other ways of managing irrigated agri-culture associated with *subak*. These entail different bundles of rights and responsibilities, norms, rules and ways of organizing, and relationships between 'religion' and 'management'. Formal exclusion of *subak* from resource management could not prevent the gradual introduction of its normative, organizational and technical characteristics in irrigation man-agement. *Subak*-related norms, arrangements and practices became the in-stitutional 'glue' in local irrigation management, at the level of the WUA wherever possible, or at lower levels of farmer organization.

The new functions of the *subak* as formal organizations for guarding and staging the religious–ritual elements of irrigated agriculture brought new interactions with the government domain, including the planning of the agricultural season, especially the determination of the date on which rice transplanting is allowed to begin. Although the schedules of government agencies and *pekaseh* are never far apart, there is some tension between the government policy of transplanting as early as possible and the Balinese stress on forbidding transplanting before the day of the ritual. The issue may also become sensitive in relation to stresses and constraints associated with another factor in agricultural planning: availability of labour for plowing and transplanting. The way in which transplanting regulations are enforced in the field shows that the formal separation of *subak* and WUA is not always clear-cut in social practice.

The forced separation of *subak* as organization from the formally defined WUA domain and the gradual reintroduction of some of its institutional elements into irrigation management have set off new processes of contes-tation of the boundaries of both WUA and *subak*. The case of a multi-ethnic WUA with increasing Balinese land ownership shows that growing Bali-nese influence, in combination with tensions about irrigation management between Balinese and Toraja farmers, brings in the factor of identity related to property and resource management. New infrastructure, organizational arrangements and rules have turned TUs and WUAs into spaces and organizations with an increasingly prominent Balinese (*subak*) identity, leading to the *de facto* exclusion of non-Balinese farmers from the WUA. At the same time, the definition of *subak* in terms of land allocated by the state has led to conflicts about the legitimacy of *subak* authority to impose *subak*-related restrictions (on transplanting) and obligations (tax payment) upon Balinese landowners outside the initial settlement area. There is no general agreement on the scope of *subak* authority regarding these issues. Causing divisions among the members, such problems weaken the *subak*.

It can be concluded that the embedding of state-allocated resources in Balinese social institutions and cultural–religious notions deeply influences local governance and irrigation management structures and arrangements. The plural character of rights and responsibilities influencing irrigated agriculture is reflected in conflicts about authority and legitimacy between competing organizations and institutions in the domain of management of irrigated agriculture (WUA and *subak*), as well as within them (*subak*). In the process, both local definitions of property rights (bundles of rights and responsibilities) and competing arrangements undergo important transformations. These transformations deeply influence both state and non-state resource governance and management arrangements, turning them into locally specific and 'embedded' institutions. Such processes, in which institutional arrangements are reproduced, transformed, or wholly discarded and replaced by new ones, are characterized by struggles about legitimacy, authority and power.

REFERENCES

Acciaioli, G. (1997) 'What's in a Name? Appropriating Idioms in the South Sulawesi Rice Intensification Program', in J. Schiller and B.M. Schiller (eds) *Imagining Indonesia: Cultural Politics and Political Culture*, pp. 288–320. Ohio University Center for International Studies, Monographs in International Studies, Southeast Asian Series, No. 97. Athens, OH: Ohio University Press.

Agrawal, A. (2003) 'Sustainable Governance of Common-Pool Resources: Context, Methods, and Politics', *Annual Review of Anthropology* 32: 243–62.

Agrawal, A. and C.C. Gibson (1999) 'Enchantment and Disenchantment: The Role of Community in Natural Resource Conservation', *World Development* 27(4): 629–49.

von Benda-Beckmann, F., K. von Benda-Beckmann and A. Griffiths (eds) (2005) *Mobile People, Mobile Law. Expanding Legal Relations in a Contracting World*. Aldershot: Ashgate.

von Benda-Beckmann, F., K. von Benda-Beckmann and M.G. Wiber (eds) (2006) 'The Properties of Property', in F. von Benda-Beckmann, K. von Benda-Beckmann and M.G. Wiber (eds) *Changing Properties of Property*, pp. 1–39. New York: Berghahn Books.

Birkelbach, A.W. (1973) 'The Subak Association', *Indonesia* 16: 153–69. (Cornell Modern Indonesia Project.)

Bruns, B.R., C. Ringler and R. Meinzen-Dick (eds) (2005) *Water Rights Reform: Lessons for Institutional Design*. Washington, DC: International Food Policy Research Institute.

Charras, M. (1982) *De la Forêt Maléfique a l'Herbe Divine. La Transmigration en Indonésie:*

les Balinais a Sulawesi (From Hostile Forest to Divine Grass). Paris: Editions de la Maison des Sciences de l'Homme Paris.

Geertz, C. (1972) 'The Wet and the Dry: Traditional Irrigation in Bali and Morocco', *Human Ecology* 1(1): 23–9.

Geertz, C. (1980) 'Organization of the Balinese *Subak*', in E.W. Coward Jr. (ed.) *Irrigation and Agricultural Development in Asia. Perspectives from the Social Sciences*, pp. 70–90. Ithaca, NY, and London: Cornell University Press.

Guermonprez, J.F. (1990) 'On the Elusive Balinese Village: Hierarchy and Values Versus Political Models', *Review of Indonesian and Malaysian Affairs* 24: 55–89.

Hann, C.M. (ed.) (1998) *Property Relations. Renewing the Anthropological Tradition*. Cambridge: Cambridge University Press.

Horst, L. (1996) 'Intervention in Irrigation Water Division in Bali, Indonesia. A Case of Farmers' Circumvention of Modern Technology', in G. Diemer and F. Huibers (eds) *Crops, People and Irrigation. Water Allocation Practices of Farmers and Engineers*, pp. 34–52. London: Intermediate Technology Publications.

Hotimsky, S., R. Cobb and A. Bond (2006) 'Contracts or Scripts? A Critical Review of the Application of institutional Theories to the Study of Environmental Change', *Ecology and Society* 11(1): 41. http://www.ecologyandsociety.org/vol11/iss1/art41/

Howe, L. (1991) 'Rice, Ideology, and the Legitimation of Hierarchy in Bali', *Man (N.S.)* 26: 445–67.

Jentoft, S. (2004) 'Institutions in Fisheries: What They Are, What They Do, and How They Change', *Marine Policy* 28: 137–49.

Jha, N. (2002) 'The Bifurcate Subak: The Social Organisation of a Balinese Irrigation Community'. Dissertation, Brandeis University. UMI Dissertation Services.

Johnson, C. (2004) 'Uncommon Ground: The "Poverty of History" in Common Property Discourse', *Development and Change* 35(3): 407–33.

Lansing, J.S. (1991) *Priests and Programmers. Technologies of Power in the Engineered Landscape of Bali*. Princeton, NJ: Princeton University Press.

Leach, M., R. Mearns and I. Scoones (1999) 'Environmental Entitlements Dynamics and Institutions in Community-based Natural Resource Management', *World Development* 27(2): 225–47.

McCay, B.J. (2002) 'Emergence of Institutions for the Commons: Contexts, Situations, and Events', in E. Ostrom, Th. Dietz, N. Dolsak, P.C. Stern, S. Stonich and E.U. Weber (eds) *The Drama of the Commons*, pp. 361–402. Washington, DC: National Academy Press.

McCay, B.J. and S. Jentoft (1998) 'Market or Community Failure? Critical Perspectives on Common Property Research', *Human Organization* 57(1): 21–9.

Meinzen-Dick, R. (2000) 'Public, Private, and Shared Water: Groundwater, Markets and Access in Pakistan', in B.R. Bruns and R. Meinzen-Dick (eds) *Negotiating Water Rights*, pp. 245–68. New Delhi: IFPRI.

Meinzen-Dick, R.S. and R. Pradhan (2001) 'Implications of Legal Pluralism for Natural Resource Management', *IDS Bulletin* 32(4): 10–17.

Mosse, D. (1997) 'The Symbolic Making of a Common Property Resource: History, Ecology and Locality in a Tank-irrigated Landscape in South India', *Development and Change* 28(3): 467–504.

Ostrom, E. (1992) *Crafting Institutions for Self-Governing Irrigation Systems*. San Francisco, CA: Institute for Contemporary Studies Press.

Ostrom, E. and E. Schlager (1996) 'The Formation of Property Rights', in S.S. Hanna, C. Folke and K.G. Mäler (eds) *Rights to Nature: Ecological, Economic, Cultural, and Political Principles of Institutions for the Environment*, pp. 127–56. Washington, DC: Island Press.

Pradhan, R. and R. Meinzen-Dick (2003) 'Which Rights are Right? Water Rights, Culture, and Underlying Values', *Water Nepal* 9–10 (1–2): 37–61.

Roth, D. (2005) 'In the Shadow of Uniformity. Balinese Irrigation Management in a Public Works Irrigation System in Luwu, South Sulawesi, Indonesia', in D. Roth, R. Boelens and M. Zwarteveen (eds) *Liquid Relations. Contested Water Rights and Legal Complexity*, pp. 66–96. New Brunswick, NJ: Rutgers University Press.

Roth, D. (2006) 'Which Order? Whose Order? Balinese Irrigation Management in Sulawesi, Indonesia', *Oxford Development Studies* 34(1): 33–46.

Schlager, E. (2006) 'Property Rights, Water and Conflict in the Western US', in F. von Benda-Beckmann, K. von Benda-Beckmann and M.G. Wiber (eds) *Changing Properties of Property*, pp. 293–308. New York: Berghahn Books.

Spiertz, H.L.J. (2000) 'Water Rights and Legal Pluralism: Some Basics of a Legal Anthropological Approach', in B.R. Bruns and R.S. Meinzen-Dick (eds) *Negotiating Water Rights*, pp. 245–68. New Delhi: IFPRI.

Sutawan, N. (1987) 'Farmer-Managed Irrigation Systems and the Impact of Government Assistance: A Note from Bali, Indonesia', in *Public Intervention in Farmer-Managed Irrigation Systems*, pp. 49–69. Digana Village, Sri Lanka: International Irrigation Management Institute.

Vandergeest, P. and N.L. Peluso (1995) 'Territorialization and State Power in Thailand', *Theory and Society* 24: 385–426.

Verdery, K. and C. Humphrey (eds) (2004) *Property in Question. Value Transformation in the Global Economy*. Oxford and New York: Berg.

Warren, C. (1993) *Adat and Dinas. Balinese Communities in the Indonesian State*. Kuala Lumpur: Oxford University Press.

Zwarteveen, M., D. Roth and R. Boelens (2005) 'Water Rights and Legal Pluralism: Beyond Analysis and Recognition', in D. Roth, R. Boelens and M. Zwarteveen (eds) *Liquid Relations. Contested Water Rights and Legal Complexity*, pp. 254–68. New Brunswick, NJ: Rutgers University Press.

Index